Critical Hermeneutics

9/8/88

Critical Hermeneutics

A study in the thought of
Paul Ricoeur and Jürgen Habermas

JOHN B. THOMPSON

The right of the
University of Cambridge
to print and sell
all manner of books
was granted by
Henry VIII in 1534.
The University has printed
and published continuously
since 1584.

Cambridge University Press

Cambridge
New York   New Rochelle
Melbourne   Sydney

Published by the Press Syndicate of the University of Cambridge
The Pitt Building, Trumpington Street, Cambridge CB2 1RP
32 East 57th Street, New York, NY 10022, USA
10 Stamford Road, Oakleigh, Melbourne 3166, Australia

First published 1981
First paperback edition 1983
Reprinted 1985, 1988

Printed in the United States of America

British Library Cataloguing in Publication Data
Thompson, John Brookshire
Critical hermeneutics.
1. Social sciences—Philosophy
I. Title
300'.1   H61   80-41935
ISBN 0 521 23932 X hard covers
ISBN 0 521 27666 7 paperback

Contents

Foreword

In recent years, there have been major changes in social theory in the English-speaking world. What could be called the old 'orthodox consensus' in the social sciences was dominated by the pre-eminence of functionalism on the level of methodology, and positivism on the level of epistemology. These ideas never went unquestioned, of course, but in past years they have come under increasing attack – so much so that they certainly no longer reign as an orthodoxy, but have become substantially discredited. One of the results of these events has been a new convergence between the social sciences and philosophy. Indeed, as John Thompson points out, some of those authors who have written under the influence of recent trends in ordinary language philosophy have advanced the view that social science can be regarded as 'a conceptual extension of philosophy'. This is not a position which Thompson accepts, but he does acknowledge the significance of the contributions that such authors have made to pressing issues in social theory at the current juncture.

In the first part of his book, Thompson analyses these contributions in a concise and elegant way. He concentrates his attention upon three main areas of analysis: problems of action, interpretation and truth. In each of these areas, ordinary language philosophy is shown to have encountered a cluster of unresolved difficulties. In attempting to illuminate how these difficulties may be approached, Thompson turns to traditions of Continental thought that are still relatively little known to philosophers in the English-speaking world. Paul Ricoeur is one of the outstanding contemporary representatives of hermeneutic phenomenology, an approach to philosophy strongly influenced by Heidegger. Ricoeur's writings cover a formidable range, and are often of considerable complexity. Thompson analyses the main elements of Ricoeur's work in a masterly way; his exposition now becomes the standard account of Ricoeur's philosophy for the English-speaking reader. Ricoeur's ideas involve interesting and significant points of contrast with the second leading tradition of

Continental philosophy Thompson examines, that of critical theory. Jürgen Habermas is today the most prominent representative of critical theory. While his writings are better known to English-speaking readers than are those of Ricoeur, in my opinion Thompson provides an analysis of Habermas's work that is much more penetrating than most others currently available. It is an independent contribution in its own right, to rank alongside his discussion of Ricoeur.

However, it would be quite wrong to see Thompson's book as simply a work of exposition, of however high a standard. Thompson has two other objectives, which his book fulfils brilliantly. One is, by bringing together the three traditions he discusses, to use each to highlight the limitations of the others. But underlying this is a more ambitious project, which is outlined in the concluding chapters – a project that the author describes, as indicated by the title of his book, as a 'critical hermeneutics'. It remains to be seen how far his ideas will be capable of further development, but for the present we can be content with the very considerable intellectual achievement which this book represents.

Anthony Giddens

Preface

I began work on this project in 1975, when I became a research student at Trinity Hall, Cambridge. The study was completed with the assistance of a research bye-fellowship at Girton College and a research fellowship at Jesus College, Cambridge. I wish to thank the fellows of these Colleges for the generous support which I have received.

I should like to express my gratitude to Professors Ricoeur and Habermas for their willingness to respond to my numerous inquiries. While defending many of their concerns, I have also tried to reflect critically on their work, to think in accordance with their ideas. I hope that the results of this attempt do justice to the richness of their thought.

Discussions with friends and colleagues have helped me to clarify my views. David Held and William Outhwaite read all of the manuscript and made many valuable comments. I have also benefited from conversations with Mary Hesse, Jonathan Dancy and Mike Barfoot. Any errors that remain are, of course, my own.

Above all, I offer my thanks to Anthony Giddens, who supervised the Ph.D. thesis upon which this study is based. There is no doubt that, without his constant encouragement and advice, I would have produced a very different and far inferior piece of work. Anyone who is familiar with his writings will recognise the magnitude of my debt.

Cambridge   J. B. T.
August 1980

Introduction

The following study is concerned with the philosophy of social science. This sphere of philosophical inquiry remains an arena of deep-rooted dispute. Since the middle of the nineteenth century, many authors have argued that the methods of the social sciences are identical in essential respects with those of the natural sciences. The latter disciplines provide, by virtue of their very success, an exemplar of what all knowledge should be: empirically grounded, universally binding, value-free. However, during the same period, many writers have rejected this view, maintaining that there is a radical discontinuity between the natural and the social domain. For the social world consists of speaking and acting subjects who constantly make sense of themselves and others, and whose meaningful and wilful activities cannot be comprehended by the methods of the natural sciences. The study of the social world requires, these writers contend, a fundamentally different approach.

The two opposing positions are reflected in the recent philosophical literature of the Anglo-Saxon world. In the 1940s and 50s, authors such as Hempel and Nagel sought to analyse the methods of the humanistic disciplines in a manner which concurred with the positivistic programme of a unified science. There has since been a strong reaction to this earlier aim, a reaction propelled by the work of the later Wittgenstein, Austin and other 'ordinary language philosophers'. Writers such as Peters, Winch and Louch have called for an account of social science which is no longer constrained by the positivistic model, and which recognises the unique and ineradicable meaningfulness of human phenomena. The analyses offered by the latter writers are penetrating and provocative, raising questions about the character of social science which cannot be ignored. Nevertheless, these authors have generally pursued their investigations within an unduly narrow perspective. The problems which they pose are trapped in traditional antinomies, and many important issues are excluded from consideration. Moreover, the investigations are commonly conducted in terms which bear little relation to the actual practice

1

of the social sciences. Indeed, it could be said that as a reaction to the reductionist doctrines of logical positivism, the recent Anglo-Saxon writings have resulted in their own form of reductionism. For just as the positivists of the Vienna Circle regarded philosophy as a logical arm of science, so too the followers of the later Wittgenstein have treated social science as a conceptual extension of philosophy.

It is with the aim of overcoming this pair of opposing positions, alternately assumed and rejected by Anglo-Saxon philosophers, that I have turned towards Continental traditions of thought. Among the latter, there are some traditions which have been deeply concerned with the nature of social inquiry. The exponents of these traditions have frequently opposed the unqualified use of naturalistic methods in the social sphere; and yet some of these authors have argued nonetheless that the study of the social world requires the use of objectifying concepts. One such tradition is that of 'hermeneutic phenomenology', which was formed through the fusion of the discipline of interpretation with the procedures devised by Husserl. The synthesis was originally effected by Heidegger and subsequently developed by Gadamer and others. A current and outstanding contribution may be found in the writings of Paul Ricoeur, who defends this approach in an intellectual milieu dominated by the ideas of Freud and Saussure. Another Continental tradition which has addressed itself to problems of social science is that of 'critical social theory'. Anchored in the writings of Kant, Hegel and Marx, this tradition was fostered by Horkheimer, Adorno and others, who sought to construct a theory of society which preserved a moment of critique. The project has been pursued by Jürgen Habermas, whose work is currently in the forefront of critical social theory.

One of the striking features of recent and widely differing contributions to the philosophy of social science is the extent to which they are infused with an interest in language. Among earlier Anglo-Saxon philosophers, the interest in this phenomenon was generally confined to the question of how the language of science could be clarified through the application of logical techniques. However, in the wake of the writings of the later Wittgenstein and others, philosophers have become increasingly concerned with the ways in which linguistic activities are constitutive of social life. Language is no longer seen as a formal structure which stands over and above the world, and which merely depicts states of affairs; rather, language is viewed as a practical medium through which individuals participate in the world. This new conception of language underpins many of the philosophical writings which have appeared in English during the last thirty years. Yet whatever the merits of this conception, its consequences for the philosophy of social science have not been wholly salutary. In the work of authors influenced by the later Wittgenstein, there is a persistent neglect of phenomena which lie beyond the linguistic realm and a pervasive tendency to treat language as the basic component of the social world. If positivistic accounts of social science have erred by giving insufficient attention to the role of language in social life, then their post-Wittgensteinian successors have been led astray by an over-emphasis on this role.

The Continental contributions which I examine are closely linked to particular conceptions of language. In this respect, the choice of the work of Ricoeur and Habermas as focal points for the study is not fortuitous. Unlike many of their predecessors, these authors have made a remark-able effort to bring the resources of their traditions to bear upon the phenomenon of language; and in so doing, they have encountered some of the recent results of Anglo-Saxon thought. However, neither Ricoeur nor Habermas has appropriated these results uncritically, and the accounts of language which they offer attest to the originality of their work. In the perspective elaborated by Ricoeur, language is conceived as a medium in which aspects of being are expressed and disclosed. The linguistic realm is therefore the first but not the final point of inquiry, for phenomenology must strive towards ontology through the interpretation of symbols and texts. In the writings of Habermas, language is regarded as one among several dimensions of social life, a dimension which may be deformed through the exercise of power. Accordingly, critical theory must seek to unveil the ideological distortions of everyday speech, con-trasting the latter with a presupposed ideal of communication free from constraint. Both Ricoeur and Habermas are thus concerned with the phenomenon of language; yet unlike many Anglo-Saxon authors, these Continental thinkers stress that language is neither the ultimate object of philosophical analysis nor the only modality of social life.

The convergence on the phenomenon of language provides a point of departure for the critical comparison of different traditions. In undertak-ing a comparative study, I hope to break down some of the barriers that continue to stand between diverse orientations and disciplines of thought. This does not mean that my aim is to produce a swift and facile synthesis: three cups of meaning, two spoons of interpretation and a pinch of power would indeed be a recipe for intellectual eclecticism. Moreover, in draw-ing together the work of Ricoeur and Habermas against the backcloth of ordinary language philosophy, I do not wish to denigrate the latter perspective and to treat it as a mere repository of Anglo-Saxon error. On the contrary, by adopting a comparative approach, I seek to show that each of the traditions offers valuable insights into a series of problems which are common to them all. These problems provide the criteria of selection for the expository sections of the study, as well as the basis for initiating a critical dialogue. Thus the critique which I develop is not purely 'immanent', in the sense of examining only the extent to which a tradition resolves the problems it has posed to itself; it is also 'comparative', in the sense of assessing the relative merits of the contributions offered by different traditions. So if I use ordinary language philosophy as a backcloth for this study, it is because I believe that shedding light on the limitations of this perspective will bring out the strength and relevance of hermeneutics and critical theory.

The problems which are common to the different traditions are centred on three principal themes. These themes pertain to the conceptualisation of action, the methodology of interpretation and the theory of reference and truth. I argue that while ordinary language philosophers have rightly stressed the meaningful and social character of human action, they have disregarded considerations such as power and repression, history and social change. The writings of Ricoeur and Habermas confront these and other issues more directly. For both authors seriously struggle with the question of the unconscious; and each makes some attempt to situate action within an historical and institutional context, even if in the end these attempts do not fully succeed. On the level of methodology, I endorse the Wittgensteinian emphasis on the problem of understanding, an emphasis which is shared by certain writers within the traditions of hermeneutics and critical theory. Yet the problem of understanding cannot be divorced from considerations of explanation and critique, as both Ricoeur and Habermas insist; and while I dispute the detail of the latter authors' views, I defend the general programme of depth interpretation which they espouse. Finally, on the epistemological plane, I maintain that the literature of ordinary language philosophy deals inadequately with various issues in the theory of reference and truth. I suggest that, although Ricoeur and Habermas do not resolve these issues, they nonetheless offer some intriguing ideas which are worthy of being pursued.

At the horizon of this comparative inquiry, there lies a constructive project. I call this project 'critical hermeneutics': the elaboration of a critical and rationally justified theory for the interpretation of human action. In this study, I do no more than sketch the barest outlines of this theory. After assessing the various contributions to the analysis of action, I try to develop an alternative account which relates action to the institutional and structural dimensions of the social world. The account forms a framework for reconsidering the questions of power, ideology and history. I then employ this framework to reformulate the methodological programme of depth interpretation. It is proposed that action may be interpreted by recourse to institutional and structural conditions, in such a way that understanding and explanation may be united with a moment of critique. I conclude by offering tentative solutions to some of the epistemological problems which are raised by this account. I indicate a few considerations which are relevant to the analysis of reference and objectivity; and I attempt to clarify the conditions under which a statement can be claimed to be true, in the hope that these conditions may provide a rational basis for a critical theory of interpretation. In every case my constructive remarks are of a programmatic character, forming nothing more than a rough guideline for further research.

The study is divided into two principal parts. The first part contains expositions of the three traditions with which I am concerned. Since the doctrines of ordinary language philosophy are familiar to many English-speaking students, the exposition of this tradition is brief. I sketch the genesis of Wittgenstein's later views and underline certain continuities with the ideas of Austin, Winch and others, with the aim of identifying some of the major contours of ordinary language philosophy. The two Continental traditions of thought are then presented. Since these traditions remain relatively unknown in the Anglo-Saxon world, I have considered it necessary to discuss their doctrines in greater detail. The second chapter opens with a short account of the origins of hermeneutic phenomenology, and then traces the evolution of Ricoeur's ideas from his early philosophy of the will to his recent theory of the text. In the third chapter, I offer an exposition of the writings of Habermas, placing his work within a tradition of thought that stems from Kant, Hegel and Marx. For the sake of brevity and clarity, the second and third chapters focus primarily on the writings of Ricoeur and Habermas. I point to some of the connections with the views of other authors in their respective traditions, but I do not pursue these connections in any depth. In all three chapters, considerable space is devoted to a discussion of the theory of language; and in the final sections of each chapter, I summarise the contributions of the relevant authors to the three themes mentioned above.

The second part of the study offers a critical and constructive analysis of the contributions presented in Part I. The fourth chapter examines the views of the authors concerned on the conceptualisation of human action. Most of the chapter is devoted to criticising these views, and I conclude by outlining an alternative approach to this theme. In the fifth chapter, the contributions to the methodology of social science are explored. At the end of the chapter, I introduce several concepts in an attempt to reformulate the programme of depth interpretation. The sixth chapter concentrates on certain questions of epistemology. I evaluate the views of ordinary language philosophers as well as those of Ricoeur and Habermas, and then offer some suggestions as to how the most pressing problems might be resolved. Each of the chapters in Part II is thus concerned with a particular set of problems which are common to the three traditions. This way of organising the study, whereby contributions presented in Part I are critically examined in Part II, runs the risk of repetition. I try to minimise this risk by a change of emphasis: in the final three chapters I pursue in depth certain issues which, in the first three, are merely situated within a broader theoretical context. I believe, moreover, that this mode of organisation has advantages which outweigh any such risks. For the reader unfamiliar with the traditions and thinkers concerned will find a systematic overview in Part I; while those well versed in this material may wish to proceed directly to the critical analyses of Part II. It is my hope that this study will thus be of interest and assistance to students of differing expertise and persuasion.

Part I

Thematic exposition

1. Ludwig Wittgenstein and ordinary language philosophy

Ordinary language philosophy may be regarded as the second stage in the development of the contemporary analytical school. The first stage in this development is represented by logical atomism and its positivistic offspring within the Vienna Circle; and it was through the critique of these early positions that the second stage emerged. The writings of Ludwig Wittgenstein figure prominently in both of these stages, as well as in the transitional phase between. Consequently, in the present chapter, I attempt to unfold the evolution of analytical philosophy by following the development of Wittgenstein's ideas. In adopting this approach, I seek neither to underrate the contributions of other analytical philosophers, nor to overrate the extent to which these philosophers agree among themselves. Rather, my aim is to facilitate the exposition of ordinary language philosophy by focusing the discussion around the writings of a single author. One consequence of this approach is that recent developments in analytical philosophy, such as those associated with the names of Quine and Davidson, will not be presented here; and although I shall refer to some of these developments in subsequent chapters, they will not form a focal point of this study.

I. Philosophical background

Logical atomism
The first stage of contemporary analytical philosophy comprises logical atomism and its audacious heir, logical positivism. The principal proponents of the former doctrine were Russell and the early Wittgenstein, who were among a handful of philosophers responsible for the downfall of British idealism. Russell's logical atomism may be viewed as an application of the apparatus developed in his mathematical investigations to the structure of language as a whole. For as he explains in 'The philosophy of logical atomism',

9

I shall try to set forth . . . a kind of logical doctrine which seems to me to result from the philosophy of mathematics . . . and on the basis of this a certain kind of metaphysic.[1]

Russell regards a proposition as a complex symbol which is capable of being true or false, and he calls that in the world which determines its truth or falsity a fact. Among the constituents of a proposition are simple symbols or names, and the meaning of such a name is the object to which it refers. However, it does not follow that all apparent names in the sentences of ordinary language are simple symbols in this sense. For the structure of ordinary language can be misleading, and it is one of the tasks of logical analysis to dispel such grammatical illusions. Russell's celebrated theory of descriptions is a paradigmatic execution of this task.[2] By means of this theory, descriptive phrases are shown to be incomplete symbols whose significance does not depend on any referent, and so the spurious ontological implications of ordinary language are defused. In this way, Russell pursues his methodological maxim that through the logical analysis of language one can disclose the 'ultimate simples, out of which the world is built'.[3]

The philosophy of the early Wittgenstein resembles in many respects the logical atomism of Russell. For both accounts incorporate the assumption that the logical analysis of language will reveal the atomic constituents of the world. However, Wittgenstein is not so concerned with the nature of these constituents and the limits of our knowledge of them, but rather with the nature and limits of language itself. Accordingly, the question which dominates the *Tractatus Logico-Philosophicus* is: what must language be for it to be capable of representing the world? The answer proposed in this epigrammatic text is that significant discourse is possible only insofar as language and the world possess the same logical form, that is, only insofar as the proposition is a logical picture of reality. For

in a proposition a situation is, as it were, constructed by way of experiment . . . One name stands for one thing, another for another thing, and they are combined with one another. In this way the whole group – like a tableau vivant – presents a state of affairs.[4]

The characterisation of the proposition as a logical picture of reality generates narrow limits to the realm of significant discourse. These limits are marked by tautologies at one extreme and contradictions at the other; and between these two extremes lie the genuine statements, all of which are truth-functions of elementary propositions. Since these propositions can only represent that which is part of reality, it follows that questions about ethics, value and the meaning of life fall outside the realm of significant discourse, as do the utterances of the *Tractatus* itself. So one must try to grasp what these utterances purport to say, and precisely in virtue of having done so, one will no longer continue trying to say such things. For in the end one will realise that 'whereof one cannot speak, thereof one must be silent'.[5]

Logical positivism

The logical atomism of Russell and Wittgenstein provided one of the philosophical foundations for the subsequent development of logical positivism. The latter movement was nurtured by the members of the Vienna Circle, and was dedicated to the twofold objective of unifying science and eliminating metaphysics. This objective was to be achieved through a synthesis of the analytical methods of Russell and Wittgenstein with the empiricist epistemology of Mach. Carnap's first major work, *The Logical Structure of the World*, is an epitome of this synthesis. For in this treatise, Carnap employs various techniques of symbolic logic in an attempt to show that scientific concepts can be reduced to, or reconstituted in terms of, the immediately given data of experience. In Carnap's view,

the main problem concerns the possibility of the rational reconstruction of the concepts of all fields of knowledge on the basis of concepts that refer to the immediately given.[6]

The rational reconstruction developed by Carnap is a sequential ordering of concepts in terms of their epistemic primacy; and the emphasis on epistemology leads him to designate the autopsychological domain as the basis of the constructional system. This designation is contested in the writings of other logical positivists, who regard its solipsistic overtones as a retreat into metaphysics. Thus, Neurath contends that the language of science is essentially intersubjective and physicalistic, a contention which Carnap was soon to accept. Neurath's standpoint firmly secures the possibility of the unification of science, and from this it follows that all attempts to distinguish sharply between natural and social sciences 'are, in the last analysis, *residues of theology*'.[7]

The views of the logical positivists burst upon the stage of English philosophy with the publication of A. J. Ayer's *Language, Truth and Logic*. In this brief but bold manifesto, Ayer concentrates on the principle of significance formulated by Carnap and attributed to Wittgenstein, which was employed by the positivists for the elimination of metaphysics.[8] In accordance with this principle, Ayer divides all genuine propositions into analytic and synthetic statements; and he asserts that a sentence which purports to express a synthetic statement is factually significant if and only if the utterer knows how to verify the statement in question. So if the putative proposition is such that no conceivable observation would affect its truth or falsity, and if it is not merely an analytic truth, then it follows from this principle that it is not a significant proposition at all. Hence,

no statement which refers to a 'reality' transcending the limits of all possible sense-experience can possibly have any literal significance; from which it must follow that the labours of those who have striven to describe such a reality have all been devoted to the production of nonsense.[9]

The task of philosophy by this account is not to formulate speculative truths or to search for first principles, but rather to engage in the meticulous clarification of linguistic expressions. This clarification is to be effected by the translation of sentences which contain a complex symbol x into sentences of symbols that are not synonymous with x, in which case x is said to be a logical construction of the latter. In this way, material objects can be analysed into logical constructions of sense-data, or political states into logical constructions of individuals;[10] and in general, philosophy as the reductive analysis of linguistic expressions can be consigned to a humble partnership with science in a world devoid of metaphysics.

II. Emergence of ordinary language philosophy

Critique of elementary propositions
Ordinary language philosophy emerged through a critique of some of the principles propounded by the logical atomists and positivists. Early indications of Wittgenstein's disquietude are evident in 'Some remarks on logical form',[11] an article which appeared in 1929. The article is concerned with the problem of how to analyse propositions which express different degrees of the same quality, for example, different shades of colour. Wittgenstein recognises that the Tractarian view, whereby the contradictory claim that 'A is red and A is blue' implies that the two conjuncts are not elementary propositions, fails to resolve the problem. So Wittgenstein suggests that elementary propositions can contain numbers, and hence that such statements can exclude one another. However innocent this solution may appear, it marks a considerable departure from the doctrine of the logical independence of elementary propositions espoused in the *Tractatus*. For on the revised account, to understand the

sense of a proposition which ascribes the degree of a quality, one must know not only what possible situations it represents, but also what situations it precludes; and one can understand what situations it precludes only if one understands its relation to other propositions ascribing different degrees of the same quality. As Wittgenstein observes in the *Philosophical Remarks*,

just as all the graduation marks are on *one* rod, the propositions corresponding to the graduation marks similarly belong together, and we can't measure with one of them without simultaneously measuring with all the others. – It isn't a proposition which I put against reality as a yardstick, it's a *system* of propositions.[12]

The literature of logical positivism abounds with similar reservations about the status of protocol sentences. It was the original opinion of Carnap and Schlick that these sentences constitute a special class of empirical statements whose validity is guaranteed by their simple reproduction of experience. In opposition to this view, Neurath maintains that protocol sentences always involve some degree of interpretation, and hence that they are just as corrigible as any other empirical statement. For Neurath, the ultimate acceptance of any sentence does not depend upon its agreement with experience, but upon its compatibility with the established system of empirical statements:

There is no way of taking conclusively established pure protocol sentences as the starting point of the sciences. No *tabula rasa* exists. We are like sailors who must rebuild their ship on the open sea, never able to dismantle it in dry-dock and to reconstruct it there out of the best materials.[13]

One consequence of such critiques is that the status of elementary propositions as the ultimate conveyors of significance, or as the absolute foundations of empirical knowledge, is radically undermined. For it is clear that in neither case can these statements be considered in complete isolation from the whole system of signs wherein they have meaning, and whereof our knowledge consists.

Reorientation of analysis

The critique of elementary propositions was closely connected with a more general reconsideration of the nature of philosophical analysis. For it was through the analysis of sentences into their constituent propositions that the determinacy of sense or the certitude of knowledge was to be secured. Wittgenstein's doubts about the notion of analysis surface in the *Philosophical Grammar*, where he acknowledges that

my notion in the *Tractatus Logico-Philosophicus* was wrong . . . because I too thought that logical analysis had to bring to light what was hidden (as chemical and physical analysis does).[14]

The Tractarian demand for determinacy engenders a conception of sense as something hidden, so that analysis assumes the form of a logical excavation. However, not only is it doubtful whether the products of this excavation could ever fulfil the original expectations, but the whole point of such an analysis is itself questionable. Thus, in the *Philosophical Investigations* Wittgenstein attacks the suggestion that the analysans of a sentence display a more complete and precise account of its sense. If instead of saying 'Bring me the broom' one were to say 'Bring me the broomstick and the brush which is fitted on to it', the addressee would probably appear puzzled; and while the latter sentence may achieve the same result as the former, it would do so only in a more obscure and roundabout way. So to say that the latter sentence is an 'analysed' form of the former, and to suggest that it alone shows what the former sentence means, is quite misleading. For as Wittgenstein insists, 'an aspect of the matter is lost on you in the *latter* case as well'.[15]

Scepticism concerning the merits of the early programme of analysis is evident in the writings of other philosophers. Ryle and Wisdom both express misgivings about the supposed achievements of reductive analysis;[16] and the legitimacy of the phenomenalistic translation of material object sentences is called into question by Austin and others.[17] The theory of descriptions itself, that paradigm of logical analysis, is submitted to critical examination.[18] The vexing question which lurks behind these reservations and rebukes is crystallised by Strawson in his contribution to *The Revolution in Philosophy*:

Why should it be supposed that the only way to gain understanding of the words which express the philosophically puzzling concepts was to translate sentences in which they occurred into sentences in which they did not occur?[19]

The recommendation made by Strawson, and earlier by Wittgenstein, Wisdom and others, is to replace the old programme of analysis by a detailed investigation into the ordinary use of linguistic expressions. For whatever the reductive analysis of sentences may have achieved, there is one thing that it did not: namely, the clarification of how those sentences are actually used in everyday discourse.

Attack on essence
A third theme that came under attack is centred upon the concept of essence. For implicit in the *Tractatus* and in many writings influenced by it

is the assumption that there must be a single characteristic which is definitive of all significant discourse; and the characteristic generally isolated by these works is that the proposition is a picture of reality, that is, a description of some possible state of affairs. However, it is clear that this demand for a single characteristic which is common to all significant synthetic statements is an a priori claim imposed upon the material from without. In contradistinction to this claim, the later Wittgenstein openly shuns the quest for essence:

Instead of producing something common to all that we call language, I am saying that these phenomena have no one thing in common which makes us use the same word for all, – but that they are *related* to one another in many different ways. And it is because of this relationship, or these relationships, that we call them all 'language'.[20]

Wittgenstein insists that one should not simply assume that there must be something common to all entities subsumed under a general term. Rather, one should look and see whether there is; and if one looks, for example, at board games, card games and so on, one finds nothing but a complicated network of similarities and relationships. Wittgenstein calls these similarities 'family resemblances', and he says that games have no essence but form a family instead. Of course, one can draw rigid boundaries around the concept if one so desires, but they would not correspond to the boundaries which it actually has. For the concept has no rigid boundaries, and it is a no less usable concept for all that.

The critique of essence is refracted throughout the writings of other analytical philosophers. Wisdom, for example, characterises the verification principle as just another piece of metaphysics;[21] and the principle is widely regarded in the literature as an excessively restrictive piece of a priori legislation. Austin too criticises the assumption that there must be something common to all objects called by a single name. For such an assumption embodies the view that every word is essentially a proper name which designates an object.

But why, if 'one identical' word is used, *must* there be 'one identical' object present which it denotes? Why should it not be the whole function of a word to denote many things? Why should words not be by nature 'general'?[22]

Austin suggests that there are many different reasons for calling things by the same name, and that it simply will not do to incorporate them into a general theory of universals. Instead, Austin urges his audience to study actual languages, not ideal ones; and thereby he concurs with Wittgenstein's descent from the slippery ice of essence to the friction of rough ground.

Critique of meaning

Finally, the conception of meaning which underpinned the early analytical philosophy was subjected to thorough critique. According to the *Tractatus*, an elementary proposition consists of a determinate configuration of simple symbols or names; a name stands for an object, and the object is its meaning. However, the later Wittgenstein recognises not only that this conception of meaning renders it difficult to understand how a language could ever be learned, but also that this conception fails to explain how a name could have meaning if its bearer ceased to exist. For suppose a person with the name 'N. N.' dies: the name 'N. N.' would then no longer stand for an existent object and so, by this conception, would have no meaning. Accordingly, the sentence 'N. N. is dead' would be senseless and would not even express the fact that N. N. was dead. Nor will it suffice in the face of such difficulties to maintain that 'N. N.' is a pseudo-name which will disappear on analysis, and that the Tractarian conception of meaning is applicable only to the genuine names which result from this analysis. For if the meanings of genuine names were identical with their bearers, then it would seem that 'meaning' and 'bearer' could be used interchangeably. Yet that is not the case: if an object called 'M. M.' moves from one place to another, then it is possible to say 'the bearer of the name "M. M." has moved', but one could not say 'the meaning of the object has moved'. Thus, as Wittgenstein concludes,

it is important to note that the word 'meaning' is being used illicitly if it is used to signify the thing that 'corresponds' to the word. That is to confound the meaning of a name with the *bearer* of the name.[23]

The attack on the denotative theory of meaning is sustained in the writings of various other philosophers. Austin's antipathy towards abstraction militates against any general identification of the meaning of a word with its bearer; and his condemnation of the 'descriptive fallacy' suggests that expressions need not report anything in order to secure their significance.[24] Similarly Strawson, in his examination of the theory of descriptions, isolates the erroneous identification of referring with meaning as the source of Russell's mistake.[25] Ryle also attacks the assimilation of the meanings of words to their alleged bearers, and captures concisely the alternative conception which supports this assault:

Meanings are not things, not even very queer things. Learning the meaning of an expression is more like learning a piece of drill than like coming across a previously unencountered object.[26]

Thus, from the collective critique of the doctrines espoused by the early analytical philosophers, there emerges an alternative theory of language; and it is the latter theory which forms the foundation for the development of ordinary language philosophy.

III. Exposition of the theory of language

Meaning and use
The theory of language which underlies ordinary language philosophy establishes a close connection between the meaning of an expression and its use. In the *Philosophical Investigations,* Wittgenstein formulates this connection by imagining that a tool is given the name 'N' and that this name is added to the simple language of a group of builders. Now suppose that the tool is broken, or that for some reason it completely disappears. Not knowing this, builder A gives builder B the sign 'N': what is B to do? So far the answer is not clear, but one can imagine a convention whereby B has to nod in reply if A gives the sign of a broken or missing tool. The name 'N' might then be said to have meaning even though its bearer has ceased to exist. Indeed, an entirely new sign could be given a place in the language in this way. Hence Wittgenstein infers that

for a *large* class of cases – though not for all – in which we employ the word 'meaning' it can be defined thus: the meaning of a word is its use in the language. And the *meaning* of a name is sometimes explained by pointing to its *bearer*.[27]

The last sentence suggests that while some words may signify in accordance with the demands of the Tractarian conception of meaning, it is inaccurate to say that all words signify in that way. For what an expression means depends upon how it is used in the language; and given the variety of ways in which expressions are used, to say simply that 'every word signifies something' is to say very little indeed. Moreover, this formal schema is misleading insofar as it implies that meaning is some sort of object, real or ideal, which is denoted by the word. To set forth in search of such an object is to chase a will-o'-the-wisp; and it is to avoid such ineffectual exercises that Wittgenstein urges philosophers to 'let the use of words teach you their meaning'.[28]

The assertion of a connection between the meaning of an expression and its use is commonplace among ordinary language philosophers. However, many of the latter have not accepted this connection uncritically, and some have attempted to render its nature more precise. Strawson distinguishes between an expression or a sentence on the one hand, and a use of an expression or a sentence on the other; and he maintains that to give the meaning of an expression or a sentence is to give 'general directions' for its use in referring to particular objects or in making particular assertions.[29] Ryle accepts that understanding a word or a phrase is knowing how to use it; but he is critical of the tendency to conflate 'use' and 'usage', and to conceive of the meaning of a sentence in the same way.[30] Similarly, one of the impulses behind the development of the theory of speech-acts is the necessity to distinguish between the various ways in which an expression can be 'used' on a particular occasion. For as Austin complains,

'use' is a hopelessly ambiguous or wide word, just as is the word 'meaning', which it has become customary to deride. But 'use', its supplanter, is not in much better case.[31]

So while the recognition of a connection between the meaning of an expression and its use is a view shared by most ordinary language philosophers, the precise nature and scope of this connection remain topics of perpetual debate.

Language-games and speech-acts

The critique of the concept of essence finds its positive correlate in the emphasis on the diversity of linguistic phenomena. In the philosophy of the later Wittgenstein, this emphasis is encapsulated in the concept of language-game. The concept of language-game may be construed in various ways, for Wittgenstein does not employ it univocally. When he introduces this concept in the *Blue Book*,[32] he speaks of language-games as primitive forms of language, wherein the ways of using signs are much simpler and easier to discern than those involved in everyday discourse. At other times, Wittgenstein regards specialised linguistic systems, or specific applicational contexts of ordinary language, as language-games in themselves. This indeterminacy in the concept of language-game is not, moreover, a mere vagary of Wittgenstein's work. For just as there are various kinds of games which have no single characteristic in common, so too there is no essence of language. Just as the significance of a piece of chess is determined by its role in the game, so too the meaning of an expression is dependent upon its use in the language-game wherein it occurs. Just as chess is played in accordance with the rules that define the game, so too the ways in which expressions are used are governed by constitutive conventions. Finally, just as a game is not a static and isolated structure but rather a process which is inseparable from human activity as a whole, so too 'the term "language-*game*" is meant to bring into prominence the fact that the *speaking* of language is part of an activity, or of a form of life'.[33]

The emphasis on the heterogeneous and dynamic aspects of language is equally evident in the writings of Austin and others. For Austin is highly critical of the traditional philosophical preoccupation with the descriptive function of language. In contrast to this concern, he focuses his attention on various expressions which share a peculiar characteristic: namely, that to utter them is to do something, and not merely to report or describe some state of affairs. For example, 'I do', uttered in the course of a marriage ceremony, is not reporting on the marriage but participating in it. Austin introduces the concept of speech-act to isolate this characteristic; and in *How to do Things with Words* he proceeds to analyse this concept into its three constituent parts. Thus, the locutionary act is the act *of* saying something, the illocutionary act is the act performed *in* saying something, and the perlocutionary act is the act performed *by* saying something. Austin concludes by generalising this scheme into a comprehensive theory of speech-acts. For stating, describing and so on do not fall within the exclusive domain of traditional grammar, but are merely further examples of everyday speech-acts. As Searle submits,

the unit of linguistic communication is not, as has generally been supposed, the symbol, word or sentence, . . . but rather the production or issuance of the symbol or word or sentence in the performance of the speech act.[34]

So although the Austinian aspiration for a comprehensive theory of language is a goal disavowed by Wittgenstein, the notion of speech-act coincides with the concept of language-game in its emphasis on the multiplicity of activities that language is used to perform.

Rules and conventions

In contrast to the early analytical view that the significance of a proposition is dependent upon its logical form alone, most ordinary language philosophers regard the utterance of a meaningful expression as a conventional or rule-governed activity. Accordingly, the concept of rule plays a central part in the later philosophy of Wittgenstein, wherein it is elucidated through the analogy with games. A rule in chess, for example, might be expressed in the claim that 'a bishop can only move diagonally'; and if someone were to observe that chess was invented in a certain year, or that it requires many hours of practice to learn, such historical and empirical observations would not belong to the list of rules which characterise this game. Similarly, in the language-game played with words of colour, a rule is expressed neither by discussing diachronic variations nor by ascertaining electromagnetic frequencies, but simply by pointing to an object and saying 'this colour is called "red"'. The rule thus expressed specifies the role of 'red' in the language-game of colour and thereby defines the meaning of that word. Of course, it does not follow that every application of a word is predetermined by rules, any more than each move in a game of chess is settled in advance. In Wittgenstein's analogical terms,

a rule stands there like a sign-post. – Does the sign-post leave no doubt open about the way I have to go? Does it show which direction I am to take when I have passed it; whether along the road or the footpath or cross-country? . . . The sign-post is in order – if, under normal circumstances, it fulfils its purpose.[35]

Moreover, just as a sign is capable of showing the way only insofar as there is a general agreement about which way an arrow points, so too a rule exists only when a certain consensus prevails. Consequently, the suggestion that one could obey a rule privately, or that there could be a language which only one person could understand, is a suggestion that is fundamentally without sense.

The concept of rule or convention occupies an equally central position in the writings of philosophers concerned with the theory of speech-acts. Austin specifies two sets of conventions that are required for the performance of a locutionary act, which he sometimes calls conventions of sense and conventions of reference.[36] Similarly Searle, although critical of many of Austin's distinctions, sustains the thesis that speaking a language is performing acts in accordance with rules:

the semantic structure of a language may be regarded as a conventional realization of a series of sets of underlying constitutive rules, and . . . speech acts are acts characteristically performed by uttering expressions in accordance with these sets of constitutive rules.[37]

Austin also invokes the concept of convention in an attempt to maintain the distinction between illocutionary and perlocutionary acts. For he allows that both kinds of acts are concerned with the production of effects, but suggests that perlocutionary acts achieve their response by non-conventional means whereas illocutionary acts are entirely conventional.[38] The inadequacy of this suggestion is revealed by Strawson, who argues that it must be supplemented by an account of intention adapted from Grice.[39] Whatever the merits of Strawson's recommendation, and however much it may diverge from the views of Wittgenstein, it nevertheless accords with the latter in its acknowledgement of the indispensable role of social convention.

Criteria and evidence

The concept of criterion is commonly employed to articulate the relation between the meaning of an expression and the rules for its use. In the *Blue Book*, Wittgenstein says that to explain the meaning of a word is to elucidate the rules for its use, and one way of effecting this elucidation is to clarify the criteria which justify the application of that word. Wittgenstein distinguishes such criteria from the symptoms of a phenomenon, for the latter are discovered in experience and justified by appeal to empirical evidence, whereas the former belong to the grammar of language and rest solely upon convention. So to say, for example, that 'he is groaning and clasping his jaw' (x) is a criterion for 'he has a toothache' (y) is not to say that whenever x was true in the past, y was also found to be true; rather, it is to say that it is part of the meaning of y that the truth of x is non-inductive, conventionally fixed evidence for the truth of y.[40] This does not imply, however, that the truth of x entails the truth of y, for any one criterion is ultimately defeasible. Nor does it imply that what counts as a criterion in any particular case is fixed for all time. For the criteria employed in a given language-game are tailored to certain conditions of normality,

and if things were quite different from what they actually are – if there were for instance no characteristic expression of pain, of fear, of joy; if rule became exception and exception rule; or if both became phenomena of roughly equal frequency – this would make our normal language-games lose their point.[41]

The concept of criterion appears in the writings of other philosophers concerned with the characteristics of ordinary language. Although Austin does not discuss this concept directly, he does observe that being angry is connected 'in an intimate way' with the whole pattern of events including circumstances, expressions and feelings.[42] In a more rigorous manner, Strawson distinguishes between M-predicates, which are applied to material bodies in general, and P-predicates, which are applied only to persons; and he maintains that it is a necessary condition of one's ascribing P-predicates to oneself that one should be able to ascribe them to others. From this it is claimed to follow that there would be no sense in talking of individuals of a type that possessed both M- and P-predicates unless there were in principle some way of telling whether an individual of that type possessed a P-predicate. So

in the case of at least some P-predicates, the ways of telling must constitute in some sense logically adequate kinds of criteria for the ascription of the P-predicate.[43]

For if this were not the case, then one could not ascribe such predicates to others, and so could not ascribe them to oneself. Strawson thereby concurs with Wittgenstein's refutation of traditional forms of scepticism through an appeal to the conditions of significant discourse.

Philosophy and metaphysics

The second stage in the development of the contemporary analytical approach is characterised by a conception of philosophy, not as the reductive analysis of linguistic expressions, but as the clarification of the ways in which words are commonly used. In the writings of Wittgenstein, the necessity for such clarification arises from the fact that when speakers follow the rules of their language-games, things do not always turn out as they may have expected. Speakers become entangled in their own grammatical conventions and this entanglement is the principal source of philosophical problems. For example, the puzzlement surrounding the metaphysical claim that 'only my sensations are real' is rooted in the failure to notice that these words are not being used in their customary ways. The metaphysician has not discovered by the common criteria that someone who said 'I feel pain' was cheating; for indeed, the metaphysician is not construing this expression in accordance with these criteria. It is the task of philosophy to make such discrepancies explicit, and thereby to resolve philosophical problems through a 'perspicuous representation' of the grammar of ordinary language. The execution of this task does not require the provision of additional factual data, or the explanation of that data already at hand. On the contrary,

philosophy simply puts everything before us, and neither explains nor deduces anything. – Since everything lies open to view there is nothing to explain. For what is hidden, for example, is of no interest to us.[44]

Wittgenstein allows that language could be reformed for particular purposes, and that terminology could be improved to prevent misunderstandings in everyday life. However, such improvements are technical matters which fall outside the legitimate domain of philosophy. For as Wittgenstein insists, 'philosophy may in no way interfere with the actual use of language; it can in the end only describe it'.[45]

Wittgenstein's emphasis on the passive role of philosophy is shared in varying degrees by other ordinary language philosophers. Austin claims that while ordinary language must be the first word, it need not be the last: 'in principle it can everywhere be supplemented and improved upon'.[46] Similarly, Strawson acknowledges the legitimacy of a revisionary as well as a purely descriptive metaphysics, even though he insists that the development of the latter is prior to and possible without the revelations of the former.

For there is a massive central core of human thinking which has no history – or none recorded in histories of thought; there are categories and concepts which, in their most fundamental character, change not at all.[47]

So while these philosophers differ in the extent to which they allow the emendation of ordinary language to be a legitimate and worthwhile task, they generally agree in maintaining that such a task is but a subsidiary and parasitical pursuit.

IV. Problems in the theory of reference and truth

Grammar and ontology

The theory of language underlying ordinary language philosophy offers solutions to a series of problems in the theory of reference and truth. The solutions are based upon a general account of the relation between language and reality; and in the writings of Wittgenstein, this account is expressed in theses concerning the autonomy of grammar and the constitution of objects. The former thesis is adumbrated in the *Philosophical Grammar*, where Wittgenstein maintains that grammatical rules are not dependent upon some extra-linguistic entity:

Grammar is not accountable to any reality. It is grammatical rules that determine meaning (constitute it) and so they themselves are not answerable to any meaning and to that extent are arbitrary.[48]

The rules of grammar are arbitrary in a sense in which the rules of cookery are not: the latter can be assessed as correct or incorrect in terms of the results which they produce, whereas if one follows different grammatical rules then one is simply playing another game. Moreover, the rules of grammar cannot be justified by an appeal to 'what is really there'; for any such appeal would have to be formulated in a grammatical way, and so would presuppose the very rules which it sought to justify. However, it does not follow from this that any rules whatsoever will suffice, since a correspondence obtains between the concepts people employ and certain 'very general facts of nature'. Nor does it follow that in philosophical discourse one is forever talking merely about words. For the world is articulated only within particular language-games, and so the rules which govern the use of an expression also constitute a specific organisation of phenomena. Consequently, a clarification of the rules of grammar is simultaneously a revelation of the structure of reality; or as Wittgenstein cryptically contends, 'grammar tells us what kind of object anything is'.[49]

Similar views concerning the relation between language and reality are evident in the writings of other philosophers. In *Sense and Sensibilia*, Austin proposes to examine the use of the word 'real' and thereby to explore 'the Nature of Reality'.[50] For as he submits elsewhere,

when we examine what we should say when, what words we should use in what situations, we are looking again not *merely* at words . . . but also at the realities we use the words to talk about.[51]

Strawson begins his essay on descriptive metaphysics with the suggestion that remarks about the way people think of the world, or concerning their conceptual scheme, are also remarks about what their ontology comprises.[52] In a more Wittgensteinian vein, Winch argues that Evans-Pritchard's attempt to distinguish scientific discourse from other types in terms of its agreement with objective reality is quite confused, for what counts as real and unreal is determined only within these various discourses.[53] Thus, in general, ordinary language philosophy can be associated with the view that the structure of reality is a projection of the grammar of language, so that an investigation into how words are used is at the same time an inquiry into what there is.

Reference and description

The general account of the relation between language and reality is complemented in the writings of ordinary language philosophers by a specific theory of reference. In his contributions to this theory, Wittgenstein observes that the rules which govern the application of expressions used to refer to particular objects or persons are neither comprehensive nor crystal clear. So if someone says 'Moses did not exist', this may mean that the Israelites did not have a single leader, or that their leader was not called 'Moses', or any number of other possibilities. For the name 'Moses' can be defined by means of various descriptions; and when some speaker S makes a statement about Moses, S need not be prepared to substitute any one of these descriptions for that name. Rather, S may have a whole series of descriptions in readiness, and some of them may fail to characterise the object in question without thereby resulting in a failure of reference.

And this can be expressed like this: I use the name 'N' without a *fixed* meaning. (But that detracts as little from its usefulness, as it detracts from that of a table that it stands on four legs instead of three and so sometimes wobbles.)[54]

However, to say that some expressions are commonly used to refer in this way is not to say that all expressions are so used. For language functions in many different ways, and not simply in accordance with the model of object and designation. Only by recognising the limited applicability of this model can one dispel the clouds of confusion surrounding concepts such as pain and joy, and thereby 'shew the fly the way out of the fly-bottle'.[55]

The suggestion that a referring expression is tied to a cluster of descriptions which characterise the object referred to is a view espoused by several other philosophers. Strawson distinguishes between an expression which is commonly used to refer to some object or person, and a particular use of such an expression; and he maintains that it is not the expression as such which refers, but that it is used on a particular occasion to refer. If the occasion is one in which the object is not sensibly present, then one may use a description or a name to refer to that object. However, in Strawson's opinion,

it is no good using a name for a particular unless one knows who or what is referred to by the use of the name. A name is worthless without a backing of descriptions which can be produced on demand to explain its application.[56]

Similarly, Searle construes reference as the performance of a speech-act; and he submits the following principle as one of the necessary conditions for successful performance: 'either the expression must be an identifying description or the speaker must be able to produce an identifying description on demand'.[57] According to Searle, even the utterance of a proper name satisfies this principle of identification. For although the referring use of such a name does not entail any specific set of descriptions, it does presuppose that the object which it is used to refer to has some describable characteristics. Insofar, then, as referring is regarded as an activity dependent upon the applicability of an indeterminate range of identifying descriptions, the problem of reference elicits some consensus among philosophers of ordinary language.

Truth and rationality
The theory of language elaborated by ordinary language philosophers can be linked to a particular treatment of truth and rationality. In *On Certainty*, Wittgenstein regards the traditional notion that a proposition is

true if and only if it agrees with the facts as an uninformative and misleading view. For just as there are many ways in which expressions may be used, so there are many grounds upon which one may decide in favour of propositions. Further, just as expressions are used only within particular language-games, so the provision of grounds is possible only within particular systems of belief. The framework of such a system is constituted by a class of statements which function like the rules of a game: although empirical in form, they are isolated from every doubt and serve as the very foundations of empirical inquiry. Yet the boundaries of this class are not rigidly fixed for all time:

> The mythology may change back into a state of flux, the river-bed of thoughts may shift. But I distinguish between the movement of the waters on the river-bed and the shift of the bed itself; though there is not a sharp division of the one from the other.[58]

When confronting a civilisation of people who do not share the basic beliefs of one's own mythology, one might be tempted to call them primitive or heretical and to say that they were foolish to believe what they do. However, one could not prove that their views were wrong, for whatever reasons one could offer might not be accepted as reasons by them. Still, if one were persistent, one might eventually be able to convert them to another point of view; and nothing more than conversion could it be, for 'at the end of reasons comes *persuasion*'.[59]

Comparable views on truth and rationality can be found elsewhere in the contemporary literature. In his critique of Austin's correspondence theory of truth, Strawson attacks the way in which the correspondence between statement and fact is characterised as a relation. Such an account fails to recognise that the word 'fact', like 'true', is inseparable from 'that-' clauses:

> Facts are what statements (when true) state; they are not what statements are about. They are not, like things or happenings on the face of the globe, witnessed or heard or seen.[60]

Strawson argues that the expression 'that's true', like 'yes' or 'it is indeed', is merely an abbreviatory device for conveying one's agreement or endorsement of the statement made, and it is not some further assertion about that statement. Hare and other moral philosophers offer a similar analysis of evaluative language, suggesting that an essential part of the meaning of words like 'good' is expressed in their capacity to commend an object for possessing the properties it does.[61] Yet one consequence of the latter suggestion is that the assertion of value judgements involves the invocation of synthetic moral standards which lie beyond the realm of rational justification. Thus, just as Strawson's attack on the correspondence theory of truth resembles Wittgenstein's critique of the traditional view, so too the Harean analysis of evaluative language reproduces a Wittgensteinian paralysis of rational argumentation.

V. Problems in the analysis of action

Voluntary action

The analysis of concepts pertaining to human action is a common preoccupation among ordinary language philosophers. One such concept is that of volition; and in the writings of Wittgenstein, the problem of voluntary action is raised by this provocative question:

> Let us not forget this: when 'I raise my arm', my arm goes up. And the problem arises: what is left over if I subtract the fact that my arm goes up from the fact that I raise my arm?[62]

It is a traditional temptation to reply to such a question by appealing to an act of volition, which supposedly serves as the inner source of all voluntary action. Yet in Wittgenstein's view, this temptation is just another manifestation of the illusion that all words function in accordance with the model of object and designation. Those who succumb to this temptation assume that the expressions with which we characterise human action refer to some act or process in the hidden recesses of the mind, and this assumption blinds them to the surrounding circumstances in which these expressions are actually used. To borrow two examples from the *Brown Book*, suppose that one is lying in bed in the morning, postponing the inevitable moment of exertion, and then one finds oneself getting up. Alternatively, imagine that one is standing near a wall, pressing the back of one's hand against the surface, and then one steps away and finds one's arm rising. In the first case, the act would be commonly described as voluntary, and in the second case as involuntary. There are, of course, many differences between the two examples, such as the complete absence of surprise in the former case. However, as Wittgenstein repeatedly asserts, there is no single characteristic which distinguishes voluntary from involuntary acts as such; and only when one accepts this assertion can one be cured of that 'general disease of thinking which always looks for (and finds) what would be called a mental state from which all our acts spring as from a reservoir'.[63]

The rejection of an internalist interpretation of voluntary action is evident in the writings of other philosophers. Following faithfully in the footsteps of Wittgenstein, Melden observes that any act of volition would itself be an act, and hence subject to the very same problems of analysis which it was invoked to resolve.[64] Ryle proffers a similar argument in defence of his claim that the doctrine of volitions is yet another variation of the myth of the ghost in the machine.[65] However, these writers are careful to point out that the extirpation of this doctrine does not render the epithets 'voluntary' and 'involuntary' inapplicable. For as Ryle remarks, these epithets do have a use in everyday life, namely

as adjectives applying to actions which ought not to be done. We discuss whether someone's action was voluntary or not only when the action seems to have been his fault.[66]

In accordance with this everyday use, Austin proposes to approach the study of voluntary action through an inquiry into the ways in which acts break down, and the ways in which such breakdowns are commonly excused.[67] So for Wittgenstein, Austin, Ryle and others, the problem of voluntary action is not to be resolved through the introspective elucidation of some inner act of volition, but rather by studying the concrete circumstances in which the relevant expressions are ordinarily employed.

Intentional action

The concept of intention is submitted to a similar analysis in the writings of ordinary language philosophers. Wittgenstein argues that this concept does not stand for an ephemeral experience of 'tending', any more than the notion of volition refers to some nebulous non-causal 'bringing about'. So if one were to say 'for a moment I was going to deceive him', the intention would not consist in any specific sensation that may have occurred, nor in any particular process that may have transpired. Rather, the intention would lie in the whole series of circumstances which preceded and accompanied the utterance of that expression. So if one were then to become ashamed of this incident, one would become ashamed of its entire history and not simply of some individual accompaniment. Moreover, it will not suffice to suggest that the sensation wherein intention allegedly consists is simply elusive and hard to grasp, as if one only needed to alter the adjustment of the philosophical microscope. For 'suppose', Wittgenstein retorts,

that (with a particular adjustment of the lenses) I did remember a *single* sensation; how have I the right to say that it is what I call the 'intention'? It might be that (for example) a particular tickle accompanied every one of my intentions.[68]

Wittgenstein concludes that it is nonsensical to say such things as 'I alone can know what I intend.' For what one intends lies also in what one does and in the surrounding circumstances of one's action, and not simply in some internal phenomenon accessible only to oneself.

Several other authors have contributed to the analysis of the concept of intention. Austin seeks to illuminate problems of freedom and responsibility by imagining everyday examples in which we distinguish between acting intentionally, acting deliberately and acting on purpose.[69] In a more sustained discussion, Anscombe characterises intentional actions as those to which a certain sense of the question 'why?' is applicable; and she proceeds to elucidate this sense by considering cases in which the question does not apply. For example, the question is refused application by the answer 'I was not aware I was doing that', or by 'I knew I was doing that, but only because I observed it.' Moreover, since one's knowledge of what one is doing depends upon how the action is described, it follows that an action may be intentional under one description and unintentional under another. For as Anscombe insists,

the only events to consider are intentional actions themselves, and to call an action intentional is to say it is intentional under some description that we give (or could give) of it.[70]

Thus, according to Anscombe, the intentionality of an action is dependent upon its description; and so the occurrence of some internal performance is relevant to that intentionality only insofar as it affects the way in which that action may be described.

Meaningful action

The interconnections of language, action and surrounding circumstances may be highlighted by raising the problem of meaningful action within the context of ordinary language philosophy. Although Wittgenstein does not confront this problem directly, one may speculate about what his solution would be. For just as with the meaning of an expression, so with the meaning of an action: there is no single, simple phenomenon, and consequently no mental process or experience, wherein this meaning consists. 'Nothing', Wittgenstein reproves, 'is more wrong-headed than calling meaning a mental activity!'[71] Rather, whether an action is meaningful or not, and what its meaning is, depends upon its role within particular language-games. In *Zettel*,[72] Wittgenstein suggests that in some cases an action may function as a conventional device which supplements or replaces a verbal expression, as the wave of a hand may be substituted for the utterance of 'good-bye'. In other cases, however, an action is not so far a move in the language-game, but only the criterion of such a move. Thus, the behaviour of a person pacing back and forth across the room, occasionally checking the time and peering out the window, may be called meaningful action insofar as it is describable as an instance of 'expecting someone to come'. In neither case does the significance of the action in question depend upon the occurrence of some mysterious mental event, but rather upon the surrounding circumstances in which that action is performed. As Wittgenstein observes,

a coronation is the picture of pomp and dignity. Cut one minute of this proceeding out of its surroundings: the crown is being placed on the head of the king in his coronation robes. – But in different surroundings gold is the cheapest of metals, its gleam is thought vulgar. There the fabric of the robe is cheap to produce. A crown is a parody of a respectable hat. And so on.[73]

The conventional character of meaningful action is emphasised in the writings of several philosophers influenced by Wittgenstein. Peters identifies the rule-following purposive pattern of behaviour as the paradigm of human action, and claims that 'man in society is a chess-player writ large'.[74] Melden draws attention to the role of convention in the designation of a bodily movement as, for example, an act of signalling.[75] More generally, Winch maintains that the distinctive characteristic of human action is that it commits the agent to behaving in one way rather than another in the future; and he claims that one can be committed in this way only if one's present act is the application of a rule. Consequently,

the analysis of meaningful behaviour must allot a central role to the notion of a rule; . . . all behaviour which is meaningful (therefore all specifically human behaviour) is *ipso facto* rule-governed.[76]

Thus the notion of rule-governed behaviour, which is implicit in the writings of Wittgenstein, is presented by Winch and others as the defining criterion of meaningful action.

VI. Problems in the methodology of social science

Understanding

The work of ordinary language philosophers generates a distinctive approach to various problems in the methodology of social science. One such problem is centred upon the concept of understanding or *verstehen*, a concept which featured prominently in the methodological disputes of late nineteenth-century Germany.[77] These disputes left the concept of *verstehen* tinged with the spirit of Romanticism, and as such it was quickly cast into disrepute by the empiricist fervour of logical positivism. With the work of the later Wittgenstein, however, a foundation is provided for the philosophical resurrection of this notion. For just as 'meaning' does not refer to some mysterious process buried within the mind, so too 'understanding' does not stand for the empathic excavation of such a process. Rather, the grammar of the word 'understand' is related to that of 'can', 'is able to', 'know'; and in many cases, 'understanding an expression' means 'knowing how it is used' or 'being able to apply it'. Hence Wittgenstein exhorts:

> Try not to think of understanding as a 'mental process' at all. – For *that* is the expression which confuses you. But ask yourself: in what sort of case, in what kind of circumstances, do we say, 'now I know how to go on'?[78]

So one criterion of understanding an expression or an action is whether one can demonstrate its function in the language-game of which it is part; and if that language-game is played by a people very different from one's own, its constituent expressions or actions can be understood only insofar as one can elucidate their role in the life of that people as a whole. In his 'Remarks on Frazer's *Golden Bough*',[79] Wittgenstein suggests that the possibility of such an elucidation is secured by the universal centrality of phenomena like birth, death and sexual life, a suggestion later encapsulated in his occasional allusions to 'the common behaviour of mankind'.[80]

The implications of Wittgenstein's analysis of understanding for the methodology of social science are elaborated by Winch. The latter's identification of meaningful action with rule-governed behaviour implies that to understand what someone is doing is to grasp the rule which is being followed. Winch furthermore points out that the criteria by which various events are judged to be the same are relative to some rule, and so any discipline which purports to provide statements of regularities presupposes rules in accordance with which judgements of identity are made. In the case of the sociological investigation of a specific human activity, the rules which specify the criteria of identity are the very rules which govern that activity itself. So the sociologist

> has to take seriously the criteria which are applied for distinguishing 'different' kinds of actions and identifying the 'same' kinds of actions within the way of life he is studying. It is not open to him arbitrarily to impose his own standards from without.[81]

Winch concedes that this requirement does not prevent the sociologist from introducing technical notions to facilitate a study; but he insists that such notions imply a prior understanding of, and hence remain 'logically tied' to, the concepts which belong to the activity under investigation. If that activity is part of a way of life quite foreign to the sociologist, Winch too suggests that the sociologist might dispel the perplexity by appealing to certain fundamental notions which 'the very conception of human life involves'.[82] For although the particular institutions in which these notions are embedded may vary from one society to the next, their centrality within the organisation of any society will forever remain the same.

Explanation

A closely related problem in the methodology of social science is concerned with the concept of explanation. Various attempts have been made to link this concept to the notion of understanding; but the uneasy syntheses proposed by Max Weber and others soon succumbed to a positivistic emphasis on explanation at the expense of any reference to understanding. The philosophy of the later Wittgenstein tends to reverse this trend, insofar as it disputes the relevance of explanation for the understanding of human phenomena. In the *Blue Book*, Wittgenstein distinguishes between two senses of the question 'why?': it may be used to ask for a reason or for a cause. To offer a reason for something one said or did is to appeal to some accepted rule that shows a way which leads to that action; a rule, in other words, which justifies the utterance of that expression or the performance of that action. To provide a cause, on the other hand, is to adduce a statistical regularity, or to trace a mechanism, or to sketch an historical genesis. In no case, however, would the provision of such a cause further elucidate the significance of what is said or done, any more than it would clarify the meaning of what is believed:

The causes of our belief in a proposition are indeed irrelevant to the question of what we believe. Not so the grounds, which are grammatically related to the proposition, and tell us what proposition it is.[83]

So while Wittgenstein does not deny that the causes of a particular phenomenon may be interesting for some purposes, he does contend that the causal explanation of that phenomenon in no way contributes to the comprehension of its sense.

The antithesis between reason and cause, or between understanding and explanation, pervades the literature of post-Wittgensteinian philosophy. Peters maintains that a sufficient explanation of human action, as opposed to mere bodily movement, can only be given in terms of the rule-following purposive model and not in causal terms; for there is, he claims, 'a logical gulf between nature and convention'.[84] Similarly, Melden argues that insofar as 'cause' is being used in a Humean sense, causal explanation is irrelevant to everyday accounts of human action. For when we offer such accounts, we provide motives or reasons for doing the action; and since the description of a motive necessarily refers to the action which it is a motive for, it cannot be a Humean cause of that action.[85] Winch also observes that relations between ideas are 'internal relations'; and since social relations between individuals exist only in and through their ideas, social relations are just another species of internal relations. 'It follows', Winch infers,

that social relations must be an equally unsuitable subject for generalizations and theories of the scientific sort to be formulated about them. Historical explanation is not the application of generalizations and theories to particular instances: it is the tracing of internal relations.[86]

For Winch, an appeal to statistical regularities concerning the occurrence of an action is quite irrelevant to the understanding of that action, just as a formulation of probabilistic laws about the appearance of an expression in no way facilitates its comprehension. What is required in both cases is a fuller grasp of the rules which govern the performance of the action and the utterance of the expression, not the invocation of some account which is completely different in kind.

Role of critique

Finally, the problem may be posed concerning the extent to which a social science informed by the writings of ordinary language philosophers could incorporate an element of critique. There are passages in which Wittgenstein clearly displays a critical concern, for example his remark that 'in psychology there are experimental methods and *conceptual confusion*'.[87] Yet such passages seem to restrict the role of critique to the censorship of philosophers, social scientists and others for misrepresenting their subject matter. Thus Wittgenstein reproaches philosophers for imposing preconceived demands upon language, or for abstracting words from the everyday language-games in which they are used. Similarly, Wittgenstein criticises Freud for his aspiration to uncover the essence of dreams, and for the distortions engendered by his attempt to explain oneiric symbols in sexual terms:

Freud called [a] dream 'beautiful', putting 'beautiful' in inverted commas. But *wasn't* the dream beautiful? I would say to the patient: 'Do these associations make the dream not beautiful? It was beautiful. (This is what is called beautiful.) Why shouldn't it be?' I would say Freud had cheated the patient.[88]

Fraser too is reproved for explaining ritual practices as primitive and mistaken stages in the historical progress towards a scientific world outlook. Insofar, then, as one distorts or mishandles the subject matter in question, one is liable to the strictures of a Wittgensteinian critique. Beyond this, however, the critical function of a social science inspired by Wittgenstein would seem to be of little avail; for as regards the subject matter itself, Wittgenstein insists that his approach 'leaves everything as it is'.[89]

In the writings of some of his successors, the critical element of Wittgenstein's work is transformed into an attack on the pretensions of social science to exceed the explanatory adequacy of philosophy and common sense. In Peters's account, this attack is crystallised in the claim that a sufficient explanation of human action can only be given in terms of the rule-following purposive model, so that any theory couched in alternative terms *ipso facto* cannot explain an action.[90] Winch maintains that since social relations are internal relations constituted by ideas, and since the clarification of ideas is a conceptual task, it follows that 'any worthwhile study of society must be philosophical in character'.[91] Whereas Winch thereby subsumes social sciences under the custodial canopy of philosophy, Louch relegates it to the realm of ethics; and while Louch is critical of Winch's a priorism, he is contemptuous of social scientists' attempts to offer anything other than *ad hoc* moral explanations of human action. Moreover, Louch suggests that insofar as one recognises the sole legitimacy of the latter, one

must also see that the government and law of . . . society requires the flexibility of judgment and attention to unique needs of particular situations. It cannot rest on a monolithic conception of the state served by scientific experts.[92]

Thus, the theory of language elaborated by Wittgenstein and others is employed in the writings of authors indebted to them, both as a philosophical foundation for a critique of the social sciences, and as a philosophical weapon for an attack on the totalitarian state.

In conclusion, it might be helpful to summarise the central themes of this chapter. Ordinary language philosophy may be regarded as the second stage in the development of the contemporary analytical school, and its emergence may be traced through a rejection of various doctrines espoused by the earlier phase. Accordingly, the later Wittgenstein, Austin and others no longer attempt to analyse the structure of language as a potential system of representation, but rather focus on the ways in which expressions are actually used in everyday life. The theory of language that underlies this reorientation has implications for a wide range of philosophical problems. Doubt is cast upon the model of object and designation which dominated the theory of reference, as well as on the widely held correspondence theory of truth. The traditional obsession with mental acts and processes is exorcised from the theory of action, and attention is redirected towards the concrete circumstances in which human actions are performed and described. Similarly, the problems of understanding, explanation and critique in the methodology of social science receive fresh illumination. It must be emphasised, however, that these various implications are not accepted by all of the writers who have been influenced by Wittgenstein, Austin and others, and the literature abounds with endogenous critiques. Nevertheless, it has been the object of this chapter to demonstrate that sufficient consensus prevails within the limits of ordinary language philosophy to permit a systematic exposition of some of its central themes.

2. Paul Ricoeur and hermeneutic phenomenology

Hermeneutic phenomenology may be regarded as a philosophical tradition created by the synthesis of two Continental orientations. One of these orientations, that of hermeneutics, has a long and distinguished history which includes the work of authors such as Schleiermacher and Dilthey. The other orientation, that of phenomenology, stems largely from the investigations of Husserl, who clothed its contents in a transcendental guise. The key figures in the synthesis of these orientations are Martin Heidegger and Hans-Georg Gadamer. In recent years, an outstanding contribution to this tradition has been made by Paul Ricoeur. However, the nature of Ricoeur's contribution can be fully appreciated only if it is placed within the wider context of his voluminous work. My aim in this chapter, therefore, is to present some key ideas of hermeneutic phenomenology by tracing the evolution of the philosophy of Ricoeur. This approach necessarily underplays the contributions of other authors within this tradition, as well as those writings of Ricoeur which are not immediately relevant to the topic concerned. Nevertheless, and in spite of these limitations, I assume that a short and selective exposition of Ricoeur's philosophy will provide a clear and coherent image of hermeneutic phenomenology.

I. Philosophical background

Hermeneutics

Hermeneutics is a discipline that has been primarily concerned with the elucidation of rules for the interpretation of texts. The development of this discipline may be traced from the Homeric disputes of the Greek Enlightenment, through the struggle between rival theological schools in the first century A.D., to the biblical controversies of the Reformation.[1] However, it was not until the eighteenth century that the foundations were laid for the theoretical unification of these discrete historical developments. The principal proponent of this unification was the German

36

theologian Schleiermacher, who approached the art of interpretation in the general spirit of Kantian philosophy. Thus Schleiermacher sought to reach behind the various interpretative activities and to uncover the primordial act of understanding which renders these activities possible. This act of understanding is the inverse of the process whereby the expression to be understood is produced; and

just as every speech has a twofold relationship, both to the whole of the language and to the collected thinking of the speaker, so also there exists in all understanding of the speech two moments: understanding it as something drawn out of language and as a 'fact' in the thinking of the speaker.[2]

In accordance with these two moments of understanding, Schleiermacher establishes two dimensions of interpretation. Grammatical interpretation corresponds to the linguistic aspect of understanding; this dimension is tied to the hermeneutical circle of part and whole, for it involves a consideration of the relation between an isolated expression or work and the pre-given totality of language or literature. Psychological interpretation, on the other hand, is a divinatory dimension that attempts to recover the individuality and originality of the speaker or writer, to recreate the creative act. Through this twofold process of interpretation, one is able, Schleiermacher suggests, to make explicit the assumptions in accordance with which the original expression was produced, and thereby 'to understand an author as well as and even better than he understands himself'.[3]

The generalised hermeneutics of Schleiermacher provided the point of departure for Wilhelm Dilthey, who sought in this discipline an epistemological foundation for the human sciences. Between Schleiermacher and Dilthey stood the great historians of nineteenth-century Germany, Leopold von Ranke and Gustav Droysen. In the wake of their work, the text to be interpreted was no longer a mere fragment of classical or Christian literature, but rather history itself as the document of the achievements and the failures of humanity. Dilthey was critical, however, of the Romantic overtones of the German historical school; and while he wished to endow historical inquiry with a scientific character, he was unsympathetic to the indiscriminate importation of positivistic methods into the human sphere. Whence the principal task of Dilthey's hermeneutics:

to counteract the constant irruption of romantic whim and sceptical subjectivity into the realm of history by laying the historical foundations of valid interpretation upon which all certainty in history rests.[4]

The possibility of historical understanding is secured by the fact that the subject matter of the human sciences is objectifications of life. What historians seek to understand is what they themselves have produced. Ideas, actions and works of art are among the initial objects of understanding, which proceeds through the implementation of quasi-Kantian categories towards the life experiences from which these objects arose. In his later writings, Dilthey emphasises the relative autonomy of expressed phenomena, whose structures of signification can be subsumed under the Hegelian canopy of 'objective mind'. Yet Dilthey retains the reproduction of experience as his goal, anchoring the possibility of such reproduction in a vitalistic philosophy of life. So while understanding may be initially concerned with objectified expressions, its final task remains the 'rediscovery of the I in the Thou'.[5] Thus, in spite of Dilthey's attempt to establish a firm foundation for the human sciences, the philosophy of life to which he adhered tends to return this attempt to the Romantic medium of experiential empathy.[6]

Phenomenology
Contemporaneous with the later writings of Dilthey, Edmund Husserl embarked upon an ambitious programme of transcendental phenomenology. The primary aim of this programme was to elucidate the essential meaning of objects of experience through an investigation of the modes of their appearance. This investigation was to be conducted in a manner free from all presuppositions, including any presuppositions concerning the existence of material objects. Accordingly, Husserl opens *Ideas* with a phenomenological 'reduction' of the spatio-temporal world:

We put out of action the general thesis which belongs to the essence of the natural standpoint, we place in brackets whatever it includes respecting the nature of Being: this entire natural world . . . is a 'fact-world' of which we continue to be conscious, even though it pleases us to put it in brackets.[7]

What remains after the reduction of the spatio-temporal world is pure consciousness, a continuous stream of unadulterated experiences, of thinking, of perceiving, of fancying, of feeling: in short, the Cartesian *cogito*. Yet Husserl goes beyond Descartes and adopts Brentano's doctrine of intentionality, according to which every act of consciousness is consciousness *of* something. By focusing on the 'noematic contents' of such 'intentional objects', a universal essence or 'Eidos' may be abstracted and taken as the datum of phenomenological judgements. As one walks around a red box, for example, one may be aware of one and the same object appearing amid the ever-changing patterns of colour and shape. Husserl maintains, moreover, that part of the meaning of everything contingent is that its contingency is correlative to a necessity and therewith to an Eidos. From this it follows that the facts and objects of the spatio-temporal world can be reconstituted within the phenomenologically reduced sphere of the 'transcendental subjectivity'. For in the last analysis, the entire spatio-temporal world is but a Being for a consciousness, 'a Being which consciousness in its own experience posits, and . . . over and beyond this, is just nothing at all'.[8]

The programme of transcendental phenomenology reveals its uncompromising idealism and imminent solipsism when it confronts the problem of constituting other subjectivities. Indeed, as Husserl frankly confesses in the *Cartesian Meditations*,

it is quite impossible to foresee how, for me in the attitude of reduction, other egos – not as mere worldly phenomena but other transcendental egos – can become positable as existing and thus become equally legitimate themes of a phenomenological egology.[9]

Husserl attempts to avert the solipsistic consequences of his position by introducing the notion of the 'analogical apprehension of the other'. Although the other is not experienced primordially, a form of analogy obtains between the ego and the alter ego which enables the sense of the former to be transposed to the latter. Yet however illuminating this notion may be, it does nothing to dispel the suspicion that the givenness of the other is apodictic in a purely derivative sense. Nor is the difficulty overcome by the substantial recasting of the phenomenological programme embodied in Husserl's last major work, *The Crisis of European Sciences*. In this work, Husserl locates the origins of the contemporary crisis in the positivistic dissolution of the classical idea of universal philosophy, a dissolution initiated by Galileo's mathematisation of nature. He argues that this crisis can be resolved only by returning to an investigation of the 'life-world' of pre-given meanings which the development of Galileo's project has obscured. Nevertheless, Husserl continues to insist that this investigation must proceed through the various stages of reduction, and must ultimately acknowledge 'the absolute singularity of the ego and its central position in all constitution'.[10] Thus, while striving to do justice to the presence of the other and the reality of the socio-historical world, Husserl's relentless commitment to the Cartesian ideal culminates in the cul-de-sac of transcendental solipsism.

Hermeneutic phenomenology

The epistemological problems which preoccupied Dilthey and Husserl were radically displaced by the hermeneutic phenomenology of Heidegger. For in spite of their critiques of positivism, both Dilthey and Husserl remained prisoners of a Kantian theory of knowledge, unable to free their thought from the traditional juxtaposition of subject and object. However, Heidegger maintains that before any object is posited for a subject, both of these terms are bound together by a fundamental relation of belonging to a world. So rather than searching for the conditions under which a knowing subject can understand a particular expression or constitute a particular object, Heidegger begins with an ontological inquiry into the nature of that being which is capable of such activities, that is, into the nature of 'Dasein'. As Heidegger explains in *Being and Time*,

Dasein is an entity which does not just occur among other entities . . . It is peculiar to this entity that with and through its Being, this Being is disclosed to it. *Understanding of Being is itself a definite characteristic of Dasein's Being.*[11]

Understanding is not simply a way of knowing, nor even a method of investigation distinctive to the human sciences. Rather, understanding is an ontological characteristic of Dasein's being-in-the-world. To understand, in Heidegger's primordial sense, is to understand one's position within being; and one understands one's position within being by projecting one's ownmost possibilities. 'Understanding is the Being of such potentiality-for-Being';[12] and interpretation is the subsequent development of this potentiality. Moreover, since Dasein *is* only insofar as it has projected itself, it follows that Dasein is always already ahead of itself in time. In this way, temporality is disclosed as the primitive ontological basis of being-in-the-world. Dasein stretches itself along in time, historicising itself and bestowing historicity upon the entities which it encounters. Indeed, it is only because Dasein itself is an historical being that the scientific investigation of past and present entities is possible.

The fundamental historicity of being unveiled in Heidegger's analytic of Dasein forms a central theme in the work of Gadamer. Beginning from the insight that all understanding involves the projection of possibilities, Gadamer proceeds to establish a connection between the preconceptions or 'prejudices' of understanding and the authority of tradition. For tradition is the source of the prejudices which render understanding possible. So however much human beings may aspire to rational self-determination, to a position outside or above the flow of history, such an aspiration is vain, as it is their primordial participation in tradition which defines the reality and the finitude of their being. Moreover, it follows from this view that the projection of meaning which governs understanding is not the act of an isolated subjectivity, but stems from the tradition to which one belongs. Similarly, that which one seeks to understand is not the psychological constitution of another subject, but a meaningful content which is immersed in a tradition of its own. Thus, so far from being a matter of esoteric empathy, understanding is conceived by Gadamer as an open fusion of historical horizons:

In the process of understanding there takes place a real fusing of horizons, which means that as the historical horizon is projected, it is simultaneously removed . . . the conscious act of this fusion [is] the task of the effective-historical consciousness.[13]

The fusion of horizons in understanding is an accomplishment which occurs within language. For tradition itself is linguistic in nature, and so it is by means of language that the world as an historical phenomenon is conveyed. As Gadamer concisely and cryptically remarks, 'Being that can be understood is language.'[14] Thus, however reality may be subsequently objectified by the naturalistic methods of the various sciences, there remains a prior and primitive form of understanding which is constituted within language, and through which the truth of being is disclosed.

II. Evolution of Ricoeur's philosophy

Structural phenomenology of the will
Some of the themes of hermeneutic phenomenology are defended and developed in the writings of Ricoeur. Ricoeur's concurrence with these themes has appeared gradually in the course of a long and prolific career which opened with an interest in the philosophy of the will. One of the points of departure for these early concerns is a critique of the logistic prejudice of transcendental phenomenology, whereby Husserl tends to collapse the multifarious modes in which consciousness constitutes its objects into a single theory of representation. In extirpating this prejudice, Ricoeur proposes to submit the affective and volitional processes of the will to an independent phenomenological analysis. This proposal does not necessitate, in Ricoeur's opinion, an immediate recourse to the contingencies of the life-world. For he insists that if such a recourse is not to result in a vague existential monism, then 'in the early stages at least, phenomenology must be structural'.[15] Ricoeur undertakes this structural phenomenology of the will in the first volume of a sequential study, a volume entitled *Freedom and Nature*. As the title suggests, the primary aim of this work is to explore the phenomenon of willing as both a realisation of freedom and a reception of necessity; and the principle which governs

this exploration is that of the fundamental reciprocity of the voluntary and involuntary. That is, while the involuntary may be devoid of meaning in itself, it is nevertheless accessible to phenomenological description in virtue of its relation to the voluntary. Thus,

far from the voluntary being derivable from the involuntary, it is, on the contrary, the understanding of the voluntary which comes first in man. I understand myself in the first place as he who says 'I will.'[16]

Ricoeur embarks upon the reciprocal investigation of the voluntary and the involuntary by distinguishing three primary articulations of the will. The expression 'I will' may be analysed into the following components: (a_1) 'I decide', (b_1) 'I move my body', and (c_1) 'I consent'. Moreover, in virtue of the phenomenological doctrine of intentionality, these three components may be approached through noematic analysis of their intentional objects: (a_2) the decision or project, (b_2) the action or motion, (c_2) the acquiescence or consent. Finally, in accordance with the principle of the reciprocity of the voluntary and the involuntary, these three objects may be correlated with the following realms of the involuntary: (a_3) needs, motives, values, (b_3) skills, emotions, habits, (c_3) character, unconscious, life. By unfolding the practical mediations which obtain between the intentional objects and those aspects of the involuntary which correspond to them, Ricoeur seeks to transcend the traditional dualisms which have plagued the philosophy of the will.

On the one hand, we must pass beyond self-consciousness and see consciousness as adhering to its body, to all its involuntary life and, through them, to a world of action; passing beyond, on the other hand, the objectification of this involuntary life, we must recover all this life in consciousness, under the form of motives of the will, of organs and of situation for the will. In short, we must reintegrate consciousness in the body and the body in consciousness.[17]

However, the reintegration effected by the analysis of the mediations between the structures of the voluntary and the involuntary remains a precarious one. Indeed, the unity of these structures is less a reality than a regulative idea for grasping the dramatic duality of human existence, an existence that falls short of that idea precisely to the extent that we are not perfect beings. Yet this imperfection of our being, this perilous boundedness of our will, does not imply that we are not free. For our decision, our action and our consent all manifest an aspect of our freedom, only this is 'a freedom which is human and *not* divine'.[18]

Synthetic phenomenology of the will

The second volume of Ricoeur's philosophy of the will is entitled *Finitude and Guilt.* This volume is divided into two books, and in the first book Ricoeur investigates the dimension of human fallibility that lurked in the background of *Freedom and Nature.* Fallibility is that constitutional weakness in human beings which creates the possibility of evil; it can be conceived as a fault, as an interruption or distortion of the essential structures of the will. This distortion is not subject to the principle of mutual intelligibility which governs the voluntary and the involuntary, but places this principle within a wider dialectic dominated by the idea of 'the intimate disproportion of man with himself or the antinomical structure of man, suspended between a pole of infinitude and a pole of finitude'.[19] Accordingly, the investigation of fallibility requires a transformation in the method of analysis. The object of investigation is no longer an essential structure accessible to eidetic description, but rather an internal aberration that must be approached regressively through reflection on unstable syntheses. By means of such reflection, one must attempt to specify those aspects of our being which harbour the possibility of evil, and thereby to recover philosophically our precomprehension of ourselves as flawed and miserable creatures: 'The whole movement of this book', explains Ricoeur at the outset of *Fallible Man,*

consists in an attempt to enlarge reflection step by step, beginning with an initial position of a transcendental style. At the extreme limit, pure reflection, by becoming total comprehension, would be equivalent to the *pathétique* of misery.[20]

Ricoeur conducts this reflective exercise on three distinct levels. The first and most abstract of these is the transcendental plane, whereupon the disproportion within being is rooted in the distinction between sensibility and understanding. In separating the reception of the presence of things from the determination of their meaning, reflection engenders a primal dialectic between the finitude of perspective and the infinitude of signification. The intermediate term in this dialectic is pure imagination; but pure imagination is so far only consciousness in general and not yet self-consciousness, 'not yet the unity of a person in itself and for itself'.[21] ·Reflection on the latter unity necessitates a transition from the transcendental level to the practical and affective planes. On the practical plane, the finitude of being is encapsulated in the concept of character, a concept that expresses a perspectival orientation towards a field of motivation which, taken as a whole, forms the pole of infinitude. The mediation between these two extremes is represented by the person, as a projected ideal constituted by the moral feeling of respect. The phenomenon of feeling itself is the concern of the affective level of reflection, whereupon the sensation of pleasure serves as the finite counterpole to the infinitude of happiness. This basic polarity is manifested within each of the primary passions of possession, power and worth: suspended between pleasure and happiness, each of these passions bears the threat of endless pursuit. At this level, that disproportion within being which creates the possibility of evil attains its most determinate and dramatic form. Nevertheless, between the possibility and the actuality of fault there remains a leap which the reflective method of *Fallible Man* cannot make. Hence,

to catch sight of that leap we must make a fresh start and enter upon a new type of reflection bearing on the *avowal* that consciousness makes of it and on the *symbols* of evil in which this avowal is expressed.[22]

Symbolic phenomenology of the will

The transition from the possibility of evil to the actuality of fault is the task of *The Symbolism of Evil*, which is the second book of *Finitude and Guilt*. In this book, Ricoeur removes completely the brackets which contained his previous analyses within the bounds of essential possibility, and attempts instead to explore the existential reality of human fault through a re-enactment of the confession of evil by the religious consciousness. The starting point of this endeavour is neither the speculative accounts of evil expounded in works of theology, nor the traditional myths embodied in these accounts. Rather, Ricoeur begins with the most primitive expressions of the confession of evil, expressions which disclose the blindness, the equivocalness and the scandalousness of the experience they represent. In beginning with such expressions, Ricoeur immediately distances himself from the contemporary formalisation of language and returns to a richness that has long been forgotten.

It is in the age when our language has become more precise, more univocal, more technical in a word, more suited to those integral formalizations which are called precisely symbolic logic, it is in this very age of discourse that we want to recharge our language, that we want to start again from the fullness of language . . . Beyond the desert of criticism, we wish to be called again.[23]

The primitive language of avowal in which the experience of evil is expressed is a thoroughly symbolic language, not in the sense of formal logic but in the phenomenological sense of double intentionality. That is, while every sign aims at something beyond itself, it is only in symbols that 'the first, literal, patent meaning analogically intends *a second meaning which is not given otherwise than in the first*'.[24] This double intentionality manifests itself within three distinguishable domains: the cosmic, the oneiric and the poetic. These three dimensions are interwoven in a unified symbolic structure, and the initial task of the philosopher is to unfold the experiences within each of these domains through an intentional analysis of authentic symbols.

The three primary symbols that Ricoeur analyses in depth are stain, sin and guilt. In the case of each of these symbols, evil is first read upon some aspect of the world or cosmos, for example upon the earth or the sun. This cosmic aspect is then experienced subjectively in a psychic or oneiric response, for instance in the feeling of dread or fear. Finally, these two dimensions are unified in a poetic image which gives the symbol its form and marks its emergence into language. Moreover, not only are these symbols articulated within themselves, but they are related to one another in a dynamic movement of progressive interiorisation. That is, each order of symbolism is recapitulated and preserved in the succeeding forms, thereby constituting a symbolic teleology which culminates in the concept of the servile will. Yet this concept cannot be thought directly, and must instead be approached 'through the mediation of the second-order symbols supplied by the myths of evil'.[25] Ricoeur regards the myth as a particular type of symbol, elaborated in the form of a narrative and articulated within an artificial time and space. The myths concerning the origin of evil reproduce the tension between exteriority and interiority that animates the language of avowal. For some of these myths, such as the drama of creation and the tragic myth, locate the origin of evil in a source anterior to human beings; whereas other myths, such as the Adamic myth, concentrate evil in a choice that arises from the inescapable reality of being human. This polarity is repeated within the Adamic myth itself, which enables Ricoeur to construct a dynamics of myth from the privileged standpoint of the latter. In taking this stand, Ricoeur transcends the level of comparative analysis and enters the hermeneutical circle of understanding and belief, a circle which must in turn yield to a final stage of philosophical reflection. For as Ricoeur insists,

I am convinced that we must think, not *behind* the symbols, but starting from symbols, *according* to symbols, that their substance is indestructible, that they constitute the *revealing* substrate of speech which lives among men. In short, the symbol *gives rise to* thought.[26]

Thus, interpretation is the route to philosophical reflection, to reflection premissed on the assumption that by following the indication of symbolic thought one will arrive at a deeper understanding of being. In the last analysis, it is the redemption of this stake in a deeper understanding of being that constitutes the ultimate justification for the interpretation of symbols and myths.

Interrogation of psychoanalysis

The centrality of guilt in the analysis of religious symbolism, and the role of interpretation in the transition from symbolic analysis to philosophical reflection, plunge Ricoeur into an interrogation of psychoanalysis. For just as there is no reflection without interpretation, so there is no interpretation without contestation. As Ricoeur observes,

there does not exist a general hermeneutics, that is, a general theory of interpretation, a general canon for exegesis; there are only various separate and contrasting hermeneutic theories. Thus, our initial problem continues to become more and more complicated.[27]

According to one view in this conflict of interpretations, hermeneutics is construed as the restoration of a meaning addressed to the interpreter in the form of a message. This type of hermeneutics is animated by faith, by a willingness to listen, and it is characterised by a respect for the object as a revelation of the sacred. However, according to another view, hermeneutics is regarded as the demystification of a meaning presented to the interpreter in the form of a disguise. This type of hermeneutics is animated by suspicion, by a scepticism towards the given, and it is characterised by a rejection of that respect for the object granted by the hermeneutics of faith. In the opinion of Ricoeur, it is the latter type of hermeneutics that is practised by Marx, Nietzsche and Freud. All three of these 'masters of suspicion' look upon the contents of consciousness as in some sense false; all three aim to clear the horizon of the mind for the reign of a more authentic word. *'Guile will be met by double guile'*,[28] and thus the contents of consciousness will be deciphered in a way conducive to their subsequent appropriation by the subject of reflection.

In his exhaustive study of the works of Freud, Ricoeur divides his considerations into two movements. The first movement is the reading of Freud, in which Ricoeur is concerned to sustain his claim that psychoanalysis is a type of hermeneutics. The specificity of this hermeneutics is reflected in the structure of psychoanalytic discourse, which presents itself as a mixture of statements of force and statements of meaning; and as Ricoeur repeatedly proclaims,

this mixed discourse is not an equivocal discourse for want of clarification: it grips firmly the very reality we discover when we read Freud and which we can call *the semantics of desire.*[29]

The reading of Freud provides the backcloth against which Ricoeur pursues the second movement of his inquiry. This movement is a philosophical interpretation of Freud, and the question which structures the interpretation is twofold: (1) how does the mixed discourse of psychoanalysis penetrate a philosophy that is deliberately reflective? and (2) what happens to the subject of reflection when the guile of consciousness is taken seriously? The answer to this question is crystallised in the claim that 'the philosophical location of analytical discourse is defined by the concept of the archaeology of the subject'.[30] The latter concept concedes the dispossession of immediate consciousness to the advantage of another agency of meaning, namely the emergence of desire. Yet desire is accessible only through the disguises in which it manifests itself; that is, it is only by interpreting the signs of desire that one can capture its emergence, and thus enable reflection to regain the archaic heritage which it has lost. Moreover, just as this expansion of reflection betrays an implicit *telos* as well as an explicit *archê*, so too the regressive analysis of Freudianism must be complemented by a progressive synthesis of the figures of the mind. Indeed, the internal dialectic of archaeology and teleology, of regression and progression, is merely a reflection of the overdetermined structure of the authentic symbol. So within the complex constitution of the symbol there appears the possibility of resolving the conflict of interpretations: no longer do the various hermeneutical theories represent competing views which sunder the human being in two, but rather complementary moments in a single appropriation of the whole of this being.

Confrontation with structuralism

The preoccupation with language as a medium of expression and a resource for reflection leads Ricoeur into a confrontation with structuralism. As with psychoanalysis, the focal point of this confrontation is the displacement of the primacy of the subject effected by the structuralist approach. This displacement calls into question any attempt to develop a hermeneutic philosophy informed by phenomenology, and hence Ricoeur submits that the 'detour through the science of language is not something one can choose or not choose to make: it is essential to phenomenology today if it is to survive'.[31] The contours of the confrontation are determined by the presuppositions of the structuralist approach. Taking Hjelmslev[32] as his guide, Ricoeur formulates these presuppositions as follows. First, structuralism assumes that language is an object that can be investigated scientifically. Second, structuralism distinguishes between a science of states of the system and a science of changes, and it subordinates the latter to the former. Third, structuralism assumes that in any state of the system there are no absolute terms, but only relations of mutual dependence; and so language,

> thus relieved of its fixed contents, becomes a system of signs defined by their differences alone; in such a system there is no longer any signification – if by that we mean the content proper to an idea considered in itself – but only values, that is, relative, negative, and oppositional dimensions.[33]

Fourth, structuralism treats the collection of signs as a closed and autonomous system of internal dependencies. It follows from these presuppositions that for structuralism a sign must not be defined in terms of some object for which it stands, but rather in terms of its relation to all other signs of the same level within the system of which it is part. In thus regarding language as a self-sufficient system, structuralism transforms it into an object and constitutes itself as a science.

Ricoeur maintains that in founding itself upon these presuppositions, structuralism excludes from consideration a number of fundamental phenomena. It excludes, for instance, the act of speaking, not only as an individual performance but as the free creation of new expressions. History is also excluded, for history is not simply the passage from one state of a system to another, but rather the process by which human beings produce themselves through the production of their language. Moreover, structuralism excludes the primary intention of language, which is to say something about something. For as Ricoeur emphasises, language aims at something; it has both an ideal sense, to say something, and a real reference, to say it about something. In one movement of transcendence language leaps across two thresholds, and thereby takes 'hold of reality and expresses the hold of reality on thought'.[34] The exclusion of these various phenomena from the structuralist domain is an indication of the limitations of that approach. However, so far this critique remains at the level of a sterile antinomy, and the phenomenological alternative threatens to collapse into a subjective psychologism. To move beyond this unproductive opposition, Ricoeur proposes to return to the very foundations of language and therefrom to rethink its unitary and hierarchical nature.

> What phenomenology must do, then, is to take up again the theory of meaning and put it to the test of semiology in order to proceed to a genuine dialectic of semiology and semantics at every level of the units of speech.[35]

III. Exposition of the theory of language

System and discourse

The theory of language elaborated by Ricoeur rests upon a fundamental distinction between system and discourse. This distinction is the contribution not so much of Saussure, but rather of the French linguist Benveniste.[36] According to Benveniste, language is a totality that may be articulated into a series of levels, each of which is characterised by a distinctive and constitutive unit. However, the transition between these various levels is not a continuous one. For whereas the phoneme, the morpheme, the semanteme and so on are all signs defined by their internal and oppositive relations, the sentence is not itself a sign but rather an unspecified creation of unlimited variety. In Ricoeur's words:

> We actually change levels when we pass from the units of a language to the new unit constituted by the sentence or the utterance. This is no longer the unit of a language, but of speech or discourse. By changing the unit, one also changes the function, or rather, one passes from structure to function.[37]

The qualitative break marked by the transition to the sentence creates the conditions for the possibility of a genuine science of semantics, as distinct from a semiotics of the sign. However, the relation between these two disciplines remains a close and complicated one, as attested to by the intermediary role of the word. The word is a sign in sentence position, for a sign becomes a word only when someone speaks in an instance of discourse. Yet the word is more than the sentence, for it survives the transitory moment of speech and returns to the system of signs, thereby providing the latter with a history of accumulated use-values and generating the phenomenon of regulated polysemy. Thus the word is, as Ricoeur remarks, 'a trader between the system and the act, between the structure and the event'.[38]

Ricoeur unfolds the distinctiveness of discourse in terms of an internal dialectic between event and meaning. For if on the one hand the utterance of a sentence is a transitory and ephemeral phenomenon, on the other hand a sentence may be reidentified as the same on subsequent occasions. This reidentification is possible because the sentence has a propositional content which transcends the act of utterance, such that 'all discourse is realised as an event and understood as an identical meaning'.[39] The notion of meaning has two basic dimensions, embracing both an objective aspect, or that which the sentence means, and a subjective aspect, or that which the speaker means. Ricoeur suggests that the former aspect can be clarified along Strawsonian lines, in terms of the conjunction of a singular identification and a universal predication. The latter aspect may be elucidated in terms of an Austinian theory of speech-acts supplemented by an account of intention adapted from Grice. However, this initial characterisation does not exhaust the notion of meaning. For following Frege, one may distinguish within the objective dimension between the sense of an expression and its reference; and whereas sense is purely immanent in language, reference appertains to the relation between language and the world. The referential relation is one of the most crucial characteristics of discourse, and one which is essentially inaccessible to semiotics. Consequently, Ricoeur maintains that

the two levels of sign and of discourse are not only distinct, but the first is an abstraction from the second . . . Semiotics, insofar as it remains within the closure of a world of signs, is an abstraction from semantics, which relates the internal constitution of sense to the transcendent aim of reference.[40]

Metaphor and symbol

The semantics of discourse reserves a privileged place for metaphors and symbols, whose complex structures shed light on the richness and creativity of language. According to the traditional view, metaphor is regarded as a type of trope, that is, as a rhetorical device whereby a figurative word is substituted for a literal one on the basis of an apparent resemblance. However, Ricoeur maintains that this account is incapable of explaining the process by which a novel metaphor is produced; and he claims that this difficulty can be overcome only if one accepts the view that the primary metaphorical unit is not the word but the sentence. On the latter view, metaphor presupposes the establishment of a tension between two terms in the sentence through the violation of a linguistic code. The metaphorical utterance then appears as a reduction of this tension by means of a creative semantic pertinence within the sentence as a whole. In thereby resolving a paradigmatic tension by means of a syntagmatic innovation, the metaphorical process situates itself at the point of articulation between system and discourse. As Ricoeur explains,

metaphorical meaning is an effect of the entire statement, but it is focused on one word, which can be called the metaphorical word. This is why one must say that metaphor is a semantic innovation that belongs at once to the predicative order (new pertinence) and the lexical order (paradigmatic deviation).[41]

In situating itself at this point of articulation, the metaphorical process draws upon the phenomenon of regulated polysemy. However, the former cannot be reduced to the latter, for metaphor is the very process by which the polysemy of words is expanded and transformed. This transformative capacity is attributable to the referential dimension of the metaphorical statement, that is, to its power to redescribe reality. For in the last analysis, the function of metaphor is 'to shatter and to increase our sense of reality by shattering and increasing our language'.[42]

The symbol shares a structure of double intentionality with the metaphor. However, whereas in metaphor the secondary signification is itself linguistic, the symbol opens onto a domain of experience that transcends the boundaries of language. That is,

metaphor occurs in the already purified universe of the *logos*, while the symbol hesitates on the dividing line between *bios* and *logos*. It testifies to the primordial rootedness of Discourse in Life.[43]

The symbolic intersection of language and experience may be articulated in differing ways, a possibility which may give rise to a conflict of interpretations. In psychoanalysis, for example, the symbol is the milieu in which the archaic impulses of humanity are expressed; and it is this anterior infusion which is responsible for the constitution of psychoanalytic discourse as a semantics of desire. Indeed, to fail to respect this mixed constitution, and so to reduce psychoanalysis to a mere interplay of signifiers in a structuralist manner, is to fail to realise that the double meaning of the psychoanalytic symbol 'is the mode in which the very ruse of desire is expressed'.[44] Similarly, in the phenomenology of religion, the symbol opens onto a domain of experience in which the mysterious and menacing power of the sacred is revealed. The interdependence of language and experience is thus crystallised in the interpretation of the symbol, whereby its multiple layers of meaning unveil the equivocal nature of being.

Concept of the text

Ricoeur's semantics can be expanded to incorporate a concept of the text, insofar as the text may be regarded as a work of discourse submitted to the condition of inscription. To say that the text is a work is to say, in the first instance, that it is a structured totality irreducible to the sentences of which it is composed. Such a totality is produced in accordance with a series of rules which define its literary genre, and which transform discourse into a poem, a novel, a play. In a manner analogous to the operation of transformational grammar, these literary genres serve

to mediate between speaker and hearer by establishing a common *dynamics* capable of ruling both the production of discourse as a work of a certain kind and its interpretation according to the rules provided by the 'genre'.[45]

The genre of a work is closely connected to its style. For just as a set of grammatical rules is capable of generating an individual sentence, so too a literary genre is implemented in the production of a singular work. The production of discourse as a work is thus exemplified in its composition, its genre and its style. These categories, Ricoeur observes, are categories of labour; they reflect 'so many ways of treating language as a material to be worked upon and formed'.[46]

In addition to being a *work* of discourse, the text is also a *written* work. Ricoeur emphasises that the text is not merely the inscription of some anterior speech, since speaking and writing are alternative and equally fundamental modes of the realisation of discourse. Nevertheless, the realisation of discourse under the condition of inscription displays a series of characteristics which effectively distance the text from the circumstances of speech. Ricoeur encapsulates these characteristics in the key notion of 'distanciation', which he divides into four principal forms. The first form of distanciation is the surpassing of the event of saying by the meaning of what is said. For it is the meaning which is inscribed in writing, and this inscription is rendered possible by the 'intentional exteriorisation' of the speech-act. That is, the locutionary act exteriorises itself in the propositional content of the sentence, and the illocutionary and perlocutionary acts may be realised in writing by means of various grammatical and periphrastic devices. The second form of distanciation concerns the relation between the inscribed expression and the original speaker. Whereas in spoken discourse the intention of the speaking subject and the meaning of what is said frequently overlap, in the case of writing this coincidence fails to obtain. Hence,

the text's career escapes the finite horizon lived by its author. What the text says now matters more than what the author meant to say, and every exegesis unfolds its procedures within the circumference of a meaning that has broken its moorings to the psychology of its author.[47]

The third form of distanciation introduces a similar discrepancy between the inscribed expression and the original audience. Whereas in spoken discourse the hearer is specified in advance by the dialogical situation, in the case of writing the text is addressed to an unknown audience and potentially to anyone who is able to read. The text thus 'decontextualises' itself from its socio-historical conditions of production, opening itself to an unlimited series of readings. The fourth and final form of distanciation concerns the emancipation of the text from the limits of ostensive reference. Unlike spoken discourse, in which the referential import of what is said is restricted by the dialogical situation, in the case of writing this restriction is abolished. Thus, as Ricoeur remarks in a Heideggerian vein, the referent of written literature is 'no longer the *Umwelt* of the ostensive references of dialogue, but the *Welt* projected by the non-ostensive references of every text that we have read, understood, and loved'.[48]

Theory of interpretation

The semantics of discourse in general, and the concept of the text in particular, provide Ricoeur with a foundation for the development of a general theory of interpretation. This theory seeks to integrate explanation and understanding in a constructive dialectic which is rooted in the properties of the text. In thereby linking interpretation to the text, Ricoeur reveals a shift away from his earlier preoccupation with the symbol: it is no longer the symbol but the text, written discourse as such, which defines the object domain of hermeneutics. Accordingly, the first movement of the dialectic of interpretation corresponds to the eclipse of the event of saying by the meaning of what is said, and to the severance of the latter from the intentions of the speaking subject. From these distanciations it follows that the objective meaning of a text is something other than the subjective intentions of its author, and so 'the problem of the right understanding can no longer be solved by a simple return to the alleged intention of the author'.[49] Rather, just as the resolution of the tension presupposed by a metaphor requires the construction of a new sense, so too the meaning of a text must be guessed or construed as a whole. Yet the text possesses an inherent plurivocity that allows it to be construed in more ways than one. Nonetheless, Ricoeur maintains that this possibility does not necessarily lead to arbitrariness and caprice, since

it is always possible to argue for or against an interpretation, to confront interpretations, to arbitrate between them and to seek agreement, even if this agreement remains beyond our immediate reach.[50]

So while a text may allow of several interpretations, it does not follow that all of these interpretations are of equal status; and the elimination of inferior interpretations is not an empirical matter of verification and proof, but a rational process of argumentation and debate.

The second movement in the dialectic of interpretation corresponds to the severance of the relation of discourse to the interlocutors and circumstances of the dialogical situation. The severance of this relation engenders two possible attitudes towards the text. On the one hand, the reader may remain in suspense as regards whatever non-ostensive references the text might have; that is, the text may be treated as a wholly worldless and self-enclosed entity. On the other hand, the reader may actualise those non-ostensive references of the text that are rendered possible by the situation of reading. The first of these attitudes is exemplified by the structuralist approach, which proceeds by means of a total *epoché* of the referential function. By adopting this attitude a new type of explanation may be incorporated into the analysis of the text, an explanatory type which comes not from the natural sciences but from the field of language itself. However, Ricoeur argues that any such explanation presupposes a form of understanding which cannot be reduced to structuralist analysis. To regard the latter as an exhaustive approach to the study of myth, for example, would be to reduce the theory of myth to a 'necrology of the meaningless discourses of mankind'.[51] The form of understanding thus presupposed is the object of the second attitude that the reader may assume towards the text. For the reader may seek, not something hidden behind the text, but rather something disclosed in front of it; not the internal constitution of the text, but rather that which points towards a possible world. To understand a text at this level is to move from its sense to its reference, from that which it says to that which it says it about; and Ricoeur suggests that if in this process structuralist analysis may be regarded

as one stage – albeit a necessary one – between a naive interpretation and a critical one, between a surface interpretation and a depth interpretation, then it would be possible to locate explanation and understanding at two different stages of a unique hermeneutical arc.[52]

The final movement in the dialectic of interpretation thus culminates in an act of understanding that is mediated by the explanatory procedures of structuralist analysis. These procedures ensure that the object of understanding is not identified with something felt, but rather with a potential reference released by explanation, that is, with a possible world disclosed by the text.

Hermeneutics and reflection

The theory of interpretation reinforces the connection that Ricoeur is concerned to establish between hermeneutics and philosophical reflection. The specific form that this connection assumes is an indication of Ricoeur's indebtedness to the writings of the French philosopher Jean Nabert.[53] In accordance with Nabert, Ricoeur regards reflection less as an epistemological justification of science and morality than as an appropriation of the effort to exist. Moreover, this effort cannot be grasped immediately in an intellectual intuition, but only indirectly through the mirror of the objects and acts, the symbols and signs, wherein it is disclosed. Hence Ricoeur submits that

reflection is the appropriation of our effort to exist and our desire to be, through the works which bear witness to that effort and desire . . . reflection must become interpretation because I cannot grasp the act of existing except in signs scattered in the world.[54]

This concept of concrete reflection is enriched by Ricoeur's encounter with the hermeneutics of suspicion. For reflection is necessarily self-reflection, and the latter disciplines raise afresh the question of what 'the self' might signify. Psychoanalysis, for instance, firmly castigates the pretensions of the narcissistic ego, leaving behind a wounded and humiliated *cogito*, 'a *cogito* which understands its primordial truth only in and through the avowal of the inadequation, the illusion, the fakery of immediate consciousness'.[55] Indeed, according to Ricoeur, one of the central insights of psychoanalysis is the discovery that consciousness is not a given, but rather a task to be accomplished through the long and tortuous by-way of a semantics of desire. Thus, reflection must incorporate hermeneutics not only because existence must be grasped in its external manifestations, but also because consciousness is in the first instance a realm of falsehood, so that true consciousness must be achieved by means of a demystifying and corrective critique.

The contribution which the theory of interpretation makes to the connection between hermeneutics and reflection is twofold. On the one hand, by subordinating the subjective intentions of the author to the objective meaning of the text, the theory of interpretation effects a displacement of the primacy of the subject comparable to that performed by psychoanalysis. On the other hand, this extirpation of the subject as radical origin prepares the way for the reintroduction of subjectivity in a more modest role. For the final movement in the dialectic of interpretation eventuates in an act of understanding whereby the reader appropriates the reference of the text. This act does not purport to rejoin the original intentions of the author, but rather to expand the conscious horizons of the reader by incorporating the world which the text unfolds. Indeed, appropriation is not so much an act of possession as an act of dispossession, in which the self-understanding of the immediate ego is replaced by a self-reflection mediated through the world of the text. So even if interpretation ends in self-comprehension, it cannot be reduced to naive subjectivism, for this comprehension proceeds under the objective guidance of the text. As Ricoeur observes, in the coming to understanding of signs inscribed in texts, the meaning rules and gives me a self. In short, the self of self-understanding is a gift of understanding itself and of the invitation from the meaning inscribed in the text.[56]

Moreover, just as the understanding of signs inscribed in texts is a necessary propaedeutic to the comprehension of self, so too self-comprehension is a necessary stage in the dialectic of interpretation. To eliminate this stage and to remain, for example, at the level of structural explanation is to extinguish the question of meaning as such. In a debate with Lévi-Strauss, Ricoeur thus confesses that 'if meaning is not a segment of self-understanding, I don't know what it is'.[57]

IV. Problems in the theory of reference and truth

Language and being
The theory of language elaborated by Ricoeur opens an avenue to experience and being; for as with the later Heidegger and Dufrenne,[58] ontology remains the horizon of hermeneutics. The phenomenological key to this avenue may be found in Ricoeur's conception of language as an articulated totality suspended between a teleological ideal of logicity and a prelinguistic origin of lived experience. Language cannot be collapsed into either of these limits, nor wholly abstracted from them: 'in itself it is a medium, a mediation, an exchange between *Telos* and *Ursprung*'.[59] Ricoeur attempts to reconcile this conception of language with the presuppositions of phenomenology through a reinterpretation of the notion of reduction. Accordingly, reduction may be regarded not as the withdrawal of the ego into an absolute subjectivity severed from reality, but rather as that break with the surrounding world which is the condition for the possibility of language as such. Reduction marks the emergence of the subject as a being distinct from nature, for it enables this being to relate to the real by designating it through signs. However, the subject thus born is so far only an abstract self, a mere field of *cogitationes*; and the sign thus constituted is so far only an empty sign, a mere system of differences. Yet reduction as difference may be complemented by the fulfilment of the sign in a referential act of the subject; and if the principle of difference is the negative condition for the possibility of a semiotics of language, then the principle of fulfilment is the positive condition for a corresponding semantics of discourse. By means of the principle of fulfilment, language is returned to the prepredicative structures of experience upon which it is based, and therewith to the signifying subject who expresses that experience. As Ricoeur explains,

reduction, in its full sense, is this *return to the self by way of its other* . . . the subject founded by reduction is nothing other than the beginning of signifying life, the simultaneous birth of the spoken being of the world and the speaking being of man.[60]

The structures of experience which constitute the prepredicative foundations of language cannot be grasped immediately, but must be approached indirectly through interpretation. For just as consciousness is not a given but a task, so too 'it is only within the movement of interpretation that we apperceive the being we interpret'.[61] It follows that the ontology which forms the horizon of hermeneutics is not an independent one, but is bound to the methods of interpretation through which it is disclosed. Moreover, since there is not a single but several methods of interpretation, it similarly follows that this horizon is not a total but a truncated ontology, internally divided and at variance with itself. So while psychoanalysis searches behind the subject and finds there an archaic dimension of human desire, the philosophy of the spirit looks forwards and shifts the origin of meaning towards a teleology of figures. In a more radical manner still, the phenomenology of religion locates the ontological roots of the signs of the sacred in an absolute existence which calls upon us and announces the finitude and dependency of our being. Each in its own way, these various hermeneutical disciplines point towards existence and attest to the primordial placement of the subject within being. Yet whether this being could ever be grasped in a coherent and unified ontology remains an open question. For as Ricoeur allusively remarks,

ontology is indeed the promised land for a philosophy that begins with language and with reflection; but, like Moses, the speaking and reflecting subject can only glimpse this land before dying.[62]

Orders of reference

The principle of fulfilment presupposed by the semantics of discourse provides the transcendental basis for a theory of reference. Ricoeur develops this theory on two levels, in accordance with the distinction between discourse as spoken and as inscribed. On the level of spoken discourse, the phenomenological distinction between meaning and fulfilment finds its semantic equivalent in the Fregean distinction between sense and reference. For in both cases,

what we are dealing with here is a meaning-intention which breaks the closed circle of the sign, which opens up the sign towards something, in short which constitutes language as the saying of something about something. The moment there is a turn from the ideality of the sense to the reality of the thing . . . is the moment of the transcendence of the sign.[63]

The element that accomplishes this transcendence of the sign is the basic unit of semantics, namely the sentence. It is only at the level of the sentence that language has both sense and reference, a sense which unites the functions of identification and predication and a reference which relates this unity to the world. Moreover, Ricoeur agrees with Strawson and others that a sentence has reference only in its use; and so whether a sentence succeeds or fails to refer depends upon the particular circumstances in which the act of discourse is performed, and not upon some aspect of the propositional content alone. Finally, insofar as the act of discourse which sustains the referential function is necessarily an act of someone, the sentence refers back to a speaker as well as to some situation in the world. This self-reference is effected by means of various grammatical devices, such as personal pronouns and related verbal forms, which acquire their meaning only in the instance of discourse. 'Thus it is at the same level and in the same instance of discourse that language has a reference and a subject',[64] for it is in the same movement that language conveys the intention of a speaker to say something about the world.

The inscription of discourse in the written text is accompanied by a modification of the theory of reference. For the forms of distanciation that characterise this inscription involve the severance of any relation to the dialogical situation. However, in opposition to the ideology of the absolute text, Ricoeur maintains that this severance is merely the condition for the realisation of a second order reference:

the literary work discloses a world only under the condition that the reference of descriptive discourse is suspended. Or in other words: in the literary work, discourse unfolds its denotation as a denotation of the second order, in virtue of the suspension of the denotation of the first order of discourse.[65]

The mode of realisation for this second order denotation is anticipated in the theory of the metaphor. For the resolution of the contradiction presupposed by the metaphor involves the abolition of the reference corresponding to the original and literal meaning, and the creation of a new reference which corresponds to the semantic innovation. The deployment of this new reference is regulated by the power of redescription which metaphor shares with other heuristic fictions, such as the models of science. Moreover, this power is paradigmatic for the literary work as a whole, for in the latter case as well, 'the effacement of the ostensive and descriptive reference liberates a power of reference to aspects of our being in the world that cannot be said in a direct descriptive way'.[66] Thus, it is only through the suspension of all ostensive denotation that the text is capable of realising a second order reference, of projecting a new way of being, that is, of disclosing a possible world.

Validity and truth

The theory of reference is closely connected to Ricoeur's analysis of the problems of validity and truth. This analysis is similarly conducted on two levels, this time in accordance with the two movements in the dialectic of interpretation. In the first of these movements, an attempt is made to construe the meaning of the text as an individual and articulated whole. Ricoeur allows that the plurivocity of texts renders possible a multiplicity of readings, and he concedes that there are no hard and fast rules whereby such readings may be made. However, following Hirsch,[67] Ricoeur maintains that there are methods for the validation of competing accounts, methods which are closer to a logic of subjective probability than to a process of empirical verification. Accordingly,

an interpretation must not only be probable, but more probable than another. There are criteria of relative superiority which may easily be derived from the logic of subjective probability.[68]

Ricoeur suggests that this view of validation provides an acceptable rendition of the concept of the hermeneutical circle. For while guess and validation may indeed be circularly related, this circle is not vicious since the criteria of validation are independently established and intersubjectively available. Such criteria constitute a firm foundation for a science of the individual, whether the latter be the distorted content of a recapitulated dream or the poetic texture of a work of art. For 'psychoanalysis cannot side-step, any more than exegesis, the question of the validity of its interpretations';[69] only this question is not to be resolved by the importation of the methods of verification employed in the observational sciences, but rather through argumentation among practitioners who are aware of the ineradicable meaningfulness and irreplicable uniqueness of the psychoanalytic situation.

The second level in the analysis of the problems of validity and truth corresponds to the final movement in the dialectic of interpretation. In his earlier writings,[70] Ricoeur emphasises that truth is inseparable from being; and insofar as interpretation culminates in the establishment of an ulterior reference to reality, the truth of a text may be regarded as the world which it unfolds. Moreover, since the ontological implications of any specific hermeneutical discipline cannot be abstracted from its methodological presuppositions, it follows that the truth attainable by that discipline is bound to the methods of interpretation which it employs. Thus, in contrast to the philosophical hermeneutics of Gadamer, Ricoeur proposes

to keep in contact with the disciplines which seek to practice interpretation in a methodical manner, and [to] resist the temptation to separate *truth*, characteristic of understanding, from the *method* put into operation by disciplines which have sprung from exegesis.[71]

However, just as the ontology implied by the rival hermeneutical disciplines remains a broken and truncated one, so too the truth which they disclose is internally torn and fragmented. Reflective philosophy may aspire to overcome this fragmentation, but whether it will ever succeed is a question that remains as open as the prospect of achieving a coherent and unified ontology. For as in the latter case, so too in the former: 'the unity of truth is a timeless task only because it is at first an eschatological hope'.[72]

V. Problems in the analysis of action

Descriptive discourse on action
The corpus of Ricoeur's work generates a multiplicity of approaches to the analysis of human action. The recognition of this multiplicity concurs with a general development in Ricoeur's exploration of the will. For in contrast to his earlier univocal treatment of this topic, he presently allows that 'the philosophy of the will requires at least three types of discourse, each with its own rules, kind of coherence, and mode of validation'.[73] In a similar manner, Ricoeur's work appears to offer three types of discourse on human action.[74] The first of these types, which may be called a descriptive discourse on action, embraces the contributions of phenomenology and linguistic analysis. In assessing these contributions, Ricoeur acknowledges the superiority of the latter as an initial approach to the field of action. For

linguistic analysis avoids the difficulties of all introspection, namely the recourse to brute sensation, to intuition: Wittgenstein, in questioning 'private ostensive definitions', questioned any phenomenology which presents itself as a mode of 'internal perception'.[75]

Linguistic analysis eludes the solipsistic snares of phenomenology by replacing a direct inquiry into private experience with an investigation into the public utterances in which that experience is expressed. Ricoeur distinguishes several levels at which such an investigation must be conducted. At a conceptual level, the notions with which action is described in everyday life, such as reason and motive, must be identified and elucidated. At a propositional level, the statements in which concepts of action are employed, for example in declarations of purpose or intent, must be isolated and analysed. Finally, at a discursive level, the relations between statements concerning action must be specified and formalised, in a manner analogous to the theory of games or decision theory. In these various ways, linguistic analysis can make a legitimate and significant contribution to a descriptive discourse on human action.

However, linguistic analysis does not exhaust the descriptive discourse and it must be supplemented by phenomenological investigation. For although such analysis may be a salutary starting point, in the end it is incapable of reflecting upon itself and justifying the distinctions and classifications which it makes. Ricoeur maintains that such a justification can be provided only by returning to the prepredicative experience which achieves its expression within ordinary language, and upon which the latter is based. Indeed, the analysis of ordinary language is possible 'only because, underlying language, there exists an articulated experience which is the *referent* of discourse'.[76] The phenomenological investigation of this domain is conducted in accordance with the doctrine of intentionality, which ensures that immediately lived experience is objectified and articulated in the contents of the corresponding noema. Thus, in the intricate studies unfolded in *Freedom and Nature*, Ricoeur approaches the experience of acting through an analysis of the action or motion, treating the latter as an intermediary stage between decision and consent. Decision is regarded as a type of judgement which designates a future action that depends upon the agent and is within the agent's power. Action is simply the fulfilment of this designation or project; and so the aim of action is not the physical movement itself but rather the 'pragma', or that which is to be done. Both the decision and its fulfilment are based upon various existential structures which are either relatively or absolutely involuntary, and to which the agent must consent. Yet the reconciliation of freedom and necessity anticipated by this consent remains utterly inaccessible to any analysis which restricts itself to the level of language. For in Ricoeur's view,

this methodological decision to know experience only in public expressions implies the forgetting of the question of the originary, the obliteration of the question of the origin of meaning.[77]

So while linguistic analysis may provide a laudable introduction to the descriptive discourse on action, this discourse acquires its full elaboration and justification only through a phenomenological investigation into the prepredicative structures of experience.

Dialectical discourse on action

The descriptive discourse on action may be contrasted with a second approach to this field, which may be referred to as a dialectical discourse. The latter does not proceed by distinction and classification, but through mediation and totalisation; it does not purport to be neutral and descriptive, but is unashamedly ethical and prescriptive. This discourse does not limit itself to an analysis of the motivated action of an isolated individual, but attempts to comprehend the relation between motivated and rational action, between practical and theoretical reason, between individual and collective will. A framework for the resolution of the latter antinomy is sketched in *Fallible Man*, where Ricoeur identifies having, power and worth as the principal passions of the will. He then suggests that this affective configuration presupposes a structure of objectivity in which the will as collective is realised:

If our theory of feeling is valid, the feelings which gravitate around power, having and worth ought to be correlative with a constitution of objectivity on a level other than that of the merely perceived thing . . . We must add the economic, political and cultural dimensions to objectivity; they make a human world out of the mere nature they start with.[78]

So just as there are three primordial passions in the affective constitution of the will, so too there are three fundamental dimensions in the objective structure of the social world. Moreover, just as each of these passions is a locus of affective fragility, so in each of these dimensions there dwells the possibility of human evil. Ricoeur does not suggest that an analysis of the conditions in which this evil prevails could be value-free; and he conducts his investigations with an undisguised commitment to democratic social- ism, tempered by a recognition of the essential fallibility of human beings. As Ricoeur cautiously amends: 'No longer "human, all too human": this formula still shares in the intoxication of absolute knowl- edge; but "only human". This formula protects the sobriety of humanism.'[79]

The three basic dimensions of the social world include the economy, the polity and culture. The economy comprises everything that may be regarded as an accumulation of human experience, such as tools and machines as well as their products and the knowledge with which they are produced. The polity consists of those institutions through which particular historical groups appropriate this technical and economic reality. Ricoeur maintains that while political institutions are thus closely tied to the economic infrastructure, the former cannot be reduced to the latter. For the polity is autonomous in at least two ways: it establishes specific, non-economic relations between people; and it fosters a particular form of human evil, which is realised in the phenomenon of power. 'Not that power is evil', explains Ricoeur, 'but power is one of the splendors of man that is eminently prone to evil.'[80] In addition to the economic and political domains, the cultural sphere encompasses the values and attitudes which are expressed in the mores and traditions of a society. It is within this sphere that one discovers the very core of the phenomenon of civilisation, namely that collection of images and symbols through which a society expresses its relation to reality, to other groups and to history. Ricoeur calls this collection the 'ethico-mythical kernel' of civilisation; and he suggests that if the task of humanism is socialisation in the economy and democratisation in the polity, then in the cultural sphere it can only be the re-appropriation of this ethico-mythical kernel:

Only a return to the past and a living reinterpretation of tradition can permit modern societies to resist the leveling to which the consumer society submits. We are touching here on the work of culture, more precisely, on the work of language, which our criticism of the idea of civilization entrusts to the hermeneutic problem.[81]

So while the dialectical discourse on action may begin with a series of antinomies, it ends with a theory of society in which the individual is linked to the collective will and a course of political action is explicitly prescribed.

Hermeneutical discourse on action
In underlining the necessity for a reinterpretation of the past, the dialectical discourse points towards a third approach to the field of human action. The latter approach emerges with the recognition that action itself projects a mode of being in the world, a mode which can only be grasped in 'a discourse which qualifies itself as interpretation'.[82] The possibility of this hermeneutical discourse is secured by Ricoeur's claim that action may be regarded as a text, insofar as it may be objectified in a way that embodies the four forms of distanciation. Thus, just as the fixation of speech involves the surpassing of the instance of saying by the meaning of what is said, so too the fixation of action is marked by the eclipse of the event of doing by the significance of what is done. This eclipse can occur

because the structure of action is analogous to that of the speech-act, so that action shares the intentional exteriorisation which is immanent in the latter. Ricoeur defends this assertion by suggesting that an analysis of the verbs and predicates of action, such as that undertaken by Kenny,[83] demonstrates that action has the structure of a locutionary act, for it reveals that action has a 'propositional content' that can be identified and reidentified as the same. Similarly, action exhibits a variety of 'illocutionary traits' which closely resemble those of the speech-act, so much so that a criteriology of action could be elaborated on the basis of a typology of illocutionary acts. Hence Ricoeur submits that

like the speech-act, the action-event (if we may coin this analogical expression) develops a similar dialectic between its temporal status as an appearing and a disappearing event, and its logical status as having such-and-such identifiable meaning or 'sense-content'.[84]

The objectification of action similarly shares the three forms of distanciation which constitute the semantic autonomy of the text. For just as a text is divorced from its author, so too an action becomes detached from the actor and develops consequences of its own. In this way, the meaning of an action is severed from the intentions of its agent, and human action is transformed into an institutionalised social phenomenon which constitutes the process of history. Moreover, just as the inscription of discourse shatters the narrowness of the dialogical situation, so too human action has an unlimited audience; and

in the same way that the meaning of an event is the sense of its forthcoming interpretations, the interpretation by the contemporaries has no particular privilege in this process.[85]

Finally, just as the written text is freed from the restrictions of ostensive reference, so too human action transcends the social conditions of its production. For the importance of an action may exceed its relevance to the immediate circumstances in which it occurs, and so it may be reenacted in different contexts and contribute to the creation of others. In this sense, human action is an open work, for 'a work does not only mirror its time, but it opens up a world which it bears within itself'.[86] Ricoeur maintains that these various similarities are sufficient to warrant the treatment of action as a text, and so to justify the distinctive status of a hermeneutical discourse on human action.

VI. Problems in the methodology of social science

Explanation and understanding

The recent writings of Ricoeur proffer solutions to a number of problems in the methodology of social science. One of these problems arises from the traditional debate concerning the relative roles of explanation and understanding. Ricoeur approaches this problem on the twofold assumption that meaningful action is the object of the social sciences, and that a hermeneutical discourse on such action is possible. On the basis of this assumption, Ricoeur submits that 'the paradigm of reading, which is the counterpart of the paradigm of writing, provides a solution for the methodological paradox of the human sciences'.[87] To substantiate this claim, Ricoeur attempts to show that each of the two movements in the dialectic of interpretation is applicable to the field of human action. Thus, in accordance with the first movement, Ricoeur maintains that the meaning of action has a specific plurivocity which allows it to be construed in a limited number of ways. For one understands what an action is when one can explain why the person acted as he or she did; and one can explain that when one can provide a reason or a motive for the action as opposed to a cause, that is, when one can subsume the action under a particular category of wants or beliefs. However, there is nothing definitive about this process, and it is always possible to argue for or against any specific interpretation. Consequently,

like legal utterances, all interpretations in the field of literary criticism and in the social sciences may be challenged, and the question 'what can defeat a claim' is common to all argumentative situations.[88]

Yet whereas in the legal tribunal there is an accepted point at which the procedures of appeal are exhausted, there is no such point in literary criticism and the social sciences; and if ever these procedures are exhausted in the latter disciplines, only dogmatism and violence ensue.

The second movement in the dialectic of interpretation is similarly applicable to the field of human action. For the structuralist mode of analysis is not restricted to the linguistic sphere, but may be extended to all social phenomena which have a semiological character, that is, which constitute a self-enclosed system of internal dependencies. The extension of this mode of analysis confers upon the social sciences a type of explanation quite different from that implied by a Humean account of causality, for structuralist explanation posits relations that are correlative rather than consecutive or sequential. However, Ricoeur maintains that the establishment of such correlations does not exhaust the second movement in the dialectic of interpretation. For just as language-games are forms of life, so 'social structures are also attempts to cope with existential complexities, human predicaments and deep-rooted conflicts'.[89] The institutionalised social phenomena constituted by objectified human action have a reference as well as a structure, for they point towards the *aporias* of human existence and thereby project a world in a way analogous to the non-ostensive referential function of the text. Moreover, the final appropriation of the world disclosed by the depth interpretation does not reduce the objectivity of the social sciences to the personal vicissitudes of the subject. Such appropriation has nothing to do with the empathic intuition of another psychic life, but rather involves the expansion of one's own horizon through the incorporation of a new mode of being. This is not to say that the social sciences can be wholly value-free, and Ricoeur emphasises that

this qualification of the notion of personal commitment does not eliminate the 'hermeneutical circle'. This circle remains an insuperable structure of knowledge when it is applied to human things, but this qualification prevents it from becoming a vicious circle.[90]

The hermeneutical discourse on human action thereby enables Ricoeur to reconcile explanation and understanding in the social sciences. For not only must the initial interpretation be subject to independent procedures of validation, but the final appropriation must be attained through a depth interpretation that is mediated by the explanatory methods of structuralist analysis.

Hermeneutics and critical theory

The concept of the text and the theory of interpretation also provide a basis for arbitration in the debate between hermeneutics and critical theory.[91] Ricoeur presents this debate as an antinomy between participation and alienation: hermeneutic philosophy regards tradition as a dimension of historical consciousness through which the individual participates in cultural heritage, whereas critical theory sees nothing but distortions and alienations in the same traditions, contrasting them with the regulative idea of communication free from constraint. In an attempt to resolve this antinomy, Ricoeur proposes the following two theses:

First, that a hermeneutic of traditions can only fulfill its program if it introduces a critical distance, conceived and practiced as an integral part of the hermeneutical process. And, secondly . . . that a critique of ideologies too can only fulfill its project if it incorporates a certain regeneration of the past, consequently, a reinterpretation of tradition.[92]

Ricoeur defends the first thesis by arguing that the consciousness of historical efficacy contains within itself a moment of distance. The recognition of this moment is obscured by Gadamer's account, wherein the experience which sanctions the universality of hermeneutics involves a rejection of the objectifying attitude of the social sciences. In contrast to this dichotomous view, Ricoeur maintains that the text must be taken as the primary focal point of hermeneutics; and when the text is so taken, the distanciation which Gadamer regards as an ontological fall from grace appears as the very condition for the possibility of hermeneutics. Moreover, since the referential power released by a depth interpretation of the text is capable of projecting an alternative world, this power carries within itself 'a recourse against any given reality and thereby the possibility of a critique of the real'.[93] Finally, insofar as the appropriation of the world which the text unfolds may result in an expansion of the horizons of consciousness, the process of interpretation creates the possibility for a critique of the egoistic illusions and ideological distortions of the subject.

In defence of the second thesis, Ricoeur argues that critical theory presupposes hermeneutics in a way that vitiates its claim to an independent epistemological status. This presupposition can be identified at several levels in the writings of Habermas. First, on a justificatory level, Ricoeur questions the basis for Habermas's general theoretical views, for example the notion that all scientific inquiry is guided by knowledge-constitutive interests, or the assertion that there are only three such interests. Ricoeur suggests that if a justification of these views is possible, then it can only be provided by means of a hermeneutic philosophy, such as that to be found in Heidegger's analytic of Dasein. Second, at a methodological level, Ricoeur challenges the claim that the critical social sciences are characterised by a unique integration of explanation and understanding. For it follows from Ricoeur's position that all hermeneutical disciplines, and not simply the one concerned with the critique of ideology, have the structure of a depth interpretation in which understanding is mediated by explanatory procedures. Third, at a substantive level, Ricoeur doubts whether the emancipatory interest can be clearly distinguished from the practical interest in intersubjective understanding. For the ideologies which the critical sciences seek to analyse and dispel are, after all, distortions of communication; and the goal of the interest in emancipation is nothing other than the ideal of communication free from constraint. Moreover, Ricoeur maintains that this ideal would be empty unless it could be substantiated through the reinterpretation of the past:

> Distortions can be criticised only in the name of a *consensus* which we cannot anticipate merely emptily, in the manner of a regulative idea, unless that idea is exemplified; and one of the very places of exemplification of the ideal of communication is precisely our capacity to overcome cultural distance in the interpretation of works received from the past. He who is unable to reinterpret his past may also be incapable of projecting concretely his interest in emancipation.[94]

At a fourth and final level, Ricoeur crystallises these abstract remarks in the observation that even the critical theorist does not stand outside of historical tradition. To be sure, this tradition is not the same as that from which Gadamer speaks; but it is a tradition nonetheless, namely that of the Enlightenment. Ricoeur therefore concludes that the alleged antinomy between a hermeneutics of tradition and a critique of ideology is falsely conceived. For as in a hermeneutic philosophy concerned with salvation, so in a critical theory premised on emancipation: 'eschatology is nothing without the recitation of acts of deliverance from the past'.[95]

Social science and philosophy

Ricoeur's writings establish a close connection between social science and philosophy. The nature of this connection may be summarised as follows: if on the one hand social science provides a wealth of material for philosophical reflection, then on the other only philosophy is capable of establishing the limits of validity of the various scientific disciplines. The possibility and necessity of incorporating the results of social science within philosophy is a consequence of Ricoeur's view of reflection as appropriation and consciousness as a task. From this view it follows that the expansion of consciousness through self-reflection requires the mediation of those signs in which human beings express themselves: 'that is why a reflective philosophy must include the results, methods, and presuppositions of all the sciences that try to decipher and interpret the signs of man'.[96] Accordingly, Ricoeur eschews the programme for a phenomenology of language sketched in the writings of Merleau-Ponty. For in advocating an immediate return to the speaking subject, that programme precludes any dialogue with semiology from the start. Similarly, Ricoeur hesitates to follow the route undertaken by Heidegger's analytic of Dasein. For in subsuming epistemology to an ontology of understanding, that analytic dissolves all questions concerning textual exegesis and the conflict of interpretations. So while Ricoeur seeks both a phenomenology of language and an ontology of being, his itinerary is not that of Merleau-Ponty or Heidegger. Rather, by incorporating the insights of psychoanalysis, semiology and other social sciences, reflective philosophy

takes the long and roundabout route of an interpretation of private and public, psychic and cultural signs, where the desire to be and the effort to be which constitute us are expressed and made explicit.[97]

Philosophy in turn has a function to fulfil within the domain of social science. For today that domain is fractured and fraught by the competing claims of disciplines which aspire to a total view. However, such aspirations are based upon a false conception of the limits of validity of the approaches concerned; and by tracing the methods of interpretation back to the theoretical frameworks of the respective disciplines, philosophy 'prepares itself to perform its highest task, which would be a true arbitration among the absolutist claims of each of the interpretations'.[98] Thus, in his epistemological reflections on Freud, Ricoeur attempts to show that psychoanalysis is not an observational science but a hermeneutical discipline which attains its specificity in a semantics of desire; and while this discipline may be legitimately applied to humanity as a whole, such universality is limited by the particularity of its point of view. Similarly, in his critique of Lévi-Strauss, Ricoeur allows that structuralism is a justifiable approach to the study of social phenomena, but only within the limits of validity established by the methodological presuppositions of the semiological model. These presuppositions constitute structuralism as a science but not as a philosophy, for they preclude the possibility of structuralist thought from reflecting upon itself. Yet while some reflection is a necessity for philosophy, Ricoeur agrees with Ladrière[99] that total reflexivity lies beyond its reach. Hence, in his comments on Habermas, Ricoeur emphasises that although the critique of ideology is a task that must be begun, it is in principle one that can never be completed. Moreover, just as the attainment of a coherent ontology and a unitary truth is but a promised land for philosophy, so too the final reconciliation of the conflicting hermeneutical disciplines is a synthesis that must be perpetually postponed. For as Ricoeur recites from Xenophanes:

There never was nor will there ever be any man who has certain knowledge about the gods and about all the things that I tell of. And even if he does happen to get most things right, still he himself is not aware of this. Yet all may have shadows of the truth.[100]

To conclude this chapter, it may be recalled that hermeneutic phenomenology is a synthesis of two philosophical standpoints. The synthesis was originally effected by Heidegger, and subsequently developed by writers such as Gadamer and Ricoeur. Ricoeur's contributions to this development emerge gradually in the course of his career, and eventually attain their full significance with the formulation of a semantics of discourse. This semantics provides the foundation for a general theory of interpretation which is centred on the concept of the text, and which integrates philosophy and hermeneutics through an affirmative notion of reflection. The theory of interpretation provides answers to several traditional problems of philosophy, generates approaches to specific fields of analysis, and suggests solutions to certain controversies in the methodology of social science. Once again, however, it must be stressed that these various contributions do not exhaust the resources of hermeneutic phenomenology in general, nor the writings of Ricoeur in particular. Moreover, to acknowledge these contributions is not necessarily to accept them, and their consistency and correctness will be contested in subsequent chapters.

3. Jürgen Habermas and critical social theory

Critical social theory marks a distinctive standpoint in the contemporary philosophical field. This standpoint is part of a tradition of thought which stems from the writings of Kant, Hegel and Marx, and which includes the contributions of the Frankfurt Institute for Social Research. The work of Jürgen Habermas represents an original development of several themes which preoccupied the critical theorists of the Frankfurt School. The specific nature of this development has appeared in the course of a brief but prolific career, during which Habermas has written on topics ranging from classical philosophy and student politics to the theory of social evolution. Accordingly, in the pages that follow, I attempt to sketch some of the themes of critical social theory through a selective exegesis of the work of Habermas. One consequence of this approach is that the writings of other authors who are commonly associated with the standpoint of critical theory are only cursorily discussed. Moreover, since Habermas has expressed his views on an astonishing variety of issues, and since with each new publication these views continue to be elaborated and reformed, no claim can be made to provide a comprehensive and conclusive account of his work. Nevertheless, and despite these limitations, this chapter is animated by the belief that a selective exegesis of the writings of Habermas will provide a suitable basis for the analysis of certain themes in critical social theory.

I. Philosophical background

Kant, Hegel and Marx

The concerns of critical theory are anchored in the writings of Kant, Hegel and Marx. One of the principal tasks which Kant undertook was to inquire into the nature and limits of human knowledge. In contrast to the approach of Locke and Hume, Kant insisted that such an inquiry must not be restricted to the analysis of the contents of consciousness. For these contents are already organised and interpreted by the knowing subject; and hence epistemology must be conceived as 'critique', that is, as an attempt to elucidate the forms and categories which render this cognitive activity possible. Yet the domain of experience which the Kantian categories made possible was prejudged by the ideals of mathematics and natural science; and the status of the subject whose self-reflection unfolded the forms of sensibility remained unclear. In pursuing objections such as these, Hegel placed epistemology within the context of an historical self-formative process wherein mathematics and science were mere stages in the progress towards truth. For in Hegel's view,

the truth is the whole. The whole, however, is merely the essential nature reaching its completeness through the process of its own development. Of the Absolute it must be said that it is essentially a result, that only at the end is it what it is in its very truth; and just in that consists its nature, which is to be actual, subject or self-becoming, self-development.[1]

In *The Phenomenology of Mind*, Hegel recounts the progressive path to the absolute through an immanent critique of human experience. This critique aims, not only to unveil conditions of possibility, but also to unmask illusion and error; its driving force is the dialectic, that 'portentous power of the negative',[2] which discloses the contradictions within each successive mode of experience. The dialectic reveals, for instance, that the impressions of the senses are not a primordial object of knowledge, for sense certainty presupposes a subject who attains self-consciousness through a struggle for recognition with others. When the state of self-consciousness is ultimately attained, a point is reached at which the self may be seen as an emanation of spirit, and from which the truth may be grasped in the whole.

The writings of Marx may be regarded in part as an attempt to transform Hegel's speculative idealism into a practical and historical materialism.[3] The transformation is mediated by the assumption that human beings distinguish themselves from animals when they engage in the activity of production. Hegel acknowledges this assumption insofar as he conceives of the dialectic as a process of labour; but Marx maintains that 'the only labor which Hegel knows and recognizes is *abstractly mental labor*',[4] and hence Hegel fails to grasp the concrete sensuous activity of human beings producing goods to satisfy their basic needs. In addition to the phenomenon of production, human beings also participate in the act of procreation and thereby contribute to the continuation of the species. Both dimensions of productive activity are characterised by the establishment of social relations with others, so that the production of life, both of one's own in labour and of fresh life in procreation, now appears as a double relationship: on the one hand as a natural, on the other as a social relationship.[5]

Marx infers that any given stage in the development of the material forces of production will be accompanied by a specific stage in the development of the social relations of production, and he suggests that the history of human societies may be understood in terms of the changing constellation of these two primary factors. The propellant of the historical process is the formation and resolution of contradictions between the emerging forces and the prevailing relations of production, and these contradictions are manifested in successive forms of class struggle. In capitalist society, the class struggle is focused upon capital and wage-labour, which confront one another in the sphere of large-scale industrial production. However, the nature of the relation between these classes remains concealed to their constituent members, as well as to the practitioners of the science which takes such relations as its object of investigation. Accordingly, in *Capital*, Marx undertakes an analysis of the capitalist mode of production through a critique of political economy, whose categories collaborate in the fetishism of commodities.[6] By identifying the appropriation of surplus value as the source of capital accumulation, and by locating the origins of the crises endemic to capitalism in the utilisation of accumulated capital, Marx conducts a critique which aims to guide the revolutionary practice of the proletariat.

Orthodox Marxism and revisionism
In the decades following Marx's death, the movement which sprang from his work divided into two irreconcilable camps. On the one hand, the 'orthodox Marxists' generalised historical materialism into a universal world outlook, and regarded the persistence of capitalism as a temporary stabilisation that was bound to explode in economic crises and armed conflicts. On the other hand, the 'revisionists' emphasised the evolutionary aspects of the materialist view, maintaining that the proletariat could continue to improve its economic and political position within the democratic framework of organised capitalism. Both branches of this bifurcation can be traced back to ambiguous passages in the writings of Marx, but the later work of Engels provides a more conspicuous source. Among other tasks, the ageing Engels undertook an extensive study of mathematics and natural science, in order to convince himself in detail of something that he never doubted as a whole, namely

that amid the welter of innumerable changes taking place in nature, the same dialectical laws of motion are in operation as those which in history govern the apparent fortuitousness of events.[7]

There is a clear thread of continuity from Engels's dialectics of nature, through certain writings of Kautsky and Plekhanov, to the orthodox tenets of Soviet Marxism; and the deterministic implications of this orientation are especially evident in the work of Bukharin. The latter author disavows any essential difference between the natural and social sciences, asserting that both types of discipline are concerned to elucidate laws which govern the course of events with inviolable necessity. In the case of the social sciences, these laws specify causal antecedents within the sphere of material production; and Bukharin contends that all super-structural phenomena, from politics and ethics to language and art, are 'ultimately determined in various ways by the economic structure and the stage of the social technology'.[8] In thus transforming historical material-ism into a positive science, Bukharin and others prepare the way for the subsequent integration of Marxism into a bureaucratic system whose existence is acclaimed as inevitable.

There are passages in the writings of the later Engels which are equally conducive to the development of revisionism. In his introduction to the 1895 edition of *The Class Struggles in France*, Engels concedes that the revolutionary expectations of 1848 were mistaken, since

history has shown us too to have been wrong, has revealed our point of view of that time to have been an illusion. It has done even more: . . . it has also completely transformed the conditions under which the proletariat has to fight. The mode of struggle of 1848 is today obsolete in every respect.[9]

Engels claims that the growth of social democratic parties has created a new weapon in the struggle for socialism, and it was this weapon that provided the theoretical basis for the practical politics of the Second International. Thus, in spite of Kautsky's self-professed orthodoxy, there are sections in his draft of the *Erfurt Program* which clearly approve of parliamentary activity.[10] Yet it was one of Kautsky's principal critics, Eduard Bernstein, who explicitly articulated the assumptions and conse-quences of the revisionist approach. Reflecting upon the statistics of social change, Bernstein rejects all theories of catastrophic collapse as well as the dialectical devices which underpin them, endorsing instead the slow but steady evolution of society towards democratic socialism. The latter view had been the effective policy of the German Social Democratic Party (SPD) for many years, and Bernstein was merely insisting that the

SPD appear in word what it was in fact, viz. 'a democratic, socialistic party of reform'.[11] Having firmly abandoned its revolutionary commitment, it is no surprise that the SPD mobilised its membership in defence of the homeland, and then became an agent of repression when the hour of insurrection finally arrived.

Frankfurt School

The Frankfurt Institute for Social Research was established in 1923, at a time when the socialist movement in the Weimar Republic was sharply split between a bolshevik Communist Party and a democratic Socialist Party.[12] Rather than aligning themselves with either of these factions, the leading theorists of the so-called 'Frankfurt School' returned to the foundations of Marx's thought and sought to re-examine the philosophical heritage from which it arose. In contrast to the dismissal of the dialectic by the revisionists, the Frankfurt theorists attempt to recapture the critical and holistic dimensions of classical German philosophy, and strive to mediate 'all that is individual through the objective societal totality'.[13] In opposition to the reductionist tendencies of orthodox Marxism, the Frankfurt writers contend that cultural products cannot be treated as mere epiphenomena of the economy. Instead, these writers regard such products as relatively autonomous expressions of contradictions within the social whole, and they perceive within some of these expressions both the social physiognomy of the present and the critical forces which negate the existing order. In contradistinction to both mechanistic and evolutionary conceptions of social change, the Frankfurt theorists emphasise the importance of the subjective conditions for revolutionary transformation. The advent of socialism is understood as a matter neither of causal consequences nor of progressive reforms, but rather of enlightened self-emancipation; and hence the truth of critical theory is dependent not upon confirmed predictions or gradual gains, but upon concrete social practice. Horkheimer expresses the practical aspect of critical theory as follows:

The truth about the future does not take the form of a verification of data which differ from others only in having some special importance. Rather, man's own will plays a part in that truth, and he may not take his ease if the prognosis is to come true.[14]

In the later years of the Frankfurt School, the theoretical contributions of its most eminent members crystallise in the critique of instrumental reason. The concept of instrumental reason refers to the adequacy of specified means for the attainment of predetermined ends, and it explicitly precludes any reference to the worthiness of the ends themselves.[15] This concept of reason thus contains its own form of irrationality, a contradictory conclusion which was the historical product of the Enlightenment. By identifying nature with whatever can be comprehended mathematically, and by equating the latter with truth, the Enlightenment absolutised a methodological technique which eliminated the exercise of critical thought as such. Consequently, as Horkheimer and Adorno observe, the Enlightenment engendered its own destruction:

> The reduction of thought to a mathematical apparatus conceals the sanction of the world as its own yardstick. What appears to be the triumph of subjective rationality, the subjection of all reality to logical formalism, is paid for by the obedient subjection of reason to what is directly given . . . Hence enlightenment returns to mythology, which it never really knew how to elude.[16]

The social and political implications of the triumph of instrumental reason are pursued by Marcuse in his sweeping critique of contemporary Western society. In *One Dimensional Man,* Marcuse argues that the steady expansion of 'technological rationality' has liquidated all transcendent and oppositional forces, and that the large-scale production of consumer goods has led to the 'repressive desublimation' of the masses.[17] However, given the pervasive presence of technological rationality, the possibility of finding an historical subject that could actualise critical theory through the transformation of capitalist society appears increasingly remote. Thus, many of the later writings of Marcuse in particular, and of the Frankfurt School in general, tend towards a pessimistic critique of contemporary culture which becomes progressively detached from political and economic analysis. The revolutionary optimism which emanates from the pages of Marx is only faintly reflected in the words of Benjamin: 'It is only for the sake of those without hope that hope is given to us.'[18]

II. Formation of Habermas's social theory

Theory and practice
The themes which preoccupied the theorists of the Frankfurt School serve as a point of departure for the work of Habermas. One of these themes pertains to the positivistic dissolution of the Enlightenment; and in his early writings, Habermas reinterprets this process in terms of the changing constellation of theory and practice. In the classical tradition of philosophy, politics is regarded as the doctrine of the good and just life, and the attainment of this life is seen as dependent upon the practical cultiva-

tion of character. However, the practical sphere as a whole is distinguished from *theoria*, which is reserved for the privileged contemplation
of the ideal and the divine. Habermas maintains that in the sixteenth and
seventeenth centuries, the classical conception of the relation between
theory and practice underwent a radical transformation. The transformation is anticipated in the writings of Machiavelli and More, but it achieves
its most explicit expression in the work of Hobbes. For only with Hobbes
is a technical approach to politics combined with a rigorous method of
investigation and a mechanistic conception of the world; and hence only
with Hobbes is politics fully transformed into a science. For Hobbes, the
aim of politics is to establish the general conditions for the correct order of
society and the state, so that the application of such knowledge would be
a mere technical problem. However, in thereby excluding all practical
issues from the province of politics, Hobbes disregards the dimension of
prudence which classical philosophy had provided, and anticipates the
surge of irrationality which the modern sciences have provoked. For as
Habermas observes,

to the degree to which politics is scientifically rationalized, and praxis is instructed
theoretically by technical recommendation, there is a growth of that residual
complex of problems, in the face of which the analysis of the experimental
sciences must confess its incompetence.[19]

One of the residual problems arises from the fact that the social engineers
of the allegedly correct order are simultaneously members of the existing
faulty order, and hence both subjects and objects of scientific knowledge.
This peculiarly reflexive position of social science is rendered inexplicable
by the Hobbesian view, which cannot conceive of social change as anything other than technical control. So within the philosophical framework
initially established by Hobbes, the *praxis* of active and enlightened
citizens is replaced by the *techne* of expert and manipulative administra-
tors, and consequently 'the relationship of theory to praxis can no longer
be explained theoretically'.[20]

Habermas maintains that in the eighteenth century an alternative
framework emerged within which the relation between theory and practice could be more adequately conceived. Among others, Holbach portrays the mind as confused by a veil of opinions, and holds that one can
extricate oneself from this veil only with the greatest effort. For the errors
of dogmatism are no mere figments of the imagination, but rather the
constituents of a false consciousness which is anchored in the institutions
of a traditional and authoritarian society. Accordingly, the critical extirpation of prejudice requires not only rational insight, but also the courage to

be rational: reason can dispel dogmatism only insofar as it incorporates the will to reason in its interest. In contrast to the contemplative aspects of classical philosophy, and in opposition to the technical conception of modern politics, the eighteenth century thus gave birth to a notion of reason which unites theory and practice through enlightened self-emancipation. In the work of Holbach and others,

> reason is equated unquestioningly with the talent for adult autonomy and with sensibility to the evils of this world. It has always made its decision in favor of justice, general welfare, and peace; the reason which defends itself against dogmatism is a committed reason.[21]

The notion of committed reason is preserved in the writings of Fichte, Schelling and Hegel, but only with Marx does it become fully integrated into the human self-formative process. Marx shows how human beings as labouring subjects strive to attain a form of social organisation which is free from the exercise of constraint, thereby realising the concepts of freedom and autonomy which are implicit in the notion of reason. The forces which obstruct this aspiration and falsify the contents of consciousness are sustained as historically specific ideologies, so that committed reason can be actualised as the critique of ideology. Today, however, the dominant ideology is no longer rooted directly in the processes of social labour, but rather is mediated through the objectivistic self-understanding of the sciences. Accordingly, Habermas pursues the task of committed reason on the plane of epistemology, seeking to disclose what Hegel and Marx once knew but what positivists have long since forgotten, namely that 'the methodology of the sciences [is] intertwined with the objective self-formative process of the human species'.[22]

Critique of positivism

In the investigations presented in *Knowledge and Human Interests*, Habermas attempts to show that there are three categories of scientific inquiry in which connections obtain between logical-methodological rules and knowledge-constitutive interests. The specific nature of these connections is revealed through an immanent critique of various positions in the history of the philosophy of science. Thus, in the early positivism of Comte and Mach, a certain class of phenomena is promoted to the exclusive status of reality, and in such a way that knowledge of that reality is directly linked to the possibility of technical control. However, since these writers abandon epistemological reflection for the logical analysis of scientific theories, they cannot conceptualise the relation between knowledge and technical control; and moreover, these authors are able to sustain their sharp delimitation of science only through an ontology of the factual which reinstates the very metaphysics which they seek to eschew. In Habermas's opinion, the pragmatism of Peirce overcomes the narrow scientism and naive objectivism which vitiates the writings of the early positivists. For Peirce does not reduce the role of methodology to the logical analysis of scientific theories, but identifies it instead with the elucidation of the procedures with which such theories are obtained. According to Peirce, the three modes of deduction, induction and abduction comprise the rules by which one must proceed if the process of inquiry is to generate true statements about reality. Furthermore, since for Peirce a statement is true if and only if it commands a consensus with regard to the validity of the belief which it expresses; and since a belief is valid if and only if, under given initial conditions, it can be transformed into technical recommendations; so it follows that the three modes of inference distinguished by Peirce can fulfil their function only within the behavioural system of purposive-rational action. This system forms the transcendental framework within which these modes of inference are pursued, and in terms of which the meaning of the validity of the statements obtained thereby is secured. Habermas thus concludes that in the self-understanding of the sciences attained by Peirce,

knowledge stabilizes purposive-rational, feedback-monitored action in an environment objectified from the point of view of possible technical control. The transcendental framework of the process of inquiry establishes the necessary conditions for the possible extension of technically exploitable knowledge.[23]

The generation of technically exploitable knowledge is the task of the empirical-analytic sciences, which Habermas regards as a systematic continuation of the pre-scientific learning process that proceeds within the behavioural system of purposive-rational action. Accordingly, this knowledge realises an interest which is neither wholly instinctual nor entirely severed from the objective context of life, that is, 'a *knowledge-constitutive interest in possible technical control*'.[24]

Habermas contends that the empirical-analytic sciences constitute only one among several categories of knowledge, and that the conduct of these sciences presupposes rather than precludes an alternative form of inquiry. For the subject who pursues such sciences is not an isolated monad, but an investigating community which sustains itself through symbolic interaction. In the construction of theoretical languages and in the formulation of observation statements, the members of this community follow reciprocally binding conventions and thereby assume, to borrow Apel's expression, an 'a priori of communication'.[25] Habermas claims that this communicative dimension is *sui generis*, and that it cannot be grasped by an operationalist concept of mind in the manner of Peirce. For communication is an intersubjective phenomenon that is not merely monologic but dialogic, and hence '*communicative action* is a system of reference that cannot be reduced to the framework of *instrumental action*'.[26] The presupposition of an irreducible communicative dimension is equally evident in the philosophy of science elaborated by Popper. In opposing the logical positivist solution to the 'basis problem', Popper propounds the view that the observational statements which falsify law-like hypotheses cannot be justified in any empirically conclusive way. Instead, scientists must discuss whether to accept a given basic statement, and so decide whether to apply the hypothesis to a particular state of affairs; but the application of the hypothesis is, Habermas observes, an unavoidably circular process. For one cannot apply a general rule unless a prior decision has been made about which facts are relevant, and yet these facts cannot be established as relevant prior to an application of the rule. In the eyes of Habermas,

the inevitable circle in the application of rules is evidence of the embedding of the research process in a context which itself can no longer be explicated in an analytical-empirical manner but only hermeneutically.[27]

Critique of hermeneutics

The connection between the logical-methodological rules of the historical-hermeneutic sciences and their corresponding knowledge-constitutive interest can be shown, according to Habermas, through an analysis of the writings of Dilthey. Dilthey is concerned to establish, among other things, that the *Geisteswissenschaften* have a status distinct from and complementary to that of the natural sciences. For the former disciplines subsume within their object domains only those phenomena which display the peculiar configuration of experience, expression and understanding. Dilthey accords ordinary language a central position in this configuration, as he recognises that it is the ground of the intersubjectivity within which understanding moves. Moreover, he perceives that ordinary language is not an homogeneous network of logical relations, but rather an heterogeneous composition of symbols and actions. So the interpretation of the meaningful structures which form the object of the cultural sciences cannot be reduced to the mere elucidation of meta-linguistic rules. On the contrary, hermeneutic interpretation is a circular process which requires the preliminary provision of an interpretative scheme that anticipates the final result. Through the formulation and corroboration of such schemata, hermeneutics is able to render perplexing expressions intelligible and to remove obstructions from the process of social interaction. Habermas therefore submits that

in its very structure hermeneutic understanding is designed to guarantee, within cultural traditions, the possible action-orienting self-understanding of individuals and groups as well as reciprocal understanding between different individuals and groups. It makes possible the form of unconstrained consensus and the type of open intersubjectivity on which communicative action depends.[28]

Hermeneutic inquiry is the methodical extension of a process of mutual understanding which occurs on the pre-scientific level within the tradition-bound structure of symbolic interaction. When the intersubjectivity of mutual understanding breaks down, then a condition of survival is disturbed which is as elementary as that of the technical control over objectified processes. Since this condition is the presupposition of practical engagement in the social world, *'we call the knowledge-constitutive interest of the cultural sciences "practical"'*.[29]

Although the historical-hermeneutic sciences have a distinct and irreducible status, they do not constitute, in Habermas's view, an exhaustive approach to the study of social phenomena. For these sciences are restricted by the limits of the very medium within which they are pursued, namely the medium of language. Habermas suggests that such limits may be discerned in the writings of both Wittgenstein and Gadamer. Similarly to Dilthey, the later Wittgenstein conceives of ordinary language as a complex combination of symbols and actions. Understanding a language implies being able to act, as it involves a mastery of the rules which a child acquires through didactic training. However, by emphasising the integral unity and self-sufficiency of discrete language-games, the philosophy of the later Wittgenstein is easily transformed into an a-theoretical pluralism. It is with the aim of avoiding this relativistic result that Habermas turns, along with Apel and Wellmer,[30] to the hermeneutic contributions of Gadamer. By focusing on the phenomenon of translation, Gadamer transcends the monadic isolation of language-games and brings to consciousness the inherent reflexivity of ordinary language. For only when the intersubjective validity of linguistic rules is problematicised does an interpretation come into play which restores the consensus, thereby overcoming a temporary distance and reproducing the system of rules. Hence Habermas claims that the writings of Gadamer disclose a dimension of language neglected by Wittgenstein: 'The unity of language destroyed in the pluralism of language-games is dialectically restored in the context of tradition. Language *is* only as handed down.'[31] However, Habermas criticises Gadamer's tendency to convert this historical insight into an absolutisation of cultural tradition. For such a conversion over-looks the fact that language itself is dependent upon social processes which are not wholly linguistic in nature. As Habermas insists,

> Language is *also* a medium of domination and social force. It serves to legitimate relations of organised power. Insofar as the legitimations of power relations, whose institutionalisation they make possible, are not articulated, insofar as these only express themselves in the legitimations, language is *also* ideological.[32]

The medium of language within which the historical-hermeneutic sciences move is only one moment of a social totality which also reproduces itself through the exercise of technical control and political power. To ignore the latter domains, and hence to hypostatise language in the manner of linguistic and hermeneutic philosophy, is to fall into the conservative clutches of a naive and submissive idealism.

Foundations of critical theory

The dissolution of relations of power and ideology is the task of the critical social sciences, which constitute the third category of disciplines wherein a relation can be shown between logical-methodological rules and knowledge-constitutive interests. One of the first writers to pursue these sciences systematically was Marx, who developed a critical social theory on a materialist basis. On Habermas's interpretation, Marx accepts Hegel's view that the human species constitutes itself in a process of self-formation; but Marx replaces the self-movement of the spirit through intellectual labour with the self-generation of the species through social labour. For Marx, social labour is both a natural process which creates the factual conditions for the possible reproduction of human life, and an epistemological category which creates the transcendental conditions for the possible objectivity of human experience. 'Thus in materialism', remarks Habermas in a Kantian vein, 'labor has the function of synthesis.'[33] However, Habermas maintains that the concept of social labour prevents Marx from providing an adequate philosophical foundation for his critical social theory. For this concept leads Marx to conflate the epistemological status of natural science with that of critique, a conflation in which Wellmer similarly detects the latent positivism of Marx's approach.[34] Habermas argues that by reducing the self-formative process of the human species to its self-generation through social labour, Marx is obliged to conceive of reflection on the model of production.

Hence he cannot distinguish between a science subjected to the transcendental conditions within which the species produces itself, and a critique which reflects upon the process of production and seeks to raise that process to the level of self-consciousness. Still, in his empirical investigations Marx does take into account the dimension of social interaction in which relations between societal members are institutionally established and normatively controlled. A discrepancy thus arises, in Habermas's view, between Marx's practice of inquiry and his limited philosophical self-understanding of that practice:

In his empirical analyses Marx comprehends the history of the species under categories of material activity *and* the critical abolition of ideologies, of instrumental action *and* revolutionary practice, of labor *and* reflection at once. But Marx interprets what he does in the more restricted conception of the species' self-reflection through work alone.[35]

In accordance with the empirical practice of Marx, Habermas declares that the idea of the self-constitution of the human species in history must be expanded to include both its self-generation through productive activity and its self-formation through critical-revolutionary activity. Correspondingly, the concept of synthesis must be reformulated in a way that integrates both the dimension of labour and that of interaction. Habermas finds the key to the possibility of such an integration in the metapsychological writings of Freud.

Habermas regards psychoanalysis as a type of depth hermeneutics which incorporates explanation and understanding into a science oriented towards methodical self-reflection. Following the work of Lorenzer,[36] the textual flaws which form the object of this science may be conceived as the result of repressed motives and privatised needs, which lead to the severance of symbols from the realm of public communication. The aim of psychoanalysis is to decipher these split-off symbols, and ultimately to eliminate the flaws which they produce, through the socio-psychological reconstruction of their genesis. The reconstruction is facilitated by the generalised history of infantile development, which provides the physician with the theoretical tools to combine the fragmentary information obtained in the analytic dialogue into a coherent narrative. However, the narrative can be verified if and only if the patient willingly accepts it as his or her own; that is, it can be corroborated, Habermas observes, 'only by the successful continuation of an interrupted self-formative process'.[37] Projected onto the phylogenetic plane of civilisation as a whole, the self-formative process is viewed by Freud in terms of a conflict between the necessities of self-preservation, which must be met through the collective subjugation of external nature, and the surplus potential of libidinal and aggressive needs, which can only be contained through the institutional suppression of internal nature. By conceiving of the human being as a drive-inhibited as well as a tool-making animal, Freud endows the institutionalisation and dissolution of relations of power and ideology with a more fundamental role than they have for Marx. Indeed, Habermas credits Freud with having shown

how the relations of power embodied in systematically distorted communication can be attacked directly by the process of critique, so that in the self-reflection, which the analytic method has made possible and provoked, in the end insight can coincide with emancipation from unrecognized dependencies – that is, knowledge coincides with the fulfillment of the interest in liberation through knowledge.[38]

In the process of self-reflection epitomised by the psychoanalytic dialogue, the subject overcomes an illusion and is thereby freed from dependence upon reified relations of power; and in so doing, the subject realises the interest in human emancipation which governs the critical social sciences as a whole, and which expresses the will to freedom and autonomy that characterises the eighteenth-century concept of committed reason.

Evolution and legitimation

The reformulation of the philosophical foundations of the critical social sciences provides Habermas with a basis for the reconstruction of historical materialism. Habermas regards historical materialism as a theory of social evolution, and he seeks to develop this theory through an analysis of certain key concepts in the writings of Marx. A mode of production is defined by Marx as a particular constellation of the forces and relations of production. The forces of production determine the level of possible control over the objectified processes of nature and society; and within this category Habermas includes labour power, technically utilisable knowledge and organisational information. The relations of production determine the way that labour power is combined with available means of production; and Habermas adds that these relations crystallise around an institutional order which in turn secures a specific form of social integration. The stability of a given mode of production is endangered when the development of the forces of production generates system problems which cannot be solved through the existing relations of production, so that the prevailing form of social integration must be revolutionised in order to create the capacity for alternative solutions. Habermas emphasises the inadequacy of any attempt to explain these evolutionary steps in terms of social conflict alone, or in terms of class conflict in post-primitive societies. For one must show how such conflict can lead to a new form of social integration, and this requires the assumption of endogenous learning mechanisms within both spheres of the mode of production. 'The species learns', according to Habermas,

not only in the dimension of technically useful knowledge decisive for the development of productive forces but also in the dimension of moral-practical consciousness decisive for structures of interaction. The rules of communicative action do develop in reaction to changes in the domain of instrumental and strategic action; but in doing so they follow *their own logic*.[39]

The developmental logic of the structures of interaction specifies the abstract principles of social organisation, which circumscribe the scope of possible solutions to existing system problems. Following the cognitive psychology of Piaget and Kohlberg,[40] Habermas characterises this logic as a series of stages in the growth of both individual and social consciousness. When system problems arise which overload the steering capacity of a given social formation, then progression to a higher level of consciousness, and therewith to a new principle of social organisation, is a prerequisite for the solution of these problems. Habermas therefore proposes the thesis that the development of normative structures is the pace-maker of social evolution; and he cautiously adds that however idealistic this thesis may appear, it is firmly anchored in 'the conditions of reproduction of a species that must preserve its life through labor and interaction, that is *also* by virtue of propositions that can be true and norms that are in need of justification'.[41]

The reconstruction of historical materialism forms the backcloth for a specification of the crisis tendencies in contemporary capitalism. Habermas concurs with Marx in identifying the relationship of wage-labour and capital as the organisational principle of liberal-capitalist societies. In this type of society, system problems initially appear as disturbances in the process of capital accumulation, and subsequently threaten social integration insofar as the prevailing ideology is directly dependent upon the exchange of equivalents. With the transition to the present form of advanced capitalism, this crisis complex undergoes a fundamental transformation. The state apparatus is now employed to ameliorate the crisis tendencies within the economy, both by large-scale planning and by creating the conditions for the utilisation of excess capital. Habermas maintains, however, that the repoliticisation of the economy does not eliminate the formation of system problems; rather, it merely dislocates the specific medium in which such problems are expressed:

> I do not exclude the possibility that economic crisis can be permanently averted, although only in such a way that contradictory steering imperatives that assert themselves in the pressure for capital realization would produce a series of other crisis tendencies.[42]

Pursuing the suggestions of Offe,[43] Habermas argues that the state apparatus is caught between imperatives which systematically overload its administrative capacity and generate rationality deficits. If the government fails to defray such deficits, and so fails to meet the contradictory demands that are placed upon it, then the conditions are created for a crisis of legitimation. The latter in turn presupposes a discrepancy between the motives which the state and educational system declare to be necessary, and the motivation actually supplied by the socio-cultural system. Habermas claims that the growth of this discrepancy is factually demonstrable, insofar as the socio-cultural system is becoming increasingly incapable of reproducing the syndrome of civil and familial-vocational privatism. Moreover, Habermas submits that the motivational system which replaces this syndrome may be systematically assessed, for 'the values and norms in accordance with which motives are formed have an immanent relation to truth'.[44] The explication of this immanent relation to truth, which normative no less than descriptive statements possess, is one of the principal tasks of Habermas's theory of language.

III. Exposition of the theory of language

Action and discourse

The theory of language elaborated by Habermas rests upon a fundamental distinction between action and discourse. In normally functioning language-games, the successful exchange of speech-acts takes place against an implicit and naively assumed background consensus. The consensus involves the mutual recognition of at least four validity claims which, according to Habermas, 'competent speakers must reciprocally maintain with each of their speech-acts'.[45] The four claims include the intelligibility of the utterance, the truth of the propositional content, the correctness of the performatory component, and the sincerity of the speaking subject. Each of these claims can be rendered problematic in the course of everyday communication, in which case their validity can be redeemed in specific ways. When the sincerity of someone is impugned, we ask questions like 'Is this person deceiving me?' or 'Is this person merely pretending?' Such questions can be answered only in the process of interaction, for whether or not someone is sincerely expressing intentions will eventually show itself in actions. When the intelligibility of an utterance is problematicised, we ask questions of the sort 'What does that mean?' or 'How should I understand that?' The answers to these questions are to be found in the functioning of language itself, for intelligibility is a factual condition rather than a counterfactual claim of communication. Finally, when the truth of a propositional content or the correctness of a performatory component is placed in doubt, we ask questions like 'Is it really as you say it is?' or 'Is it right to do what you have done?' Habermas maintains that these questions cannot be fully answered within the context of communicative action, for they raise validity claims which have a peculiar status. The declarative claim to truth and the normative claim to correctness are, Habermas contends,

claims of validity which can be proven only in discourse. The factual recognition of these claims bases itself in every case, even that of error, on the possibility of the discursive validation of the claims made.[46]

The realm of discourse is analytically distinguishable from the everyday context of communicative action. The participants of a discourse no longer seek to exchange information or to convey experiences, but rather to proffer arguments for the justification of problematicised validity claims. The latter process presupposes the suspension of all action constraints, in order to 'render inoperative all motives other than that of a co-operative readiness to come to an understanding'.[47] The process of justification further requires a progressive radicalisation in the levels of argumentation, so that one may extricate oneself from the context of action and strive towards self-reflection. This requirement applies both to the justification of truth claims, which is the function of theoretical discourse, and to the redemption of claims to correctness, which is undertaken in practical discourse. The stages of radicalisation within each of these realms are summarised in the table on p. 88.[48] The first step in the radicalisation of theoretical discourse is from a problematicised assertion representing an action to a statement in which a controversial validity claim is made about an object of discourse. The second step involves the theoretical explanation of the problematicised assertion through the construction of an argument within a chosen linguistic system. The third step consists in the modification of the initially chosen system or its replacement by an alternative. This leads to a fourth and final step in which the boundary between theoretical and practical discourse is

Steps of Radicalisation	Theoretical Discourse	Practical Discourse
actions	assertions	prescriptions/prohibitions
groundings	theoretical explanations	theoretical justifications
substantial language-critique	metatheoretical transformation of linguistic systems	meta-ethical transformation of linguistic systems
self-reflection	critique of knowledge	political will formation

blurred, for at this stage one is impelled to consider what should count as knowledge. The various steps in the radicalisation of practical discourse are parallel to those of theoretical discourse, leading from a problematicised prescription or prohibition to a collective formation of the will in the light of existing needs and available resources. However, unlike the results of theoretical discourse, the recommendations embodied in the practical will formation may well diverge from the norms which prevail in fact. Hence Habermas insists that

> the results of a practical discourse in which it is established that the validity claims of factually acknowledged norms cannot be redeemed, or that norms with argumentatively redeemable validity claims do not exist in fact, bear a critical relation to reality (namely to the symbolic reality of society).[49]

Logic of discourse

The outcome of a theoretical or practical discourse is a conclusion which is determined by the force of better argument alone. Habermas describes this force as 'rational motivation', and he proposes to clarify it within the framework of a logic of discourse. Unlike its propositional or transcendental counterpart, the logic of discourse is a pragmatic logic. It rejects the assumption that argumentation consists in the provision of a sequence of statements which can be formally deduced from one another. On the contrary, it regards an argument as a series of speech-acts, and it fully accepts that 'the transition between these pragmatic units of speech can neither be grounded entirely logically . . . nor can it be grounded empirically'.[50] Habermas elucidates the logical structure of discursive arguments by means of an example borrowed from Toulmin.[51] The assertion 'Harry is a British subject' (conclusion=C) is explained through the specification of a cause, 'Harry was born in Bermuda' (data=D). This explanation is acceptable insofar as it fulfils a key rule, such as 'A man born in Bermuda will generally be a British subject' (warrant=W). The plausibility of the key rule is justified in turn by considerations like 'On account of the following statutes and other legal provisions' (backing=B).

Applying this basic structure to the realms of theoretical and practical discourse, Habermas derives the elements of argumentation represented below.[52]

	Theoretical Discourse	*Practical Discourse*
Conclusion (C)	assertion	prescription/evaluation
Controversial Validity Claim	truth	correctness
Required from opponent	explanation	justification
Data (D)	causes, motives, etc.	grounds
Warrant (W)	uniformities, laws, etc.	norms, principles, etc.
Backing (B)	observations, data, etc.	interpretations of needs, etc.

The logic of discourse is concerned with those arguments in which the relation between the backing and the warrant is not deductive, and yet the backing is a sufficient motivation to make the warrant plausible. Habermas proposes that one of the prerequisites for this situation is an overall conformity between the language used for argumentation and the conceptual system within which the phenomenon to be explained is described. 'A satisfactory argument appears', writes Habermas,

only when all parts of the argument belong to the same language. Then the linguistic system anchors the ground concepts with which the phenomenon needing explanation is described, so that *on the one hand* the singular existential statements appearing in this description can be derived from D and W, and *on the other hand* B is, for anyone who can participate in a discourse, a sufficient motive to accept W.[53]

The initial choice of a linguistic system subsumes the phenomenon requiring explanation to a particular object domain. The basic predicates of the linguistic system determine which kinds of causes and motives, as well as which types of laws and norms, can be brought to bear on the described phenomenon. Accordingly, Habermas emphasises that it is only as constituents of linguistic systems that assertions and recommendations are capable of grounding. 'Grounding has nothing to do with the relation between individual sentences and reality, but above all with the coherence between sentences within a linguistic system.'[54] It does not follow, however, that the relation between a linguistic system and reality is wholly arbitrary. For Habermas suggests that the basic predicates of linguistic systems express cognitive schemata, in Piaget's sense, so that the relation between language and reality is regulated through an ongoing process of learning and development. The cognitive schemata provide a species-historical basis for the principles of induction and universalisation, which serve to justify the logically discontinuous transition from the backing to the warrant. Yet the rational motivation of argumentation cannot consist simply in the factual adaptation of a linguistic system to reality. Rather, rational motivation presupposes, in Habermas's view, that this factual adaptation can be brought to consciousness and continued as a discursive learning process:

> Whether a language is suitable to an object domain, and whether the phenomenon in need of explanation should be assigned to the object domain with which the chosen language accords – these questions themselves must be allowed to become the object of argumentation . . . The formal properties of discourse must therefore be such that the plane of discourse can at any time be changed, and an initially chosen linguistic and conceptual system can in given cases be recognised as unsuitable and revised.[55]

The characterisation of the formal structure of the discursive realm, and hence the specification of the conditions under which the force of better argument alone would prevail, is made possible by the theory of communicative competence.

Theory of communicative competence

The theory of communicative competence is concerned with reconstructing the general conditions of communication. In a manner similar to the Chomskyan programme, this theory seeks to elicit a system of formal qualifications which the competent speaker must possess in order to engage in the process of communication. However, in contrast to the monologic approach of transformational grammar, Habermas argues that there are semantic universals which are constituents of an intersubjectively produced cultural system, and that such universals need not precede all experience. Habermas distinguishes four categories into which these semantic universals may fall:[56]

	a priori	*a posteriori*
Intersubjective	dialogue-constitutive universals	cultural universals
Monologic	universal cognitive schemes	universals of perceptive and motivational constitution

Since Chomsky overlooks this multiplicity of possibilities and concentrates solely on an abstract system of generative rules, he cannot account for the structure of intersubjectivity which renders the application of linguistic competence possible. For 'it is not enough', in Habermas's opinion, to understand language communication as an application – limited by empirical conditions – of linguistic competence . . . On the contrary, in order to participate in normal discourse, the speaker must have – in addition to his linguistic competence – basic qualifications of speech and of symbolic interaction (role-behavior) at his disposal, which we may call communicative competence.[57]

In focusing on the qualifications which enable a speaker to apply grammatically well-formed expressions in concrete speech-acts, the theory of communicative competence converges with the tradition of ordinary language philosophy. Both approaches are preoccupied with the pragmatic entities of speech, and both regard intersubjectivity as an essential condition of linguistic communication. However, whereas ordinary language philosophy tends to restrict itself to the description of typical speech-acts employed in specific situations, the theoretical perspective developed by Habermas 'has to do with the reconstruction of the system of rules which underlies the ability of a subject to express sentences in *any* situation'.[58]

The writings of Austin and Searle provide an initial point of departure for the theory of communicative competence. These writings reveal that the basic pragmatic units of speech have a distinctive double structure; for as Habermas observes, 'the surface structure of the explicit speech-act satisfies the *standard form* when it consists of an illocutionary and propositional component'.[59] The propositional component of the typical speech-act is commonly differentiated-out, thereby disclosing two planes between which both speaker and hearer must move if they wish to communicate with one another: the plane of intersubjectivity, upon which they establish interpersonal relations; and the plane of objects and experiences, about which they exchange their views. Habermas contends that the characterisation of these two planes, as well as the ability to move between them, presuppose that subjects have at their disposal a series of dialogue-constitutive universals.

Without reference to these universals we could not even define the recurrent components of possible speech: namely the expressions themselves, and then the interpersonal relations between speakers/hearers which are generated with the expressions, and finally the objects about which the speakers/hearers communicate with one another.[60]

Habermas proposes several categories of expressions as candidates for the class of dialogue-constitutive universals. First, the personal pronouns and their derivatives form a reference system between potential speakers, enabling each participant to assume the roles of 'I' and 'You' simultaneously, and so securing the intersubjective validity of semantic rules. Second, the deictic expressions of space and time, as well as the articles and demonstrative pronouns, form a reference system of possible denotations, linking the plane of intersubjectivity upon which subjects interact with the plane of objects about which they converse. Third, forms of address, greeting and interrogation are communicative speech-acts which are directed at the process of speaking as such, and which specify speech as a medium in which misunderstanding, error and deception are possible. Finally, the constative, representative and regulative speech-acts form a system that enables one to make certain distinctions which are fundamental for any speech situation, such as the distinctions between being and appearance, being and essence, and being and ought to be. Habermas's claim is that while engaging in the process of communication, subjects naively and necessarily deploy these various categories of expressions, and thereby display the mastery of dialogue-constitutive universals which defines their communicative competence.

Ideal speech situation
The theory of communicative competence provides the means for the construction of an ideal speech situation. The latter situation is characterised by the absence of any barriers which would obstruct a communicative exchange between the participants of a discourse. In addition to contingent influences which are imposed upon the situation from without, such barriers include the constraints which are produced by the structure of communication itself; and Habermas proceeds on the basis of the following thesis:

the structure of communication itself produces no constraints if and only if, for all possible participants, there is a symmetrical distribution of chances to choose and to apply speech-acts.[61]

The thesis of symmetry defines the general framework of the ideal speech situation and allows the latter to be further specified in conjunction with various categories of dialogue-constitutive universals. Equality in the opportunity to apply communicative speech-acts means that all potential participants in a discourse have the same chance to initiate and sustain dialogue through questions and answers, claims and counterclaims. A symmetrical distribution of chances to apply constative speech-acts implies that all potential participants have the same opportunity to proffer interpretations, recommendations and justifications, so that no preconceptions remain excluded from consideration. An equal opportunity to apply representative speech-acts gives all potential participants the same chance to express their attitudes, feelings and intentions, creating the circumstances within which subjects become transparent to themselves and others in what they say and do. Finally, symmetry in the distribution of chances to apply regulative speech-acts entails that all potential participants have the same opportunity to order and to prohibit, to obey and to refuse, thus precluding the privileges that arise from one-sided norms. Habermas acknowledges that representation and regulation are accomplishments of speaking subjects *qua* social actors, and hence that the last two symmetries presuppose a reference to the organisation of action contexts. The construction of an ideal speech situation therefore implies a corresponding idealisation of action, for 'the emancipation of discourse from the constraints of action is possible only in the context of pure communicative action'.[62]

Habermas maintains that the ideal speech situation crystallises the conditions under which the conclusion of a discourse would be determined by the force of better argument alone. These conditions guarantee a freedom of movement between action and discourse, and between the various levels of radicalisation within a discourse. They secure the possibility of revising or replacing the initially chosen linguistic system, and so give substance to the view that discursively thematised validity claims may be rationally redeemed. Habermas suggests, moreover, that the ideal speech situation provides a theoretical reformulation of certain ideas which are central to the tradition of Western philosophy as a whole:

The symmetrical distribution of chances in the choice and execution of speech-acts, which refer (a) to statements as statements, (b) to the relation of speakers to their utterances, and (c) to the following of rules, are the linguistic-theoretical determinations for that which we traditionally seek to connect with the ideas of truth, freedom and justice.[63]

As an abstract construction implicit in the prerequisites of possible speech, the ideal speech situation has a unique and peculiar status. It is not an existing concept in the Hegelian sense, for no historical society completely fulfils the conditions of rational discourse. Similarly, the ideal speech situation is not a regulative principle in the Kantian sense, for it is necessarily anticipated in every act of linguistic communication. 'The ideal speech situation is', Habermas submits, 'neither an empirical phenomenon nor merely a construct, but rather an unavoidable reciprocal presupposition of discourse.'[64] Although this presupposition is normally counterfactual, Habermas does not exclude the possibility that, under certain institutional arrangements, the ideal speech situation could be transformed into reality. It is an open question as to whether such arrangements will ever in fact be established, or whether the ideal speech situation will remain forever a mere anticipation; and the answer to this question is, Habermas insists, no longer a speculative issue but a practical hypothesis.

Systematically distorted communication

The ideal speech situation provides a theoretical tool for the critical analysis of systematically distorted communication. The latter phenomenon may be provisionally characterised in terms of its deviation from the model of pure communicative action. First, on the level of language, distorted communication involves the use of rules which diverge from the recognised system of linguistic conventions. Second, on the level of behaviour, distorted communication is manifested in the rigid and compulsory repetition of behavioural patterns. Finally, when one considers the system of distorted communication as a whole, a discrepancy appears between the various levels of communication. The normal congruency between linguistic symbols, action patterns and expressions disintegrates, so that actions and expressions belie what is said. A barrier is formed between the publicly participating ego and the repressed realm of the unconscious, so that causally determining motives no longer correspond to linguistically apprehensible intentions. Habermas suggests that the degree of deviation from the model of pure communicative action is directly proportional to the extent of prelinguistically fixed motivations which cannot be freely converted into public communication. He further proposes that

these deviations increase correspondingly to the varying degrees of repression which characterize the institutional system within a given society; and that in turn, the degree of repression depends on the developmental stage of the productive forces and on the organization of authority, that is of the institutionalization of political and economic power.[65]

Historical situations of systematically distorted communication are stabilised by means of deceptions which conceal the mechanisms of repression. These deceptions exclude the implicitly raised validity claims from discursive thematisation, and thereby transform the reciprocal imputation of accountability into a fiction. At the same time, effective deceptions sustain this fiction in a compelling manner through a belief in legitimacy. The simultaneous disguise and defence of systematically distorted communication is, Habermas contends, 'the paradoxical result of ideologies'.[66]

The concept of systematically distorted communication provides a reformulated framework for critical theory. Among other things, critical theory is concerned to penetrate the veil of ideology and to elucidate the mechanisms of repression which characterise a particular social formation. These mechanisms are in turn dependent upon the development of forces of production and the institutionalisation of relations of power. Habermas currently propounds the view that such relations of power may be identified by comparing the prevailing normative structures on the one hand with the hypothetical system of norms which would result from a discursive will formation on the other. Accordingly, the critique of ideology may be guided by the following question:

how would the members of a social system, at a given stage in the development of productive forces, have collectively and bindingly interpreted their needs (and which norms would they have accepted as justified) if they could and would have decided on organization of social intercourse through discursive will-formation, with adequate knowledge of the limiting conditions and functional imperatives of their society?[67]

In focusing on the collective interpretation of needs within conditions that are historically defined, critical theory remains bound to the context of action in a way that preserves its continuity with psychoanalysis. For the analytic dialogue between doctor and patient satisfies a form of communication which provides both less and more than rational discourse. It provides less because the patient does not assume a symmetrical relation vis-à-vis the doctor from the outset, and hence the patient does not qualify as a full discursive participant. However, the analytic dialogue also provides more than rational discourse; for the successful self-reflection of the patient culminates in an insight which redeems not only a truth claim, but also a claim to authenticity. By accepting the theoretically mediated account of the analyst, the patient confirms an interpretation and simultaneously sees through a self-deception. Similarly, in the critical theory which Habermas seeks to establish, the societal subjects may attempt to dispel the illusions of ideology through a collective interpretation of needs under the counterfactual conditions of rational discourse. This attempt *must* be undertaken insofar as the ideal speech situation is necessarily anticipated in every act of linguistic communication; and it *can* be undertaken insofar as every competent speaker possesses the means to construct such a situation, however distorted the actual conditions of communication may be. 'On this unavoidable fiction', concludes Habermas, 'rests the humanity of relations among men who are still men.'[68]

IV. Problems in the theory of reference and truth

Interest, objectivity and truth

Habermas's recent writings on the theory of language mark a significant modification of his original views on the relation between interest, objectivity and truth. In his earlier work, Habermas accepts the phenomenological thesis that the object domains and validity claims of the objectivistic sciences are predetermined by the self-evidences of the life-world, although he rejects Husserl's claim that only a purified transcendental consciousness can overcome the naivety of the natural standpoint.[69] One of the central themes of *Knowledge and Human Interests* is that the logical-methodological rules for the conduct of the various sciences are linked to an interest structure which is rooted in the self-formative processes of the human species, and which prejudges both the possible objects of scientific analysis and the possible meaning of the validity of scientific statements. 'Thus we speak of a technical or practical knowledge-constitutive interest', Habermas explains,

insofar as the life structures of instrumental action and symbolic interaction preform the meaning of the validity of possible statements via the logic of inquiry in such a manner that, to the extent that these statements are cognitions, they have a function only in these life structures: that is to the extent that they are technically exploited or practically efficacious.[70]

The necessity and unsurpassability of these transcendental limits can be grasped only by a philosophical consciousness that has shed its own illusion of purity and acknowledged its position in the structure of human interests. For the tradition of philosophy within which Habermas places his work is oriented towards the same emancipatory goal as that which guides the critical social sciences; and philosophy pursues this goal 'not through the power of renewed *theoria*', as Husserl presumed, 'but through demonstrating what it conceals: the connexion of knowledge and interest'.[71]

The constellation of interest, objectivity and truth is transformed by Habermas's subsequent distinction between action and discourse. The constitution of scientific object domains is still predetermined by an interest structure anchored in the natural history of the human species. However, in the light of this later distinction, the possible meaning of the validity of scientific statements is now only indirectly dependent upon the spheres of instrumental and communicative action. For the statements of science, no less than those of everyday life, contain implicitly raised validity claims which can only be discursively redeemed. The realms of discourse are dissociated from the contexts of action within which scientific object domains are constituted, thereby ensuring that 'questions of validity are separated from those of genesis'.[72] Accordingly, the meaning of the validity of scientific statements is no longer specified by the interest structure which predetermines the objectivity of experience, but rather by the conditions which guarantee the discursive redemption of validity claims. As Habermas remarks,

the objectivity of a given experience is measured in terms of the controllable consequences of actions based upon these experiences. On the other hand, truth, i.e. the justification of the validity claims implicitly maintained with assertions, is not shown in successful action but in successful argumentation, with which these validity claims can be discursively *redeemed*.[73]

So whereas in his earlier work Habermas regards both the possible objects of scientific inquiry and the possible meaning of the validity of scientific statements as predetermined by the structure of human interests, in his later writings he carefully distinguishes between these two sets of problems. The elucidation of the presuppositions for the objectivity of experience remains the task of a theory of constitution, but the clarification of the conditions for the discursive redemption of validity claims requires an independent theory of truth.

Theory of constitution
The theory of constitution is concerned to elucidate the a priori of experience which predefines the structure of scientific object domains. In his recent investigations, Habermas schematically develops this theory in terms of the relation between types of experience and their corresponding forms of linguistic articulation. In the perception of things and events, one has an experience which can be expressed in statements, and there is a smooth transition from the act of observation to that of expression. In the understanding of meaning, on the other hand, there are two distinct and discontinuous levels. The first level pertains to the non-objectivating attitude which must be assumed by the participants of a dialogue, since one can grasp the sense of an utterance only insofar as one has established an interpersonal relationship with another. The second level is concerned with that which one understands by means of the non-objectivating attitude, namely the propositional contents of the uttered expression. Habermas claims that this level represents a notable departure from the first, for the communicative experience 'becomes strangely objectivated once it is made the content of a proposition'. [74] These

differential relations between experience and expression enable Habermas to distinguish between 'descriptions', which reproduce the contents of observation, and 'narrations', which render the results of understanding. Both descriptions and narrations contain denotative and predicative components, implying a minimum content of properties which identifiable objects must possess. This minimum content constitutes a categorial framework which may be analysed in terms of cognitive schemata, and which makes possible the objectivation of experience as such. However, when the common categorial framework is applied to the respective object domains of sensory and communicative experience, the resultant objectivations differ in important respects. As Habermas observes,

> descriptions rendering sensory experience are made in a different language than narrations rendering communicative experience. In the first case, denotative expressions of language must be able to identify things and happenings; in the second case, they must also be able to identify persons and utterances (or cultural objects), thus differentiating classes of permissible referents.[75]

The differentiated domains of sensory and communicative experience bear an a priori relation to human action. Habermas suggests that this relation could be demonstrated either through conceptual analysis or immanent critique, as both types of inquiry would disclose that observable objects are at the same time instrumentally manipulable bodies, and understanding persons are simultaneously participants in linguistically mediated interaction. In the final instance, it is the a priori relation between action and experience which preserves the continuity between the constitution of scientific object domains and the practical activities of everyday life.

In the reformulated theory of constitution, knowledge-constitutive interests are allocated to the role of linking the domains of action-related experience to the realms of theoretical and practical discourse. The structure of interests thus manifests itself in the nature of the facts which can be asserted in scientific statements. For the referential syntaxes of scientific languages contain primitive terms which categorise only certain classes of experiential objects, and the statements formulated in such languages can only be tested by methods of a specific kind. These methods determine the means by which action-related experiences may be extracted from their primary life context and utilised for the purpose of discursive argumentation, thereby transforming everyday occurrences into scientific data. Correspondingly, statements corroborated in the realm of discourse may be translated back into life contexts in only certain ways. Statements about the object domain of things and happenings may be retranslated into orientations governing purposive-rational action, whereas statements about the object domain of persons and utterances may be transformed into orientations for communicative action. Habermas holds that in thereby predetermining the relations between practical activities and scientific results,

the interests which direct knowledge preserve the unity of the relevant system of action and experience vis-à-vis discourse; they retain the latent reference of theoretical knowledge to action by way of the transformation of opinions into theoretical statements and their retransformation into knowledge oriented toward action.[76]

The interest in emancipation performs a similar role in the methodological structure of the sciences concerned with critique. However, unlike the feedback relation established by the technical and practical interests, the circuit installed by the emancipatory interest is peculiarly reflexive. For the experience of systematically distorted communication arises 'only at the point where I become analytically conscious of, and try to *dissolve*, the pseudo-objectivity which is rooted in unconscious motives or repressed interests'.[77]

Theory of truth
The clarification of the conditions for the discursive redemption of validity claims is the task of the consensus theory of truth. In attempting to formulate such a theory, Habermas concurs with Strawson's view that it is statements and not utterances which are true or false, and that what a true statement asserts is a fact.[78] This view entails the rejection of all ontological theories of truth which hypostatise facts as things, and it leads to the dismissal of any transcendental or redundancy theory which conflates the domains of experience with the realms of discourse. In contrast to these traditional theories, Habermas maintains that truth is a validity claim which is connected with constative speech-acts. A statement is true when the validity claim of the speech-act with which it is asserted is justified; and the validity claim is justified, Habermas submits, if and only if the statement would command the consent of anyone else who could enter into a discussion with the speaker.

In order to distinguish true from false statements, I refer to the judgement of another – and indeed to the judgement of all others with whom I could enter a conversation (whereby I counterfactually include all of the conversational partners which I could find if my life history were coextensive with the history of humanity). The condition for the truth of statements is the potential consent of all others . . . Truth means the promise to attain a rational consensus.[79]

However, if the attainment of a rational consensus is to be accepted as the criterion of truth, then one must specify the conditions under which a factually achieved consensus would hold as rational. Habermas regards this as both a possible and a legitimate task, for the requisite conditions are none other than those of the ideal speech situation. 'The ideal speech situation is characterised by the fact that every consensus which can be attained under its conditions may hold *per se* as a true consensus';[80] and hence the unavoidable anticipation of this ideal provides an a priori guarantee that a factually attained agreement may be linked with the notion of truth.

The consensus theory of truth has important implications for the nature of evaluative judgements and the status of critical theory. Habermas rejects the assumptions underlying classical natural rights, which hold that normative statements may be true or false in the same sense as descriptive statements, as well as the presuppositions of orthodox empiricism, which assert that normative statements are wholly incapable of corroboration. Habermas is equally critical of the intermediate positions of Weber, Popper and Hare, who, he argues, are led to a decisionistic treatment of the value problem through their failure to perceive that normative statements imply validity claims which can be argumentatively redeemed. Such argumentation is undertaken within the realm of practical discourse, wherein an attempt is made to establish a rational consensus concerning the validity claims of problematicised norms. The formal properties of the discursive situation ensure that a rational consensus can be attained only on the basis of generalisable interests; and hence Habermas suggests that the pluralism of individual ends can be transcended without recourse to an external moral principle:

The problematic that arises with the introduction of a moral principle is disposed of as soon as one sees that the expectation of discursive redemption of normative-validity claims is already contained in the structure of intersubjectivity and makes specially introduced maxims of universalization superfluous.[81]

The epistemological status of a critical theory is more complicated. For such theories incorporate a dimension of reconstruction as well as an element of self-reflection, and so their validity must be assessed on at least two levels. Insofar as critical theory is reconstructive, it implies a claim to truth which can only be redeemed through the normal processes of scientific argumentation. However, insofar as critical theory is reflexive, it entails a validity claim which 'can only be realized in the successful processes of enlightenment, which lead to the acceptance by those concerned, free of any compulsion, of the theoretically derivable interpretations'.[82]

V. Problems in the analysis of action

Types of action

The corpus of Habermas's work rests upon a distinction between two types of action. This distinction is drawn in a number of different ways, and the types themselves are variously labelled 'work', 'labour' or 'purposive-rational action' on the one hand, and 'interaction', 'symbolic interaction' or 'communicative action' on the other. Habermas initially formulates the distinction in his study of Hegel's Jena lectures on the philosophy of mind. In Habermas's opinion, these lectures occupy a unique position in the development of Hegel's thought, for they provide an original but subsequently abandoned foundation for the formative process of the spirit. In contrast to the self-reflection of the solitary ego posited by Kant, and unlike the idealistic reductionism entailed by Hegel's later philosophy of identity, the Jena lectures offer a conception of the constitution of the self as a dialectical product of language, labour and interaction. 'Labour' refers to the use of tools for the satisfaction of human needs, whereas 'interaction' denotes the process whereby the subject comes to see itself through the eyes of others and thereby attains self-consciousness. Habermas is especially interested in Hegel's account of the relation between the latter two dimensions, for the account is presented in such a way that 'a reduction of interaction to labor or derivation of labor from interaction is not possible'.[83] However, this view is largely absent from Hegel's later writings; and although Marx recovered it in his distinction between the forces and relations of production, he tended to resolve the self-formative process into the self-movement of production. In opposition to these subsequent tendencies, Habermas maintains that the dimensions of labour and interaction must be rigorously separated. For the expansion of the technical forces of production is not identical with the development of norms which would sustain an interaction free from domination. As Habermas insists,

liberation from hunger and misery does not necessarily converge with *liberation from servitude and degradation,* for there is no automatic developmental relation between labor and interaction.[84]

Habermas develops the distinction between labour and interaction in his critique of the concept of rationalisation in the writings of Weber and Marcuse. 'Rationalisation', for Weber, means the growth of societal sectors subject to the criterion of means–ends efficiency, as well as the industrialisation of social labour which promotes this process. Since the resultant transformation of social institutions leads to the destruction of old forms of legitimation, this process is accompanied by a progressive secularisation and a growing 'disenchantment' of traditional world views. Marcuse maintains, however, that Weber's concept of rationality is an excessively narrow and implicitly ideological one; and hence the process which Weber calls 'rationalisation' does not realise rationality as such, but merely a specific type of unacknowledged political domination.[85] The domination is facilitated by the institutionalisation of scientific and technological progress, for Marcuse claims that the 'material a priori' of science renders its results utilisable for the legitimation of the existing order. Accordingly, the latter writer suggests that the emancipation of human beings from the contemporary form of domination is conditional upon a revolutionary transformation of science and technology.[86] It is the possibility of such a New Science and Technology which Habermas is concerned to dispute. For in Habermas's view, the development of science and technology follows a logic that necessarily unfolds in the dimension of purposive-rational action or work; and so the critique of the prevailing form of science and technology does not lead to some new and mysteriously humanised scientific-technological project, but rather 'to an alternative structure of action: to symbolic interaction in distinction to purposive-rational action'.[87] On the basis of this distinction, Habermas differentiates between the institutional framework of a society, which consists of norms that govern symbolic interaction, and the subsystems of purposive-rational action that are embedded within it. Just as each of these types of action is irreducible to the other, so each of these societal spheres is characterised by a peculiar form of rationalisation; and whereas the latter process may accord with the Weberian account within the subsystems of purposive-rational action, this is not the case within the institutional framework of society. For Habermas contends that rationalisation at the institutional level

does not lead per se to the better functioning of social systems, but would furnish the members of society with the opportunity for further emancipation and progressive individuation. The growth of productive forces is not the same as the intention of the 'good life.' It can at best serve it.[88]

Purposive-rational action

The concept of labour or purposive-rational action can be clarified further by distinguishing between instrumental action and rational choice. The latter are both forms of purposive-rational action, and as such are both concerned with the realisation of predefined goals under specified conditions. However, instrumental action is governed by technical rules which incorporate empirical knowledge and which imply conditional predictions about observable events. Rational choice, on the other hand, is governed by strategies which incorporate analytic knowledge and which imply deductions from preference rules and decision procedures. Habermas expresses this distinction in the following way:

> while instrumental action organizes means that are appropriate or inappropriate according to criteria of an effective control of reality, strategic action depends only on the correct evaluation cf possible alternative choices, which results from calculation supplemented by values and maxims.[89]

The validity of the technical rules and strategies which govern the two forms of purposive-rational action depends upon the truth of empirical statements and the correctness of analytic deductions. Purposive-rational action is associated with language insofar as such statements and deductions are well-formed sequences of signs; but since the signs are removed from the context of everyday communication, this use of language is monologic and abstract. The relevant rules and strategies are not acquired through social interaction, but through specialised learning mechanisms which transmit technical skills and professional qualifications. If an individual violates such rules and strategies, the behaviour is regarded as incompetent. The individual is punished not by the invocation of public sanctions, but merely by the inefficacy of the action: 'the "punishment" is built, so to speak, into its rebuff by reality'.[90]

The rationalisation of purposive-rational action may apply to either instrumental or strategic behaviour. In the former case, the rationalisation of action involves the technical application of empirical knowledge. In the latter case, rationalisation is concerned with the internal consistency of value systems and decision maxims for the derivation of particular choices. Both forms of rationalisation result in a socially significant implementation of knowledge, which engenders an increase in the social forces of production. For in Habermas's view, production includes both the goal-directed transformation of raw material and the social co-ordination of this transformative process; and hence not only technical rules, but also 'the *rules of strategic action*, in accord with which cooperation comes about, are a necessary component of the labour process'.[91] However, the augmentation of the social forces of production is not the only process of rationalisation which is relevant to the explanation of social change. Marx was certainly aware of another process, as evidenced by the emphasis which he placed on class conflict; but

in conceiving of the organized struggle of oppressed classes as itself a productive force, he established between the two motors of social development – technical-organizational progress on the one hand and class struggle on the other – a confusing, in any event an inadequately analyzed, connection.[92]

Communicative action

The concept of communicative action can be elucidated through an analysis of the regulating norms. Such norms define reciprocal expectations about behaviour, and they must be understood and acknowledged as binding by at least two acting subjects. Since the meaning of consensual norms is objectified in ordinary language communication, it follows that communicative action presupposes the validity basis of speech. In Habermas's words:

The universal validity claims (truth, correctness, sincerity), which the parties concerned must at least implicitly maintain and reciprocally acknowledge, make possible the consensus which carries the collective action.[93]

The presupposition of the validity basis of speech distinguishes communicative action from its strategic counterpart. For in the case of strategic action, sincerity in expressed intentions is not expected and the correctness of underlying norms is not necessarily assumed. Rather, each acting subject follows his or her personal preferences and decision maxims, irrespective of whether other subjects concur with these choices or not. However, as soon as a system of strategic action requires that several subjects come to some agreement about a specific preference, then it demands a normative fixation or institutionalisation of action; and 'institutionalization again means the organization of consensual action resting on intersubjectively recognized validity claims'.[94] Social institutions consist of norms which govern communicative action, and the latter in turn functions to sustain such institutions. The norms are acquired in the process of socialisation, primarily through the internalisation of successively encountered roles. Failure to comply with consensual norms is indicative of deviant action, which is censured through sanctions that are founded on convention.

The rationalisation of communicative action proceeds within the dimension of practical accountability. Whereas the rationalisation of purposive-rational action is linked to the accumulation of empirically true knowledge, 'the rationalizable aspect of communicative action has to do not with propositional truth, but rather with the sincerity of intentional expressions and with the correctness of norms'.[95] It follows that the degree to which communicative action has been rationalised is dependent upon two factors. First, it is dependent upon the extent to which a subject sincerely expresses intentions in actions, or merely deceives himself or herself, as well as others, through the formation of internal and unconscious constraints. Second, it depends upon whether the validity claims connected with the norms of action are indeed valid, or merely stabilised through the establishment of intersubjective barriers to communication. The rationalisation of communicative action thus means, according to Habermas, the dissolution of internal and external obstructions which systematically distort the process of communication, and which sustain communicative action on the basis of a pseudo-consensus:

Rationalization here means extirpating those relations of force that are inconspicuously set in the very structures of communication and that prevent conscious settlements of conflicts, and consensual regulations of conflicts, by means of intrapsychic as well as interpersonal communicative barriers.[96]

The rationalisation of communicative action is reflected in successive forms of social integration and psychological identity formation. These forms in turn mediate the development of social movements and the dynamic of class conflict, which have an historically autonomous and theoretically dominant role in the process of social evolution. Some of the characteristics which thus distinguish communicative from purposive-rational action may be summarised in the following table.[97]

	Labour	*Interaction*
Rules	technical	normative
Language	monologic	dialogic
Implication	predictions	expectations
Acquisition	instruction	socialisation
Function	problem solving	institutional maintenance
Sanction	inefficacy	punishment
Rationalisation	productivity	emancipation

VI. Problems in the methodology of social science

Depth hermeneutics
The writings of Habermas make an important contribution to a number of problems in the methodology of social science. One of these problems is concerned with the relation between explanation and understanding,

which has been a topic of continuous controversy since the seminal work of Dilthey. Habermas's principal contribution to this controversy is based upon his use of psychoanalysis as a model for critical theory. As a form of 'depth hermeneutics', psychoanalysis employs explanatory hypotheses in order to understand initially incomprehensible expressions. The hypotheses are derived from general interpretations which define the self-formative process as a law-like sequence of systemic states, and which attribute distortions of communication to the confusion of successive phases of symbol organisation. It is only by recourse to this generalised history of infantile development that the physician is able to reconstruct the repressed contents of the patient's past, and thereby to decipher the behavioural manifestations which are deformed by the mechanisms of repression. Thus Habermas observes that

the What, the semantic content of a systematically distorted manifestation, cannot be 'understood,' if it is not possible at the same time to 'explain' the Why, the origin of the symptom scene with reference to the initial circumstances, which lead to the systematic distortion itself.[98]

The logic of general interpretations places psychoanalysis in a peculiar methodological position. On the one hand, insofar as scenic reconstructions assume the form of explanatory hypotheses, psychoanalysis bears an affinity to the empirical-analytic sciences. On the other hand, since the reconstruction is itself an interpretation, and since the ultimate criterion of verification is the patient's act of recollection, it follows that the psychoanalytic procedure is similar to the methods of the historical-hermeneutic disciplines. The peculiar position of psychoanalysis is epitomised by its concept of causality, which pertains not to the connections between observable events but rather to the consequences of split-off symbols and repressed motives. Echoing Hegel, Habermas calls this the 'causality of fate'; and in contrast to a science which employs causal relations for the extension of technical control, psychoanalysis aims at the abolition of these relations as such. The latter discipline 'proves its explanatory power in self-reflection, in which an objectivation that is both understood and explained is also overcome'.[99]

Habermas maintains that the methodological structure of psychoanalysis is paradigmatic for a critical science of society. For just as psychoanalysis seeks to go beyond the patient's limited self-understanding, so too a critical social science cannot rest content with an account of social action in terms of motives which coincide with the actor's interpretation of the situation. 'A sociology', remarks Habermas in an early work, which conceptualises the motivation of action in this way, must restrict itself to an interpretative explication. The explanations which it can give coincide with linguistic description and hermeneutic exegesis; it must abandon causal explanation.[100]

To abandon causal explanation is simultaneously to ignore those dimensions of the social world which determine and distort the medium of language and tradition, namely the dimensions of labour and power. The development of the forces of production is a precondition for the formation of human motives and needs, and the specific content of the latter depends upon the stage of development. Moreover, the consciousness of motives and the interpretation of needs are subject to the sanctions of prevailing norms; and insofar as these norms express asymmetries of political power, they allow only certain motives and needs to be publicly articulated. A critical social science, in Habermas's view, must try to disclose that which is suppressed, and to dispel the illusions which legitimate the mechanisms of suppression. Such a science must have at its disposal a systematically generalised history in the form of a theory of social evolution, which would generate explanatory hypotheses concerning the origins and functions of specific institutions and ideologies. Yet a critical science of society cannot remain at this objectivistic level, as if it were merely an historicised form of functionalism. For no less than psychoanalysis, critical social science aims at the emancipation of a subject through the elucidation of meaning; and as Habermas insists in his debate with Luhmann, 'the meaning of meaning cannot be conceived in a monological reduction, be it to the phenomenology of experience or to the mode of selection of a complexity-reducing system of action'.[101] So while Habermas allows that the elucidation of meaning may be facilitated by the causal explanation of its genesis, he claims that such an elucidation cannot be wholly replaced by explanation, for meaning is an irreducible component of the social world.

Reconstruction and critique
A second methodological problem which the writings of Habermas address is concerned with the respective roles of reconstruction and critique. In *Knowledge and Human Interests*, these roles are effectively assimilated within the framework established by the concept of self-reflection. The latter concept derives from the philosophy of Kant, wherein it refers to the clarification of the conditions of possible knowledge. It was Hegel, however, who destroyed the foundations of Kant's transcendental consciousness and developed the experience of reflection within

the dimension of a self-formative process. Hence it was Hegel who first showed, in Habermas's eyes, how

critical consciousness, after initially hastening forward, must work itself up to its present position through stages of reflection that can be reconstructed through a systematic repetition of the experiences that constituted the history of mankind.[102]

The concept of self-reflection elaborated by Kant and Hegel is preserved in the work of Freud. In basing the interpretation of symptoms on the generalised history of infantile development, the analyst employs a theoretical reconstruction to reveal the repressed experiences of an interrupted self-formative process. The recollection of those experiences by the patient, and the eventual elimination of the symptoms which they produce, is the ultimate aim of analysis – 'a word', Habermas notes, 'in which critique as knowledge and critique as transformation are not accidentally combined'.[103]

In his more recent studies, Habermas explicitly distinguishes between the two aspects of reconstruction and critique which are united in the concept of self-reflection. Reflection in the sense of reconstruction refers to the quasi-Kantian exercise of elucidating the conditions which make possible a form of knowledge or a mode of action. In recent years, this type of reflection has been rehabilitated on a linguistic basis, assuming the form of a rational reconstruction of systems of rules which render the transcendental subject superfluous. Reflection in the sense of critique, on the other hand, is concerned with a subjectively constituted illusion which objectively constrains the social actor. Unlike the anonymous systems of rules which are the object of rational reconstruction, these illusions appertain to the particular self-formative process of an individual or group; and the dissolution of such illusions through a theoretically induced enlightenment leads to the emancipation of the subject from previously unconscious constraints. As Habermas explains,

criticism is characterized by its ability to make unconscious elements conscious in a way which has practical consequences. Criticism changes the determinants of *false* consciousness, whereas reconstructions explicate correct know-how, i.e. the intuitive knowledge we acquire when we possess rule-competence, *without* having *practical* consequences.[104]

The explicit distinction between reconstruction and critique does not imply, however, that these two types of self-reflection are unrelated. On the contrary, a social science which aspires to a critical stance cannot avoid, in Habermas's view, the exercise of rational reconstruction. For if critique 'accepts as its task the explanation of a systematically distorted communication, then it must have mastery of the idea of undistorted communication or reasonable discourse';[105] and unfolding the idea of undistorted communication is the reconstructive project of the theory of communicative competence.

Social science and philosophy

Throughout his work, Habermas attempts to establish a close and constructive relation between the social sciences and philosophy. This relation is reciprocal, for just as the social sciences require philosophy, so too the latter can no longer be pursued independently of the former. There are, according to Habermas, at least four respects in which the social sciences may require the services of philosophy. The first respect concerns the self-understanding of the social sciences, which suffers from the same scientistic prejudice that colours the comprehension of the natural sciences. The struggle against this prejudice demands a philosophical consciousness which has retained the epistemological mode, but which has renounced all claims to the absolute. For Habermas submits that

science can only be comprehended epistemologically, which means as *one* category of possible knowledge, as long as knowledge is not equated either effusively with the absolute knowledge of a great philosophy or blindly with the scientistic self-understanding of the actual business of research.[106]

The positive counterpart to an epistemological critique is the development of theoretical strategies which serve to stimulate the progress of science without succumbing to the atomistic and inductivist tendencies of orthodox empiricism. The fulfilment of this task provides a second role for philosophy, which 'is the irreplaceable master of a claim to unity and generalisation that will be redeemed either scientifically or not at all'.[107] The social sciences require philosophy in a third way insofar as the latter discipline can clarify the conditions for the rational redemption of validity claims. The accomplishment of this task provides the means for specifying the legitimate objectivity of science, as well as the basis for criticising the ideological utilisation of scientific knowledge. Finally, since the critique of ideology creates the possibility of an alternative social identity which must be sustained by reason alone, the critical social sciences may establish a role for philosophy which could outlast their own.

Habermas contends that in our contemporary scientific civilisation, philosophy can be meaningfully pursued only in conjunction with the sciences. The primordial unity of philosophy and science was destroyed by the development of modern physics, and philosophy has long since forfeited its claim to be the only guardian of apodictic knowledge. Hence it is reactionary, in Habermas's opinion, to attempt to renew that claim through a retreat into the phenomenological sphere of indubitable experience:

> Insofar as we understand by philosophy the attempt to conceive the unity of the world with methods that are not taken from the self-reflection of the sciences, but rather which claim a dignity before or beside the sciences, it is no longer possible to vindicate philosophically the rational content of the philosophical tradition.[108]

If philosophy is to survive the collapse of its claim to the absolute in a way that preserves its rational core, then what is required is not an approach which surreptitiously reintroduces that claim in a subjectivist style, nor an attitude which simply surrenders philosophical thought to the progress of science. Rather, what is necessary is a philosophy which is capable of reflecting upon the sciences in a twofold sense: a philosophy which is able to reconstruct the conditions of scientific knowledge, and one which is capable of criticising the scientistic self-understanding and ideological application of that knowledge. Such a critique would help to remove the obstructions which preclude a discursive formation of the will, so that the pursuit of philosophy would not be free from political consequences. Indeed, philosophical thought would form one more moment in the process of renewing that problem with which the writings of Habermas are pre-eminently concerned, namely 'the problem of the peculiar relation of theory to practice, which since the eighteenth century has arisen whenever the logic of research implied the intention of enlightenment'.[109]

In this chapter the work of Habermas is regarded as part of a tradition of thought which stems from the writings of Kant, Hegel and Marx, and which incorporates the contributions of the Frankfurt School. Some of the doctrines of the latter School are pursued by Habermas throughout his work, and in his most recent studies they are placed within the context of a theory of language. This theory, which is based upon a distinction between action and discourse, seeks to formulate the conditions for the discursive redemption of validity claims. The conditions constitute an ideal speech situation which secures the possibility of a rational consensus concerning problematicised statements and norms, and which provides a rational criterion for the analysis of systematically distorted communication. The writings of Habermas thereby reformulate the tasks of critical theory and contribute to the resolution of a number of problems in philosophy and the methodology of social science. Whether this reformulation is acceptable, and whether these solutions are adequate, are questions that will be pursued in Part II.

Part II

Constructive critique

4. Problems in the analysis of action

The previous chapters have shown that the analysis of human action is a theme which is common to the traditions of ordinary language philosophy, hermeneutic phenomenology and critical social theory. Ordinary language philosophers focus on the everyday usage of the words with which actions are described, and Winch in particular elaborates an account of meaningful action which is based on Wittgenstein's later theory. As an exponent of hermeneutic phenomenology, Ricoeur develops a mode of discourse in which action may be treated as a text, so that it may be subsumed under the auspices of a general theory of interpretation. Habermas approaches the problem from the standpoint of critical social theory, proposing an analysis of action which may serve as a basis for the critique of ideology. In this chapter, I should like to begin the critical discussion of these three traditions by assessing the strengths and weaknesses of their contributions to the analysis of action. I shall try to show, first, that ordinary language philosophers do not provide an adequate account of the connection between language and experience, of history and social change, and of meaningful action and social relations. These shortcomings are avoided to some extent by Ricoeur and Habermas, but the writings of the latter authors contain difficulties of their own. Thus, in the second part of the chapter, I argue that Ricoeur does not present a compelling case for his distinction between modes of discourse, nor does he offer a satisfactory defence for his conception of action as a text; and I further maintain that the work of Ricoeur does not yield a coherent account of the relation between action and structure. In the third part, I suggest that Habermas's typology of action is unsound, that his notion of systematically distorted communication is problematic, and that his speculations on the connections between ontogenesis and phylogenesis leave many issues open. In the wake of these critical remarks, I sketch an alternative approach to action which seeks to build upon the strengths while avoiding the weaknesses of the analyses examined in this chapter.

115

I. Ordinary language philosophy

Language and experience

The writings of Austin, Ryle and the later Wittgenstein deal extensively with the language of intention and volition. By concentrating on the surrounding circumstances in which this language is used, these writers justly sever any simplistic connection between intentional concepts and private mental states. Moreover, their work generates firm semantic grounds for the view that the self-ascription of experience presupposes a dimension of intersubjectivity, so that the apprehensions of the solipsist collapse into unspeakable silence. Yet while the perspective of ordinary language philosophy offers an instructive counter to psychological intuitionism, I shall argue nonetheless that it disregards several important problems. For to focus on the circumstances in which intentional utterances are used is to obscure the process by which experience is articulated and expressed in these utterances. The obfuscation of this process is especially evident in Wittgenstein's doctrine of avowals, which treats first-person psychological sentences as similar to primitive forms of behaviour. So long as such sentences are assimilated to cries and shrieks, it is difficult to explore the specific modes whereby experience is brought to language, as well as the peculiar mechanisms which obstruct the channels of expression.

Wittgenstein encounters the problem of expression in the course of his critique of the Tractarian conception of meaning. In contrast to the view that all genuine words must stand for some object, the later Wittgenstein argues that the components of language function in a variety of ways. Accordingly, it must not be assumed that sensation words, for example, are the names of discrete experiences which transpire in the privacy of the mind. On the contrary, Wittgenstein contends that such words are not names at all, but rather 'are connected with the primitive, the natural, expressions of the sensation and used in their place'.[1] This so-called 'doctrine of avowals' is employed by Wittgenstein and some of his followers in their commendable critique of the analogical argument for the existence of other minds.[2] Moreover, the doctrine rightly repudiates an overly voluntaristic view of language use, for it draws attention to the fact that utterances are sometimes wrenched rather than released from the speaker's lips. Nevertheless, I shall maintain that the doctrine of avowals is untenable, and that it reveals a tendency in Wittgenstein's thought which has unhappy consequences. In the first place, it is implausible to propose that first-person psychological sentences in the present tense are of the same 'logical status' as groans and grimaces, a proposal intimated by Wittgenstein and explicitly endorsed by Malcolm.[3] For it seems that such sentences could be true or false, even if the question of their truth or falsity may seldom arise. Second, there appear to be cases in which first-person psychological sentences are used as descriptions of the speaker's feelings or experiences.[4] Wittgenstein occasionally acknowledges the latter point, insisting that while 'a cry is not a description', nevertheless 'there are transitions. And the words "I am afraid" may approximate more, or less, to being a cry.'[5] Yet Wittgenstein does not pursue this observation in any depth, and so the difficulties which such a description might entail remain unexplored. Third, the doctrine of avowals is, I suggest, indicative of a *naturalistic tendency* which permeates Wittgenstein's thought, concealing some of the most crucial characteristics of language. For in speaking a language one says something which transcends the level of mere action or reaction, and which attests to the primordial separation of language and life. This separation, which Ricoeur has highlighted in his remarkable reinterpretation of the phenomenological reduction, creates the void through which experience must be brought to expression, and wherein this process may be impeded by forces originating outside of the realm of language.

The disruption of the process of expression by non-linguistic forces is one of the central themes of psychoanalysis. The neglect of this theme by ordinary language philosophers is thus reflected in their attitude towards Freud, whose work is commonly regarded as a veritable labyrinth of conceptual confusion. Moore recalls, for example, how Wittgenstein treated Freud's study of jokes as 'a very good book for looking for philosophical mistakes'.[6] This opinion is shared by MacIntyre, who detects a 'systematic confusion' in Freud's discussion of the unconscious.[7] For the latter concept incorporates an element of redescription as well as an aspect of explanation; and Freud uses the concept legitimately, according to MacIntyre, only insofar as he employs it as an adjective to redescribe a pattern of behaviour. MacIntyre's critique of the concept of the unconscious is consistent with the general approach of ordinary language philosophy, since he is concerned to elucidate the public criteria for the ascription of a particular predicate. However, this concern leads MacIntyre to the conclusion that the concept of the unconscious is primarily descriptive; and hence the forces that produce the behaviour so described, forces which Freud anchored in the unconscious, are thereby excluded from view. Just as the proponents of the doctrine of avowals dissolve the problem of how experience is brought to expression, so too

MacIntyre dismisses the mechanisms which obstruct and distort this process. In this respect, MacIntyre's critique shares the most serious shortcomings of the structuralist interpretation of Freud. For as Ricoeur rightly observes, the attempt to account for repression in terms of the disjunction between signifier and signified says nothing about the forces that effect this disjunction. An adequate rendition of psychoanalysis must follow Ricoeur's lead and seek to explicate the energetic dimension of the unconscious which impinges upon language and disrupts the universe of meaning. Similarly, on the level of social theory, an attempt must be made to clarify the institutional and structural factors which intervene in the expression of social experience, precluding the public articulation of interests and needs. So long as the problem of expression is obscured by a reductionistic doctrine of avowals or a wholly linguistic transcription of the unconscious, then the pursuit of such tasks is fettered from the very start.

History and social change
The problems of history and social change receive some recognition in the works of ordinary language philosophy. In contrast to the a-historical formalism of logical atomism, ordinary language philosophers emphasise the active and creative aspects of language, as well as the regularity which is essential to its use. 'We are talking about the spatial and temporal phenomenon of language', the later Wittgenstein reminds his readers, 'not about some non-spatial, non-temporal phantasm.'[8] Such remarks tempt a few of Wittgenstein's commentators to situate his work within a tradition of metaphysics stretching from Kant to Husserl and Heidegger.[9] However, while there is undoubtedly a temporal element to Wittgenstein's later thought, this does not, I believe, amount to an adequate account of the dimension of history. The source of this inadequacy may be found in Wittgenstein's analysis of rule-following behaviour, which terminates the process of application in the phenomenon of didactic training. The termination of this process is avoided to some extent in the writings of Winch, who emphasises the problematic character of linguistic use. Nonetheless, I shall argue that Winch fails to fill the lacuna in Wittgenstein's work, for Winch lacks a satisfactory conception of social change.

The temporal dimension of Wittgenstein's later work is evident in his discussion of linguistic rules. As the critique of the possibility of a private language makes clear, it is not sufficient for an expression simply to have a use. For the use must be consistent or regular, which means that it must be repeatable in accordance with a publicly established rule. These rules are social conventions; they are created by human beings, and by human beings they may be changed. Moreover, linguistic rules are neither comprehensive nor exhaustive, and they do not bind the use of an expression in every respect. The question thus arises as to how one can follow a rule, for rules would seem to be interpretable in a variety of ways. In reply to this question, Wittgenstein suggests that there is a manner of grasping a rule which is not an interpretation, but rather a form of action or reaction which the individual is trained to perform. The inculcation of a rule is a primordial phenomenon which lies beyond justification, since it is the point at which the provision of reasons comes to an end. 'If I have exhausted the justifications I have reached bedrock, and my spade is turned. Then I am inclined to say: "This is simply what I do." '[10] So Wittgenstein invokes the didactic model to resolve a problem which is well known within the hermeneutic tradition; and it is this solution which prevents the temporality of Wittgenstein's later work from unfolding into the historicity of hermeneutics. For on the one hand, the model of didactic training emphasises the prodigious diversity of language-games, ignoring whatever historical unity they may possess. Children are taught the use of expressions in multifarious circumstances, and it is to the various details of such circumstances that Wittgenstein urges his readers to return. On the other hand, the didactic model links the rules of language to elementary processes of human behaviour, so that the acquisition and application of these rules appears as a quasi-natural phenomenon. 'What we are supplying', Wittgenstein tellingly declares, 'are really remarks on the natural history of human beings.'[11] The naturalisation of linguistic activity obscures the extent to which following a rule is an inherently problematic process, in which rules are continuously modified and transformed in their very application. The latter point is one of the central theses of Gadamer's hermeneutics, which in this respect advances beyond the position of the later Wittgenstein. As Habermas convincingly shows, Gadamer's emphasis on the problem of translation brings out the reflexivity of ordinary language, whereby disturbances in communication may be overcome through an act of interpretation which reproduces the system of rules. Wittgenstein's withdrawal from the hermeneutical circle into the realm of didactic training conceals this reflexivity, conspiring to deprive his philosophy of an adequate account of the historical process.

The writings of Winch are more explicitly concerned with the problems of history and social change. In some respects, Winch's contributions merely reiterate the accentuations and limitations of Wittgenstein's later thought. Thus, the twofold emphasis on the diversity and naturalness of language-games reappears in the uneasy tension between relativism and trans-culturalism which characterises Winch's work. Moreover, as many critics rightly complain,[12] both Wittgenstein and Winch tend to exaggerate the self-sufficiency of language-games and cultural formations, which seldom subsist in untainted isolation. However, here I wish to draw attention to a point where Winch's discussion seems to diverge significantly from the views of his mentor. The point pertains to the following of rules; and Winch maintains, in apparent contrast to Wittgenstein, that this process necessarily involves a reflective decision which determines how the rule is to be applied in particular cases. Accordingly, Winch rejects the suggestion that all aspects of social life, including the historical dimension, could be explicated in terms of habit or custom. For human history is not simply a register of changing habits; rather, 'it is the story of how men have tried to carry over what they regard as important in their modes of behaviour into the new situations which they have had to face'.[13] The emphasis on the problematic nature of rule application brings Winch's work strikingly close to the position of Gadamer. Nevertheless, the work of Winch does not, I think, provide an adequate basis for the analysis of history and social change. In the first place, Winch offers little clarification of the notion of reflection which is so central to his account, and which sits so uncomfortably alongside the preoccupation with practical ability that characterises ordinary language philosophy as a whole. Second, Winch does not give sufficient consideration to the creative aspects of human action, aspects which constitute action as something more than a reflective repetition of the past. Third, to pre-empt a point which will be discussed below, it may be noted that Winch's idealisation of social relations renders him incapable of accounting for the genesis of the conditions within which individuals make their 'reasoned decisions'. Finally, the view of the historical process offered by Winch is patterned on the model of linguistic change, where the rules of language are modified and transformed in their application. However, this is quite misleading as a model of social change, for the transformations which occur in the social sphere are often more abrupt and revolutionary than such a view would suggest. So while the contributions of Winch may compensate for some of the weaknesses of Wittgenstein's work, they still fall short of a satisfactory conception of history and social change.

Meaningful action and social relations

Ordinary language philosophy establishes a close connection between linguistic activity and social life. In the writings of the later Wittgenstein, this connection is reinforced with the idea that meaningful expressions must be used in rule-governed ways; and the existence of a rule presupposes a community of followers whose agreement alone can determine what counts as a regular use. As Wittgenstein insists, 'to obey a rule, to make a report, to give an order, to play a game of chess, are *customs* (uses, institutions)'.[14] The intimate link between language and social life provides a convenient point of departure for authors such as Peters, Winch and Louch, who are concerned to elaborate the implications of Wittgenstein's later philosophy for the methodology of the social sciences. In this section, I critically discuss some of the implications proclaimed by Winch. In particular, I argue that his concept of meaningful action and his analysis of social relations are seriously deficient, so that a sound social theory must rest upon foundations other than those laid down by Winch.

The clarification of the concept of meaningful action is one of the central concerns of Winch's work. This clarificatory task is pursued through an extension of Wittgenstein's later theory of meaning to non-linguistic activity. Accordingly, Winch maintains that the decisive characteristic of meaningful action is that it commits the actor to behaving in one way rather than another in the future; and an actor can be so committed if and only if the action is governed by a rule. So just as an expression has sense only when it is used in a regular way, so too an action is meaningful only if it is performed in accordance with a rule. One corollary of this account is that Weber's distinction between action which is merely meaningful, and action which is both meaningful and social, is untenable; for in Winch's view, meaningful action is *ipso facto* social action. In spite of such commendable consequences, I believe that Winch's account of meaningful action is inadequate in at least two respects. First, the account simply shifts the weight of analysis onto the notion of rule, which in turn does not receive a satisfactory elucidation. Wittgenstein is notoriously vague about this notion, allowing 'rule' to range over phenomena as diverse as teaching aids, official regulations and observed uniformities.[15] In an attempt to eliminate such vagueness, Winch suggests that 'the notion of following a rule is logically inseparable from the notion of *making a mistake*',[16] since to act in accordance with a rule is to act in a way that is potentially incorrect. It seems clear, however, that this suggestion does not render the notion of rule-following behaviour much more precise.

Acting in a way that is potentially incorrect may be a necessary condition of such behaviour, but it is by no means sufficient, for there are many ways of making a mistake which are not transgressions of a rule. One may, for example, be mistaken in believing that there are twelve planets in the solar system, without thereby contravening a rule in some sense. This points to the second respect in which the account proffered by Winch is inadequate. To analyse the concept of meaningful action into the notion of following a rule, and the latter into the idea of making a mistake, is to exclude as senseless many actions which one might otherwise regard as meaningful. As MacIntyre justifiably objects,[17] it is not clear what it means to say that one may be going for a walk incorrectly or scratching one's nose mistakenly, and yet such actions are not *prima facie* senseless. Winch might well reply to this objection by appealing to the attitude or awareness of the actor concerned. For he maintains, by way of example, that the weary reader who inserts a slip of paper into a book is acting meaningfully 'only if he acts with the idea of using the slip to determine where he shall start re-reading'.[18] However, the relation between 'acting with ideas' and 'following rules' or 'making mistakes' is not elucidated; and the claim that the meaningfulness of an action may depend upon the ideas of the agent is not particularly persuasive, as Winch himself admits. So although Winch is correct to concentrate on the concept of meaningful action, it must be said that he fails to analyse this concept in a clear and compelling way.

The views of the later Wittgenstein provide Winch with a distinctive approach to the nature of social relations. Since the meaning of an expression is specified by the intersubjective rules which govern its use, it appears to follow that a modification of meaning would entail an alteration of the social relations established by such rules. Winch observes, for instance, that the introduction of the concept of proper names in a society where people had been called hitherto by numbers would greatly affect the system of personal relationships. Such observations lead Winch to the conclusion that 'the social relations between men and the ideas which men's actions embody are really the same thing considered from different points of view'.[19] However, Winch's conclusion does not follow from his Wittgensteinian premises. For even if all concepts presuppose social relations, in the sense that their meaning depends upon intersubjectively established rules, it does not follow that all social relations presuppose concepts; and it certainly does not follow, as Winch contends, that 'social relations between men exist only in and through their ideas'.[20] On the contrary, there are social relations of considerable importance in a society, such as those of domination and subordination, which may remain unarticulated or even concealed by the prevailing concepts and ideas. Moreover, social relations are conditioned by structural factors which may require elucidation on a theoretical plane. There are passages in Winch's work where he appears to acknowledge such possibilities, allowing that he may be 'over-intellectualizing' social life. Nevertheless, Winch continues to hold that behaviour which 'expresses discursive ideas' is paradigmatic for that which does not, for 'that which does not is sufficiently like that which does to make it necessary to regard it as analogous to the other'.[21] Winch does not explain why it is necessary to regard non-linguistic activity in this way, and in due course I shall defend a very different view. Here I shall simply suggest that it is the illegitimate extrapolation from the characteristics of language which is at the source of Winch's idealism, and which renders his account of social relations unsuitable as a foundation for social theory.

II. Hermeneutic phenomenology

Modes of discourse

The tradition of hermeneutic phenomenology includes various works which are concerned with the study of human action. The writings of Ricoeur are an outstanding example of this concern, as his first constructive project was a phenomenological inquiry into the nature and limits of voluntary action. Ricoeur has broadened his perspective in subsequent publications, allowing for the possibility of alternative approaches to the analysis of action. Although Ricoeur has never explored these alternatives in a systematic manner, his recent writings appear to offer three distinct approaches. I have presented these as the descriptive discourse on action, which includes the contributions of linguistic analysis and phenomenology; the dialectical discourse, which attempts to mediate between the individual and collective will in a manner that is overtly prescriptive; and the hermeneutical discourse, which proceeds on the basis of action considered as a text. Ricoeur may be right to suggest that the analysis of human action can be approached in several ways, and that these may be quite compatible with one another. Nevertheless, I shall argue that the threefold articulation elicited from the writings of Ricoeur cannot be satisfactorily sustained. For the descriptive and dialectical discourses both presuppose a hermeneutical moment, as Ricoeur occasionally concedes; and the attempt to establish sharp boundaries between these discourses obscures a number of important issues. In short, I shall maintain that the threefold articulation of modes of discourse results in a detrimental fragmentation of the field of action.

The formal distinction between three modes of discourse is undermined by Ricoeur's more substantive work. For instance, the phenomenological dimension of the descriptive discourse appears to be hermeneutical in at least two senses. First, the diagnostic relation of *Freedom and Nature*, whereby the results of the objectivating sciences are reintegrated into the contents of consciousness, is a hermeneutical relation.[22] For the facts disclosed by the empirical disciplines are regarded as decipherable signs or indications of an experiential stream in which the *cogito* is submerged, and upon which it must mediately reflect. Second, and more importantly, phenomenology itself is not a direct inquiry into lived experience, but rather an interpretative process in which the articulated contents of intentional objects or noemata are systematically unfolded. Ricoeur renders this hermeneutical moment of phenomenology explicit in a recent essay, where he maintains that the latter discipline must conceive of its method 'as an *Auslegung*, an exegesis, an explication, an interpretation'.[23] Similarly, there are passages in Ricoeur's writings where the dialectical discourse is translated into the language of hermeneutics. In the closing pages of *Freud and Philosophy*, the psychoanalytic interpretation of the economy, the polity and culture is complemented by a progressive synthesis of these spheres of objectivity, and this synthesis is regarded as a contemporary hermeneutical rendition of the Hegelian philosophy of spirit. Moreover, Ricoeur relegates the cultural task of creatively reappropriating the past, a task prescribed within the dialectical discourse, to the province of hermeneutics. So even within the compass of Ricoeur's own work, a clear distinction between the three modes of discourse is difficult to sustain.

The threefold articulation of discourse on action has several undesirable consequences. In the first place, to distinguish the dialectical discourse in terms of its overtly prescriptive character is to suggest that the descriptive and hermeneutical discourses are less laden with elements of value. Yet this suggestion disguises the extent to which the investigation of ordinary language is an implicitly normative activity, as well as the degree to which the interpretation of everyday action is an ineluctably evaluative exercise. Second, the circumscription of the prescriptive aspect prematurely excludes the possibility, raised by Habermas, of establishing a normative foundation for an interpretative theory in the semantic structure of ordinary language. The necessity of providing such a foundation is underlined by the dialectical discourse of Ricoeur, whose avowed commitments, however commendable they may be, stand without substantial justification. Third, the distinction between the descriptive and hermeneutical discourses deprives Ricoeur's theory of interpretation of an important insight. For the interpretation of human action is just as concerned with description as is the analysis of concepts and noemata, even if the objects and methods of description may differ in each case. Finally, to situate the constitution of the economic and political spheres within the dialectical discourse is to conceal the pervasive effects of social structure and political power. The ways in which concepts are employed cannot be wholly severed from such factors, and the interpretation of human action must rest upon their explicit thematisation. Thus, whatever the merits of distinguishing different approaches to the analysis of action, the threefold articulation suggested by Ricoeur's work would seem to be untenable.

Model of the text
The hermeneutical discourse on action is supported by a series of arguments which are worthy of more detailed consideration. The focal point of these arguments is the concept of the text, which Ricoeur employs as a model for the analysis of human action. This employment is justified, according to Ricoeur, insofar as action may be objectified in a way that embodies the four forms of distanciation. Accordingly, action may be conceived as a delineated pattern that confronts the observer as an object to be understood, and no longer as an ongoing and continuously fluctuating process. One of the merits of this view is that it places action within the scope of a general interpretative theory, thereby highlighting the similarities between disciplines which are too often held apart. Ricoeur rightly emphasises that concepts elaborated in philosophy or literary criticism may be relevant to the social sciences, and I do not wish to deny that the text may be one such concept. However, I believe that Ricoeur's proposal to conceive of action as a text is unsatisfactory. For the arguments which he adduces in defence of this proposal are inadequate, and some of the consequences which follow from it are unacceptable. In the course of substantiating these objections it will become clear that the source of Ricoeur's mistake is similar to that of Winch's, as both writers are guilty of an illegitimate generalisation from the linguistic sphere.

The first series of arguments for the possibility of treating action as a text concern the fixation and inscription of human action. Ricoeur contends that the process of trans-action is characterised by an 'intentional exteriorisation' which facilitates the detachment of the meaning of the action from the event of its performance. However, the notion of the intentional exteriorisation of action is obscure, and the writings of those authors cited by Ricoeur do not provide the requisite clarification. The most that Kenny shows, for instance, is that actions may be described in terms of sentences which have certain irreducible grammatical characteristics;[24] and if anything may be said to have a 'propositional content' that can be identified and reidentified as the same, then it is surely these sentences and not the actions which they describe. Indeed, Ricoeur's argument for the intentional exteriorisation of action seems to be little more than an over-extended analogy, in which characteristics ordinarily ascribed to sentences or statements are attributed to actions and justified by a liberal use of inverted commas. In opposition to Ricoeur, it must be stressed that meaning is not something inherent in an action, a 'noematic structure which may be fixed and detached from the process of interaction'.[25] Rather, as I shall argue more fully below, the meaning of an action is closely linked to its description, such that the meaning may be specified by the manner in which the action is described. This alternative view avoids Ricoeur's reification of the concept of meaning, as well as his allusive account of the 'substratum' wherein the meaning of action is 'inscribed'. Ricoeur suggests that the meaning is recorded in the 'course of events' which constitute the 'social time' of 'history': 'history is this quasi-"thing" *on* which human action leaves a "trace", puts its mark'.[26] Yet while human action does play an essential role in the process of history, it seems inadequate to view this role as an objectification which results in a tableau of reified traces. Such a view involves an hypostatisation of history which is reminiscent of structuralism, an approach so effectively criticised in earlier essays by Ricoeur. Thus, there are good grounds to suppose that Ricoeur has failed to provide a clear and convincing defence of the notion that action may be detached and inscribed in a manner analogous to the text.

The second series of arguments for the possibility of treating action as a text concern the emancipation of human action from the circumstances and participants of the trans-actional situation. Ricoeur maintains that just as a text is freed from the restrictions of ostensive reference, so too the importance of an action transcends its relevance to the original circumstances of its production. 'An important action', Ricoeur remarks, 'develops meanings which can be actualised or fulfilled in situations other than the one in which this action occurred.'[27] Once again, however, the force of this analogical argument is dependent upon the equivocal use of key expressions. For 'meaning' is not the same as 'importance', nor is 'reference' identical with 'relevance'; and so even if a clear sense could be given to the notions of the importance and the relevance of an action, it would remain to be shown that the relation between these two notions is the same as that between the meaning of a text and its reference. Moreover, whatever the merits of this analogy, it is implausible to suggest that the meaning of an action is independent of the circumstances in which it is performed.[28] For the meaning of an action is linked to its description, and how one describes an action is deeply affected by circumstantial considerations. This point is particularly important for the theory of interpretation, for it creates the possibility of reinterpreting action in the light of institutional arrangements and structural conditions. The tendency to abstract from such issues is equally evident in Ricoeur's final claim that human action is an open work. Ricoeur contends that the meaning of an action is accessible to anyone who can 'read', and that 'the interpretation by the contemporaries has no particular privilege in this process'.[29] However, to say that the meaning of an action is universally accessible is to underplay the extent to which an action may remain opaque to competent actors. Ricoeur's rendition of psychoanalysis rightly emphasises that subjects are not transparent to themselves; and yet if that is so, then the interpretation of action may require a theoretical elucidation of the unacknowledged conditions under which it is performed. Finally, while it is surely correct to say that contemporaries do not have the only word in the interpretation of an action, it is misleading to say that they have 'no particular privilege' in this process. For it is precisely because contemporaries do have a privileged position that there are methodological problems concerning the relation between the everyday descriptions of lay actors and the theoretical accounts of external observers, and concerning the relation between the latter accounts and the subsequent courses of action pursued by reflective and informed agents in the social world. Lay actors may not have the first word in the interpretation of their action, but they do, in a fundamental epistemological sense, have the final word. To conceive of action as a text in accordance with Ricoeur's hermeneutical discourse is to eliminate such problems by a premature piece of conceptual legislation.

Action and structure
The problem of the relation between action and social structure receives some attention in the writings of Ricoeur. In spite of the phenomenological origins of his work, Ricoeur is acutely aware of the limitations of a theory of action which disregards the institutional context. He rightly

insists that 'the abstract character of analytic efforts cannot be forgotten',[30] and he suggests that the theory of action must be developed into a general philosophy of practice. The seeds of this development are evident in each of the three discourses distinguished by Ricoeur, insofar as each of these discourses incorporates some recognition of the social dimension of human action. In the descriptive discourse, the exercise of the will is mediated by the structures of the involuntary, some of which are socially produced. In the dialectical discourse, the three primordial passions presuppose a framework of objectivity that comprises the economy, the polity and the cultural sphere. In the hermeneutical discourse, the exteriorisation of action creates the possibility of its inscription in the temporal texture of history, thereby constituting social institutions as rule-governed regularities of objectified action. Yet while Ricoeur thus progresses beyond many analytical theories of action, I shall argue that he does not provide an adequate thematisation of the relation between action and social structure. The inadequacy is especially marked in the very discourse which seeks to resolve the antinomy between the individual and collective will, namely the dialectical discourse. The latter remains the least developed of Ricoeur's discourses, and it is pitched at a level of abstraction which sheds little light on the ways in which actions are situated in the social world. Accordingly, in the following discussion, I shall explore the insights into the relation between action and structure which may be found in the descriptive and hermeneutical discourses alone.

The descriptive discourse raises the possibility of grasping the relation between action and structure in a way that transcends the classical dichotomy between freewill and determinism. For Ricoeur's attempt to understand the reciprocity of the voluntary and the involuntary is a systematic attack on the dualism of an autonomous self-consciousness exiled from an objective world which it regards as its other. Ricoeur pursues this attempt through a detailed demonstration of how each moment of the will comprises both a voluntary and an involuntary aspect, the ultimate unity of which remains an unattainable ideal. Thus, a decision presupposes a motive which inclines the will by depicting for it a good, and which is based upon needs that are both organically and socially induced. Among the social sources of such needs are the 'collective representations' discussed by Durkheim and his followers. Ricoeur justly criticises these writers for their tendency to treat social psychology as a type of mental physics; but he wholly applauds their observation that society 'must finally act out its role in the individual consciousness'.[31] However, the view that collective representations are one among several sources for the non-organic needs upon which motives are based does not in itself do justice to the totality and ubiquity of the social sphere. Moreover, the phenomenological bias of Ricoeur's analysis tends to reduce the results of the empirical disciplines to diagnostic indications of hidden realms of subjectivity, rather than regarding them as evidence for the determination of objective social conditions. Finally, despite Ricoeur's laudable attempt to transcend the freewill and determinism debate, his critique of Durkheim remains bound to the opposition between motive and cause. The latter opposition is mitigated in his discussion of the second moment in the triple articulation of the will. The fulfilment of a project presupposes the body as the organ of an action, and this organ is pre-formed through the prior acquisition of practically effective schemata. 'All that I know intellectually and that we indicate by the general term "knowledge"', explains Ricoeur, 'is a schema, a flexible method rather than rigid association.'[32] The notion of a schema as a flexible framework for action is a provocative idea, but Ricoeur does not pursue it in any depth. So while Ricoeur's descriptive discourse contains a number of remarkable insights into the relation between action and social structure, it fails to provide a comprehensive thematisation of this relation.

The social dimension of human action is explored more thoroughly in the hermeneutical discourse. In defending the conception of action as a text, Ricoeur maintains that just as discourse frees itself from the intentions of the speaker and is inscribed in the written work, so too action transcends the intentions of the agent and is sedimented in social time. 'Thanks to this sedimentation in social time, human deeds become "institutions"'; and accordingly, 'the object of the social sciences is a "rule-governed behaviour"'.[33] However, the precise nature of the process whereby human action is transformed into social institutions is far from clear, and simply to call it 'sedimentation in social time' is hardly adequate. Furthermore, the representation of social institutions as rule-governed regularities succumbs to the same difficulties that vitiate the views of Winch, to whom Ricoeur somewhat misleadingly alludes. Finally, no attempt is made to elucidate the concept of social structure, and hence the relation of this concept to the notions of action and institution remains uncertain. In spite of such limitations, Ricoeur's hermeneutical discourse contains several suggestions that are worthy of being pursued. In his critique of structuralism, Ricoeur sketches a relation between structure and event which is relevant to the theory of action, and to which I shall return at a later point. Similarly, in his discussion of the text, Ricoeur notes that one of the traits which characterise this entity as a work is its production in accordance with rules that define its literary genre. 'To master a genre', submits Ricoeur, 'is to master a "competence" which offers practical guidelines for "performing" an individual work.'[34] The idea of a 'generative grammar' which would provide a common dynamic for the production and interpretation of texts is a stimulating proposal, and it is unfortunate that Ricoeur does not develop it in any detail. Yet such suggestions serve to offset the weaknesses of the hermeneutical discourse, which alone does not yield a satisfactory account of the relation between action and social structure.

III. Critical social theory

Types of action

Within the tradition of critical social theory, the writings of Habermas make the most significant contribution to the analysis of human action. The contribution is premised upon a fundamental distinction between labour or purposive-rational action on the one hand, and interaction or communicative action on the other. The ramifications of this distinction are evident on every level of Habermas's work, from the most abstract issues of epistemology and methodology to the most concrete questions of practical politics. Moreover, the distinction helps to counter an over-emphasis on technical and instrumental considerations, an over-emphasis too often found within contemporary forms of social theory. Yet in spite of its centrality and merit, the precise status of the distinction between labour and interaction remains obscure. In a recent attempt to clarify some of his ideas, Habermas claims that in drawing the distinction, he is seeking merely to '*analyze* a complex, i.e. dissect it into its parts'.[35] This appeal to the analytical status of the distinction may appear somewhat implausible in view of the substantive role which it plays in the corpus of Habermas's work, and one may well suspect that what is presented as a dwarf by daylight is working like a giant after dark. Moreover, the import of this appeal is ambiguous, and Habermas's claim vacillates between a stronger and a weaker thesis. According to the stronger thesis, labour and interaction designate two distinct types of action which could in principle be instantiated independently, although in fact one may rarely find a pure instance of either. The weaker thesis asserts that labour and interaction do not designate two types of action but merely two tables of characteristics, so that it makes little sense to suppose that either could be instantiated in any way. In the critical comments which follow, I assume that Habermas endorses the stronger of these two theses. For Habermas explicitly refers to labour and interaction as two 'types' of action, and there are occasional passages in which he cites relevant examples. Furthermore, it is difficult to see how the substantive role of this distinction could be sustained on the basis of the weaker thesis alone. I shall therefore attempt to demonstrate the untenability of Habermas's distinction through a critique of the stronger thesis implied by his analytical defence.

The principal points of contrast between labour and interaction may be summarised in the following way. Labour is governed by technical rules or strategies formulated in a monological language, and it is sanctioned through the failure to attain some predetermined end. Interaction, on the other hand, is governed by intersubjectively binding norms which are objectified in ordinary language, and which incorporate conventional sanctions for the punishment of whoever fails to comply. Summarised in this way, the analytical distinction may not fully clarify what labour is; but as McCarthy aptly observes,[36] the distinction does seem to specify what labour is not: namely, it is not governed by intersubjectively binding norms, it does not involve a dialogical use of language, and it is not sanctioned by means of convention. However, it is difficult to find a clear case of an action which would conform to this negative characterisation, and which would thereby instantiate the proposed type. Consider, for example, the action of a chemical engineer who is concerned to activate a quantity of polyester resin. The engineer proceeds to combine various chemicals in accordance with the following rule:

(R) X cc of catalyst activates Y litres of resin at $N°$ centigrade

The rule might appear to be purely pragmatic, governing the action of the engineer in a way that is entirely free of normative force. However, this appearance is almost certainly an illusion. For there are other ways of activating polyester resin, such as lowering the temperature and adding an accelerator; and the fact that the engineer followed (R) instead is a matter that may require explanation by reference to conventions. Furthermore, it is difficult to see what it could mean to say that a rule like (R) involves a use of language that is 'monologic'. Of course, (R) contains expressions which are uncommon in everyday discussion, and which form the vocabulary of a specialised language; but the latter is a language nonetheless, and insofar as it is used to exchange information and ideas within a community of individuals, it is in some sense 'dialogic'. Finally, the suggestion that failure to comply with technical rules is sanctioned through inefficacy rather than convention seems to be only partially correct. If the engineer were to add less than X cc of catalyst to Y litres of resin at the appropriate temperature, then this mistake may be paid for by the inactivity of the material. However, the desired result could be obtained in ways other than that specified by (R), and these alternative courses may be blocked by conventional sanctions alone. So in lieu of a more favourable example, the assertion that labour is a type of action which may be clearly distinguished from interaction is a claim that must be treated with due suspicion.

Habermas's attempt to elucidate a concept of interaction which is entirely free from purposive-rational elements is equally problematic. Indeed, the very attempt may appear somewhat surprising, since everyday action is thoroughly infused with the pursuit of individual ends. It may be the recognition of this commonplace which is responsible for Habermas's growing concern with the notion of strategic action, which he regards as a purposive-rational form of social action. Yet Habermas continues to maintain that interaction may be distinguished from all forms of purposive-rational action, insofar as interaction alone presupposes the validity basis of speech. In strategic action, by contrast, sincerity in expressed intentions is not expected and the correctness of underlying norms is not assumed; each acting subject follows his or her personal preferences and decision maxims, irrespective of whether other subjects agree with these choices or not. However, it is difficult to find an example of social action which would not be in some sense strategic, and which would fall unequivocally within the category of interaction. Habermas suggests that when strategic action is placed within an institutional framework like the Hague Convention, then its purposive-rational character is eclipsed by an implicit consensus which constitutes the action as communicative. This suggestion is a welcome example in an argument that is all too abstract; but nevertheless, it fails to provide a clear instance of the proposed type of communicative action. For negotiations concerning war and peace are generally undertaken in pursuit of particular goals, so that even if certain assumptions must be commonly shared for these negotiations to be possible, the goals themselves need not be. Moreover, the assumptions which underlie such action are presumed to be correct in a manner that is no more than contingent. For the normative procedures of an international agreement are binding upon the parties concerned if, but only if, they wish to play the negotiating game; and there is no shortage of historical catastrophes which attest to this conditional character. Finally, in cases where momentous issues and great sacrifices are at stake, one rarely expects the participants to express their intentions sincerely. On the contrary, one assumes that each party will submit excessive and impractical claims, so that the discussion must progress through a prolonged process of guile and counter-guile. In these various respects, war and peace negotiations are not substantially different from playing chess, which Habermas treats as the paradigm of strategic action. Where these two examples obviously differ is in the role of language, which is not a central feature of the game of chess. However, the centrality of language does not suffice to differentiate communicative from strategic action. For Habermas allows that communicative action can be non-linguistic, and he holds that strategic action can be pursued through the medium of ordinary language. Thus, just as Habermas has failed to specify a concept of labour which would be clearly distinct from communicative action, so too he has yet to elucidate a notion of interaction which would be wholly devoid of purposive-rational elements. It must be concluded, therefore, that the stronger thesis implied by the analytical distinction stands without satisfactory support.

Systematically distorted communication

The concept of systematically distorted communication provides one of the key links between Habermas's theory of action and the critique of ideology. The nature of this nexus is established by the model of psychoanalysis, which shows how one can elucidate the significance of behaviour that has been deformed by the exercise of repression. Psychoanalysis assumes that the occurrence of an unbearable conflict is followed by the exclusion of the relevant object from public communication, creating a gap in the semantic field which is filled by a privatised symbol. The latter appears as a symptom which deviates from the rules of ordinary language, remaining unintelligible until its genesis has been reconstructed and explained. Similarly, on the level of social analysis, ideologies may be regarded as collective fantasies which are removed from public criticism, and which serve to legitimate the suppression of generalisable interests. The emphasis on the notion of ideology must be regarded as a major strength of Habermas's work, as this notion is too often neglected in other traditions of thought. Habermas is also correct to insist that the meaning of an expression or action may not be immediately transparent, so that a satisfactory interpretation may require recourse to a theoretical explanation. I shall attempt to show nonetheless that systematically distorted communication is an ambiguous and questionable concept. I shall further argue that the extension of this concept from a psychological to a social plane is rife with difficulties. In the end I shall suggest that while the notion of ideology is fundamental for social theory, the clarification of this notion can be accomplished outside the conceptual confines of systematically distorted communication.

Habermas proposes three criteria for defining the scope of systematically distorted communication. Such communication involves a deviation from the recognised system of linguistic conventions; it is manifested in the rigid repetition of behavioural patterns; and it betrays a discrepancy between the various levels of communication, so that actions and expressions belie what is said. However, this provisional characterisation does not fully clarify what systematically distorted communication is being contrasted with. Since Habermas is attempting to distinguish 'scenic understanding' from semantics and orthodox hermeneutics, and since he effects this distinction in terms of the deviation of the object of scenic understanding from the 'system of rules of public language',[37] it seems that systematically distorted communication is being contrasted with the ordinary intercourse of everyday life. Yet insofar as Habermas maintains that scenic understanding presupposes a conception of non-distorted communication, and insofar as he regards the latter as a construction analogous to the ideal speech situation, it appears that systematically distorted communication is being contrasted with a 'model of pure communicative actions [which] is included in the design of pure intersubjectivity'.[38] Whichever of the two alternatives one accepts, the implications of this provisional characterisation are not wholly consistent with Habermas's overall project. For if, on the one hand, systematically distorted communication is conceived as a deviation from the ordinary intercourse of everyday life, then the latter domain becomes inaccessible to the interpretative procedures of depth hermeneutics. This implication is surely unacceptable for a critical theory incorporating these procedures, for such a theory must not preclude the possibility that everyday life is the very locus of ideology. On the other hand, if systematically distorted communication is regarded as a deviation from the model of pure communicative action, then scenic understanding can no longer be distinguished from semantics and orthodox hermeneutics in terms of the nature of its object, since no empirical interlocution is likely to accord with the model of pure communicative action. The latter implication suggests that the depth-hermeneutical dimension of critical theory should not be defined in terms of an object domain which is constituted in some exceptionally complex way, as Habermas seems to suppose. On the contrary, depth hermeneutics should be defined in terms of a methodological structure which renders it applicable to all forms of human action; and hence the object of scenic understanding need not be an initially incomprehensible phenomenon, as is amply illustrated by Freud's classic analysis of parapraxes. So however one construes the concept of systematically distorted communication, there is reason to believe that this concept will not suffice to specify the object domain and interpretative method of critical theory.

The extension of the concept of systematically distorted communication to the level of society as a whole is focused upon the notion of ideology. For in Habermas's view, ideology is a form of systematically distorted communication, one which functions simultaneously to disguise and defend the suppression of generalisable interests. Just as psychoanalysis attempts to eliminate behavioural symptoms through the scenic understanding of privatised symbols, so too critical theory seeks to dissolve systems of power through the interpretation of ideologies which restrict the realm of public debate. The adequacy of the analogy between psychoanalysis and critical theory will be discussed at length in the following chapter; here I shall simply note three discrepancies which are of some consequence for the analysis of ideology. First, whereas psychoanalytic symptoms are produced by the exclusion of an emotionally charged object from the sphere of public language, ideologies are concerned with the suppression and legitimation of social interests. Although Habermas acknowledges a connection between ideology and interests, he provides no detailed clarification of the latter notion; and hence the extent to which such interests resemble the repressed contents of the unconscious remains unclear. Moreover, it is not easy to see how Habermas could provide a clarification which would concur with his theory of action. For the notion of interest seems to be linked to the purposive-rational pursuit of specific ends, whereas Habermas regards ideology as a form of communicative action, albeit a distorted form. Second, even supposing that a precise meaning could be given to the psychoanalytic concept of a privatised symbol, it seems doubtful whether this concept would provide a suitable exemplar for ideology. On the contrary, the efficacy of ideology presupposes that it is widely shared and at least partially understood, so that the sense in which the object of critical theory is an 'initially incomprehensible symbol' is even more attenuated than in the case of psychoanalysis. The third and most important discrepancy concerns the relation between the problematic symbol and the force of repression. It is a peculiar characteristic of psychoanalysis that the repression of the contents of the unconscious is overcome by the subject's eventual acceptance of the analyst's interpretation. The situation is quite different for critical theory, where both the interpretation of ideology and the acceptance of the interpretation are not dissolutions but mere disclosures of power relations; and the final transcendence of such relations is not itself a part of the interpretative process. So while Habermas is right to emphasise the importance of ideology in the social world, there are good grounds to suspect that the concept of systematically distorted communication does not provide a satisfactory framework for the analysis of this phenomenon.

Action and structure

The relation between human action and social structure is a recurrent theme in Habermas's work. The specific way in which Habermas explores this theme varies throughout the course of his career, in accordance with his changing conception of the connection between onto-genesis and phylogenesis. In his earlier writings, the theme is probed from a psychoanalytic perspective, whereby social institutions and ideologies are seen as quasi-neurotic solutions to the problem of collective defence. In his more recent studies, Habermas relies increasingly upon the developmental psychology of Piaget, which specifies a series of cognitive stages through which the individual and the species must pass. The use of these two perspectives provides Habermas with a number of stimulating insights into the complex intersection of the social and psychological planes. Moreover, the ability to draw upon such perspectives demonstrates Habermas's remarkable grasp of the contemporary literature, a grasp which few social theorists could equal. I do not think, however, that Habermas offers a satisfactory account of the relation between action and structure within either of these approaches. Furthermore, Habermas does not confront the substantive objections which may be levelled against these perspectives, nor does he attempt to integrate the two frameworks in a systematic way.

Habermas's early work examines the relation between action and social structure in the light of Freud's writings on the theory of civilisation. These writings show, in Habermas's view, how the social gratification of needs proceeds under conditions of scarce resources and limited productivity, so that excess demands must be suppressed by compulsory norms and appeased by compensatory fantasies. The needs which are thereby suppressed are excluded from the realm of public communication and transformed into causally effective motives; and since these motives no longer coincide with linguistically apprehensible intentions, the behaviour of the agent is a deviation from the model of pure communicative action. 'The greater the share of prelinguistically fixed motivations which cannot be freely converted in public communication', proposes Habermas, 'the greater the deviance from the model of pure communicative action.'[39] Habermas further suggests that these variations are directly dependent upon the degree of repression characterising the institutional system of society, and that such repression depends in turn upon the developmental stage of the forces and relations of production. This suggestion is intriguing, but so far it remains vague and unrefined. Habermas does not elucidate, for example, the way in which the suppression of excess demands leads to the formation of causally effective motives, so that the extent to which his suggestion presupposes the dubious content of Freud's theory of civilisation is left unclear. Moreover, Habermas's hypotheses on the correlations between deviant behaviour and institutional repression are abstract and imprecise. To say that the extent of deviation 'depends on' the degree of repression, and that the latter in turn 'depends on' the developmental stage of society as a whole, is to say neither what ranges of variation are involved, nor wherein these dependencies consist. Finally, even if the requisite clarifications could be provided, it seems unlikely that this approach could provide a wholly adequate account of the relation between action and social structure. For psychoanalysis may well illuminate the social constitution of motives, but the light which it sheds on the structural and institutional factors which effect this constitution is of a highly questionable colour. So whatever the merits of Habermas's initial contributions to social psychology, it must be said that they are provisional and partial at best.

Habermas's current ideas on the relation between action and structure are unfolded within the framework of Piaget's developmental psychology. In accordance with his theory of action, Habermas maintains that the human self-formative process occurs within two basic dimensions: the dimension of purposive-rational action, which is controlled by technical rules and strategies; and the dimension of symbolic interaction, which is governed by intersubjective norms. The structures which specify the possible constellations of intersubjective norms may be reconstructed as a sequence of developmental stages. On the ontogenetic level, these stages correspond to those elucidated by Piaget and Kohlberg in their studies of cognitive capacity and moral consciousness. On the level of phylogenesis, a similar sequence of stages is reflected in the progressive decentralisation of world outlooks, from the magical and mythical

conceptions of paleolithic and clan society to the rationalised and reflective orientations of more recent cultures. There is a close connection
between the development of individual consciousness and the evolution
of forms of collective identity. As Habermas observes, 'the reproduction
of society and the socialization of its members are two aspects of the same
process; they are dependent on the same structures'.[40] The work of Piaget
thus provides Habermas with a refurbished foundation for the theory of
social evolution; but this foundation is unstable at crucial points. First,
Habermas does not offer a convincing justification for the projection of
ontogenetic stages onto the phylogenetic plane. The claim that the level
of maturity attained by the action competencies of people of earlier
epochs was restricted to pre-conventional or conventional stages of development is a highly questionable assumption.[41] Second, Habermas
does not attempt to meet any of the substantial objections which may be
levelled against Piaget's approach. Many psychologists have argued that
Piaget's stages are incorrectly formulated, and some have claimed that
the concept of stage is itself unsound.[42] Such objections strike to the core
of Habermas's recent work, leaving the basic tenets of his evolutionary
theory in a precarious position. Third, Habermas has yet to show the
extent to which his recent reliance on Piaget is consistent with his apparent retention of certain Freudian themes. The question of consistency is
especially acute in the case of the unconscious, a concept which acquires a
very different connotation in the writings of Piaget.[43] Whereas the Freudian unconscious is a reservoir of infantile experiences which retain their
identity and efficacy through time, Piaget conceives of the unconscious in
terms of operational schemata which are oriented towards equilibrium
with the environment. Whatever the merits of the latter conception, it
cannot be readily reconciled with the view that action may be systematically distorted by motives which are constituted in the past, rather than
merely modified by schemata which are continuously adapted to the
present. Fourth, while the theory of cognitive development may generate
social-psychological insights within the symbolic sphere, it seems less
capable of accounting for the ways in which this sphere is conditioned by
other aspects of social life. Habermas is fully aware of this limitation, and I
shall return to his supplementation at a later stage. Here I shall simply
suggest that the supplementation remains incomplete, insofar as the
notion of an organisational principle is never systematically integrated
with the concept of a mode of production. As a fifth and final point, it may
be noted that even if these difficulties could be overcome, it seems
doubtful whether the work of Piaget could provide an adequate

framework for the thematisation of the relation between action and social structure. For although his structuralism is explicitly 'genetic', Piaget conceives of genesis as merely the transition from one structure to another;[44] and hence the process whereby social structure is sustained and transformed by human action is excluded from view.[45] However important developmental psychology may be, therefore, it seems clear that Habermas's importation of Piaget's ideas into the realm of social theory is in need of considerable qualification and defence.

IV. Towards a theory of action

Language and action

The development of a satisfactory social theory must begin with a re-examination of the relation between language and action. The path for this re-examination is prepared by the traditions discussed above, since their respective exponents emphasise the centrality of language in social life. However, this emphasis is frequently overstated, as is especially evident in Winch's account of meaningful action and social relations. Although authors within Continental traditions are concerned to stress the limitations of linguistic analysis, they also succumb to the tendency to treat language as a general paradigm of human action. Such a tendency is reflected in Ricoeur's conception of action as a text. The tendency is averted to some extent in the work of Habermas, but even Habermas is inclined to regard communicative action as the most important component of the social world. Moreover, while Habermas may be right to distinguish different forms of human action, the specific way in which he effects this distinction seems to be mistaken. In Habermas's view, communicative and purposive-rational action appear as mutually exclusive types, which may be represented roughly as follows:

PR = purposive-rational action
CA = communicative action

or, more accurately:

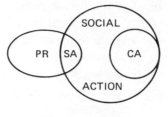

SA = strategic action

Many of the difficulties encountered by Habermas's theory of action could be overcome by rejecting the strict separation of his two basic types. I propose, therefore, that the peculiar form of activity which involves the speaking of a language should be regarded not as an autonomous type, but rather as a sub-category of human action as such:

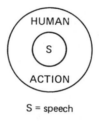

S = speech

This proposal concurs with the remarks of Austin and others, who repeatedly stress that speaking is a way of acting. However, it also indicates that there are ways of acting which do not share all of the characteristics of speech; and hence, rather than generalising from the features of language in the manner of Winch or Ricoeur, this proposal suggests that one commence with an analysis of the wider category of human action. In this section, I make an initial contribution to such an analysis by defending the following theses:

(1) An action is an event which can be described as something that someone (or group) does, and not simply as something that happens to someone.

(2) The meaning of an action is generally specified by the manner in which it is described.

(3) An action presupposes a subject, as the agent (individual or collective) which actualises the relevant event.

(4) The meaning of an action is not decided by the intentions of the subject, for the subject may be unaware of the full sense of what he or she is doing.

In the next section, I attempt to situate action within an overall context of social institutions and structural conditions. Finally, in the closing section of the chapter, I seek to show how this general framework can be developed to incorporate considerations of power, ideology and history.

The performance of an action may be conceived as an event which is describable in a variety of ways. This conception generates an approach to the problem of meaningful action which might avoid the limitations and reifications of the accounts proffered by Winch and Ricoeur. For this conception eliminates the need to proliferate rules that govern the occurrence of every meaningful act, or to attribute to meaningful action a propositional content that can be reidentified as the same. On the contrary, the conception I wish to defend regards an action as an event which satisfies a range of possible descriptions, so that the meaning of the action is generally specified by the way in which it is described. The idea that actions are events demands a more precise specification which would identify the peculiarity of the action-event. As an initial approach to this problem, I suggest that an action is an event which can be described as something that someone (or group) does, and not something that happens to someone. This suggestion may well be insufficient, since it would appear to include some events, such as snoring or sneezing, which one may be reluctant to regard as actions. One may therefore be tempted to follow the analysis recently offered by Davidson,[46] who maintains that action requires the possibility of a description which would render it as the intentional outcome of an agent. However, this account seems to me to be mistaken, for there are many accidental, absent-minded and habitual actions which are performed quite unintentionally under any description.[47] Someone may spill a cup of tea, and under certain circumstances that may be a poignantly meaningful action, even though the person did not intend to do anything at all. As an alternative to the Davidsonian analysis, I propose to refine my initial suggestion by supplementing it with a counterfactual clause, adding that an action is an event which can also be described as something that the agent could have avoided doing. This clause points to a fundamental link between action and knowledge, for the agent might have avoided performing a particular action if he or she had known something which, in the actual circumstances, he or she did not know. I shall not, however, develop these considerations here, restricting my present comments to several issues which arise from the proposed account. It should be noted, first, that by treating an action as an event, I do not wish to imply that there are no differences between the action-event and events which transpire in the non-human world. For not only does the action-event presuppose a subject, but it is also interwoven in a complex manner with the language employed both by that subject and by others. Second, by conceiving of an action as an event which may be described in various ways, this account transforms the traditional problem of meaningful action. The task is no longer to identify some essential feature of action which endows it with meaning, whether that feature be a governing rule, a noematic structure or an animating intention. Rather, the principal task that must now be confronted is to clarify the ways in which an action may be described and to elucidate criteria for the evaluation of alternative descriptions. The third issue which arises from the proposed account concerns the relation between the theory of meaning and the theory of action. By regarding the meaning of an action as specified by the expressions with which it is described, this account renders the relevant meaning susceptible to semantic analysis. Once an action has been satisfactorily described, then the description may in turn be submitted to analysis within a general theory of meaning. The specific nature of such a theory is, of course, a matter of considerable controversy, and I shall return to this question in the final chapter. For the moment it will suffice to draw some initial distinctions and intersections, so as to avoid the confusions which have arisen from an erroneous presentation of the problems concerned.

The performance of an action presupposes a subject, as the agent who utters the expression or executes the act. This general thesis is accepted by both Ricoeur and Habermas, as well as by many Anglo-Saxon philosophers. Moreover, the thesis may be supported by various grammatical considerations, as proper names and personal pronouns are an ineliminable part of the language in which action is described. Such considerations also suggest that the agent need not be an individual, but may be a group or collectivity instead. I shall not pursue this suggestion in any depth, for I wish to focus on a particular set of issues which concern the constitution of the subject. The issues may be approached by inquiring into the relation between the agent's intentions in performing an action and the meaning of the action thus performed. In opposition to the views espoused by certain contemporary writers,[48] I shall maintain that the agent's intentions are not decisive for determining the meaning of an action, and that their role in the process of description is secondary and derivative. The first of these claims is frequently acknowledged in everyday life, insofar as it is accepted that an agent may intend to do something quite different from what he or she does. Of course, there may be some description of the action in which the agent would recognise what he or she intended to do; but as I argued above, the possibility of such a description is not a necessary condition for the event to qualify as an action. Moreover, even if an intentional description were available, it would not necessarily be the most appropriate or legitimate characterisation of the action. For one can imagine a case in which the act of shooting a prince could be equally or more informatively described as the overthrow of a monarchy, even though the assassin had no revolutionary intentions whatsoever. This intentional under-determination of meaning is further attested to by the fact that an agent may be quite unclear as to what his or her intentions are when acting in a particular way. In such cases, so far from the agent's intentions providing the key to the meaning of the action, it may be said that the description of the action opens the pathway to the elucidation of the agent's intentions. Thus, in accordance with the hermeneutical theory elaborated by Ricoeur, I shall regard the interpretation of action as a relatively autonomous process in which the subject is not naively enthroned, but rather systematically and critically unveiled.

Action and structure

The performance of action must be situated within a wider context of social institutions and structural conditions. The analysis of this context has been sadly neglected by ordinary language philosophers, whose recognition of the social nature of language has seldom led beyond a supercilious nod towards the social sciences. Such neglect is less evident within the tradition of hermeneutic phenomenology, and the writings of Ricoeur contain many valuable insights into the relation between action and structure. Thus, at one point, Ricoeur suggests that the structuralist mode of analysis may be extended from textual entities to 'all social phenomena which may be said to have a semiological character'.[49] Such an extension can be found in the writings of Barthes and others,[50] who seek to study the spheres of fashion or cuisine as systems of interdependent signs. The semiologists assume that the structure of social spheres is sufficiently similar to the structure of language, so that the categories introduced by Saussure and other linguists can be legitimately applied to social life. However, the assumed analogy between social structure and the structure of language is unsatisfactory in several respects. First, the analogy cannot easily account for the exercise of power and the occurrence of conflict, as Barthes occasionally concedes. Second, social life is characterised by the possibility of swift and radical change, which would appear to have few parallels in the linguistic realm. Third, the semiological approach may be able to analyse ideology as a disjunction between systems of signification,[51] but it can shed little light on the social mechanisms which effect this disjunction. Thus, just as the attempt to conceive of meaningful action on the model of an utterance or a text must be rejected, so too the conception of social structure as analogous to the structure of language cannot be sustained as such. The latter conclusion is endorsed in the recent writings of Giddens, whose work on the relation between action and structure must be regarded as one of the most important contributions to this theme.[52] Giddens rightly insists that the linguistic exemplar is a provocative but limited case, for there are aspects of social life which cannot be accommodated within the framework of semiology. However, by regarding the problem of reproduction as primary, Giddens tends to establish an overly close connection between action and social structure. He conceives of social structure as an assortment of 'rules and resources' which actors 'draw upon' in their everyday routine activities. This conception results, in my opinion, in an undesirable dilution of the concept of social structure, since 'structural properties' are apparently defined by each and every 'rule' which actors employ; and there would seem to be no grounds intrinsic to this conception for regarding some 'rules' as more fundamental than others. Moreover, this conception leaves no room for a *structural* analysis of the conditions and limits within which particular clusters of rules and resources are possible. I therefore suggest that Giddens's concept of social structure may be more suitably seen as a notion of social institution, which pertains to the networks of social relations in which agents are enmeshed. An alternative conception of social structure must account for the profound stability of structural features amid the ever-changing institutional contexts in which they appear.[53]

In an attempt to develop a more adequate thematisation of the relation between action and structure, I shall distinguish three levels of abstraction. The first and most immediate level is that of action itself, whereby agents participate and intervene in the social world. Action commonly involves the implementation of specific means for the attainment of particular ends, which may be privately or publicly defined. However, as I argued above, the meaningfulness of an action is not dependent upon the aims or intentions of the agent, nor do such intentions provide the decisive criterion for the appropriate description of the action. The second level of abstraction is that of social institutions. Institutions may be viewed as specific constellations of social relations, together with the reservoirs of material resources which are associated with them. One is concerned with social institutions when one inquires into the authority relations and capital resources which constitute, for example, the enterprise of Fords, or the University of Cambridge. Institutions must be analytically distinguished from a third and more abstract level, that of social structure. I propose that social structure may be conceived as a series of elements and their interrelations, which conjointly define the conditions for the persistence of a social formation and the limits for the variation of its component institutions. This conception bears a certain resemblance to the views proffered by Habermas in his theory of social evolution, as well as a remote affinity to some of the ideas recently propounded by Godelier.[54] In order to render this conception more precise, I shall uphold a distinction between two categories of structural elements. On the one hand, there are those elements which must be present in any social formation, since they represent necessary conditions for the persistence of social life as such. Within this category one might include, for instance, the element of production, whereby raw materials are transformed into consumable goods for the satisfaction of human needs. On the other hand, there are those elements which are necessary conditions, not for the persistence of social life as such, but rather for the continuation of a particular type of social formation. These elements specify the limits for the variation of social institutions, beyond which they would cease to be characterised by the same structure. So whereas production may be a necessary component of any social formation, production by means of capital and wage-labour is not; and it is the interrelations between the latter elements which define the institutions of a social formation as capitalistic. Social structure is thus a theoretical construct which is capable of accounting for the essential similarity which underlies the apparent diversity of social institutions.

The connections between the three levels of abstraction are multiple and complex. I shall attempt to clarify some of these connections by observing that within an institutional context, certain courses of action are open while others are relatively closed. Knowing how to act in such a context is, among other things, knowing the range of possible actions which are permitted by the relevant institutions. This knowledge may be conceptualised in terms of flexible schemata, as suggested by Ricoeur in an early and unelaborated remark. Schemata are practically effective principles which the agent acquires during the gradual initiation into an institution, and which provide the agent with general parameters for acting in new and unanticipated situations. In this respect, the concept of schema is similar to the notion of habitus introduced by Bourdieu, which the latter author defines as 'the durably installed generative principle of regulated improvisations'.[55] It must be stressed, moreover, that action is an essentially creative and potentially transformative process. For the application of an institutional schema is an inherently problematic process, and not all action is strictly schematised in this way. Indeed, in certain circumstances an agent may act in a way that directly contravenes an institutional schema, thereby placing either the agent's career or the continuation of the institution at risk. This possibility points to one of the crucial connections between action and social structure. In the second sense distinguished above, social structure consists of a series of interrelated elements which define the conditions for the variation of social institutions. Insofar as the institutions of a social formation satisfy the same conditions, they may be said to be structured in a similar way; and to undertake a structural analysis of an institution is to investigate the extent to which it fulfils these conditions. So long as the transformative capacity of action does not propel institutions beyond the limiting conditions, then action may be said to reproduce social structure. However, one cannot preclude the possibility that these conditions may be exceeded by the cumulative consequences of collective action, a possibility which I shall discuss in the following section. Thus, so far from action and structure forming mutually exclusive dimensions of the social world, it is precisely their complex interconnection through the schematised medium of social institutions which must be grasped and explored.

Power, ideology and history

The thematisation of the relation between action and structure provides a general framework for the analysis of power, ideology and history. Both Ricoeur and Habermas emphasise the centrality of power in social life, but neither author conceptualises this phenomenon with sufficient care. In order to rectify this deficiency, it may be helpful to consider the accounts which predominate in the literature of social science.[56] Such accounts tend to fall into one of two alternative positions. On the one hand, taking the locution 'power to' as basic, some authors construe power as a facility for the attainment of predetermined goals. On the other hand, focusing upon the expression 'power over', other writers analyse power into a particular type of intersubjective relation. However, the framework sketched above suggests that these two views are neither wholly incompatible with one another, nor jointly sufficient to account for the phenomenon of power. I shall maintain that the principal locus of power is the level of institutions, for power is primarily an institutionally endowed capacity for the pursuit of specific ends. Since institutions are partially constituted by social relations, the exercise of this capacity commonly thrusts the agent into a network of relations with others. Such relations may be either conflictual or consensual, depending upon the nature of the objectives pursued. This account implies that power may exist without being actualised in a particular relation, for the capacity may remain merely potential. Moreover, it follows from this account that the exercise of power is not necessarily repressive, for the objectives may be commonly shared by the parties concerned. Finally, the proposed account suggests that power, as a capacity endowed by institutions, is always limited by social structure. Just as the range of possible institutions is restricted by structural conditions, so too the scope for the provision and exercise of power is structurally circumscribed. Thus, however efficacious the exercise of power may be, it would be illusory to suppose that this phenomenon is in some sense autonomous and unconstrained.

The problem of ideology is situated at one of the major intersections between the theory of language and the theory of action. Once again, it may be helpful to approach this problem by distinguishing two senses which the notion of ideology has assumed.[57] According to the first sense, the notion of ideology refers to the lattice of ideas which permeate the social order, constituting the collective consciousness of an epoch. This sense has its origins in the transcendental subjectivity disclosed by Kant and historicised by Hegel; and it is elaborated and sustained by the Heideggerian ontology of being, whereby all understanding involves the projection of 'prejudices' which are continuously modified in the process of interpretation. The second sense of ideology pertains not to the constitution of consciousness as such, but rather to a consciousness which is in some way 'false', one which fails to grasp the real conditions of human existence. Ideology in this sense is closely linked to the rise of the positive sciences, which originally sought to dispel the idols of tradition through a systematic study of the natural and social world. The antithesis of science and ideology is to some extent preserved in the writings of Marx, whose critique of political economy may be seen as the demystification of a discipline which falls short of a scientific status. It seems to me, however, that each of these two senses of ideology is inadequate. The first sense is inadequate because it is too wide: by anchoring ideology in the very nature of consciousness, it conceals the specificity of the ideological phenomenon and renders the latter unsurpassable. The second sense, on the other hand, is too narrow: by defining ideology in opposition to science, it precludes the possibility that science itself may be ideological. In the hope of avoiding these two extremes, I shall regard ideology as a system of signification which facilitates the pursuit of particular interests. Structural conditions generally ensure that certain groups occupy the dominant institutional positions, so that the prevailing ideology is commonly a legitimation of the status quo. Insofar as subordinate groups accept such legitimations, they lack a counter-ideology through which divergent interests may be articulated and pursued. The subordinate groups participate in a system of ideas which expresses interests other than their own, and hence their consciousness may be described in one sense as false. Of course, this account presupposes that the concept of interest can be given a clear and justifiable meaning, and I shall return to this task in a subsequent chapter. Moreover, this account emphasises that the social mechanisms which obstruct the articulation of interests play a crucial role in the phenomenon of ideology, a point which is cogently and extensively illustrated in studies inspired by Habermas.[58] Finally, in contrast to the views espoused by Ricoeur and others,[59] the foregoing account does not imply that ideology is a necessary feature of social life. For the particular interests which nurture ideology may be eclipsed by interests which are general and commonly shared; and in such circumstances, the system of signification which facilitates the pursuit of these interests would cease to be ideological.

A sketch for a theory of action would be incomplete without a brief consideration of the dimension of history. This dimension is inadequately explored by Wittgenstein and his followers; and while it is discussed by both Ricoeur and Habermas, it remains in need of further thought.[60] As a proposal for directing such thought, I shall suggest that action is the ultimate fount of social change. In performing an action, the agent produces an event which is inescapably temporal. The element of temporality is clearly reflected in the language with which action is described, for such descriptions are always cast in a particular tense.[61] Moreover, insofar as action is the application of an institutional schema, it is a re-petition of events which transpired in the past. Action thus shares with speech that inter-play of identity and non-identity which Derrida crystallises in the concept of difference.[62] Yet action is not merely a repetition of the past, since institutional schemata are continuously modified and occasionally rejected by the acting subject. So even when the past is not present in the application of a schema, it lingers as a backcloth through which action irrupts into the future. The reproductive and transformative capacities of action are manifest not only on the level of institutions, but also on the plane of social structure. The interrelated elements of social structure may possess a distinctive dynamic, in the sense that they may be sequentially ordered in a specific way. However, from this it does not follow that the intersection of social structure and history can be adequately conceptualised in terms of a 'physiological morphology', as Godelier and other structuralists suggest.[63] On the contrary, a social structure 'functions' only insofar as agents reproduce established institutions, thereby reconstituting the structural conditions for institutional persistence. If, on the other hand, institutions are propelled beyond the limiting conditions by the transformative capacity of action, then social structure is no longer reproduced but replaced. In the last analysis, therefore, both social institutions and social structure are sustained and transformed by human action, which is the indispensable basis of history and social change.

Let me recapitulate, in conclusion, the general argument of the chapter. I try to show how some of the limitations of the analyses of action found within the literature of ordinary language philosophy are overcome in the writings of Ricoeur and Habermas. I suggest nonetheless that the contributions of the latter authors are unsatisfactory in certain respects. In an effort to improve upon their views, I repudiate the tendency to treat language as a paradigm of human action and focus instead on the latter, proposing several theses concerning meaningfulness and subjectivity. I attempt to situate action within a wider social context through a thematisation of the relation between action and structure. Finally, I seek to integrate considerations of power, ideology and history into the framework provided by this account. I have no doubt that these constructive remarks leave much to be desired, and there are many issues which could not be raised in so confined a space. Nevertheless, these remarks will have fulfilled their task if they succeed in providing a foundation for the methodological and epistemological investigations which follow.

5. Problems in the methodology of social science

The methodology of social science is a topic which attracts the attention of writers within the traditions of ordinary language philosophy, hermeneutic phenomenology and critical social theory. As an exponent of ordinary language philosophy, Winch offers an analysis of the idea of understanding which effectively eliminates explanation from the sphere of social science. The hermeneutic phenomenology of Ricoeur adopts a more complementary approach, seeking to integrate understanding and explanation into a systematic theory of interpretation. The latter approach is shared by Habermas, who employs depth hermeneutics as a framework for critical social theory. In the present chapter, I continue my critical discussion of the three traditions by evaluating these various contributions to the methodology of social science. I maintain, first, that Winch's characterisation of the concept of understanding is untenable, and that his treatment of the problems of adequacy and critique is unsound. Second, I suggest that Ricoeur's recent views on the relation between motive and cause are in need of development; that his theory of interpretation faces a number of difficulties; and that his mediation in the debate between hermeneutics and critical theory raises problems which he has yet to resolve. In the third part of the chapter, I try to show that Habermas's proposals for the programme of depth hermeneutics and the conduct of critique are unsatisfactory in certain respects, and that his desire to forge a unity of theory and practice remains unfulfilled. Finally, I conclude with a few constructive remarks on these themes, in the hope of pointing towards a methodology which would build upon the strengths while avoiding the weaknesses of the foregoing contributions. It may be helpful to point out that my initial criticisms will be focused primarily on the writings of Winch, since his work represents the most original and provocative encounter with social science that has emerged from the tradition of ordinary language philosophy. My constructive remarks will again be cursory and incomplete, dealing with a mere handful of the issues which arise from the critique of the contributions concerned.

I. Ordinary language philosophy

Understanding

The tradition of ordinary language philosophy provides a distinctive analysis of the concept of understanding. The details of this analysis are closely connected to Wittgenstein's later theory of meaning, whereby the sense of an expression is specified by the criteria which justify its use. To say that someone understands a mathematical formula, for example, is not to attribute a private intuition or idea, harboured in the hidden recesses of the mind. Rather, it is to acknowledge a public capacity or technique, which is exemplified in the correct employment of the formula in question. The rules which govern such employment are integrated into a wider form of life, so that understanding is inseparable from an ongoing mode of human existence. The ontological dimension of the concept of understanding marks one of the basic convergences between Wittgenstein's later philosophy and the hermeneutics of Heidegger, who treats *verstehen* as a definitive characteristic of 'Dasein'. Moreover, just as Gadamer attempts to unfold the consequences of Heidegger's work for the foundations of the *Geisteswissenschaften*, so too the methodological implications of Wittgenstein's philosophy are elicited in the writings of Winch. In this section, I examine some of Winch's conclusions concerning the nature and role of the concept of understanding. I hope to show that while Winch is right to underline the importance of this concept, he nevertheless fails to develop a satisfactory framework for the interpretation of human action.

The extension of Wittgenstein's theory of meaning to the sphere of human action provides the basis for Winch's analysis of understanding. Since an action is meaningful only if it is performed in accordance with some rule, so it seems to follow that one understands an action only insofar as one comprehends the conventions which govern its performance. One can understand the behaviour of Chaucer's Troilus, for example, only by reference to the conventions of courtly love; as Winch insists, 'understanding Troilus presupposes understanding those conventions, for it is from them that his acts derive their meaning'.[1] I shall argue, however, that Winch's analysis cannot be sustained, since the elucidation of conventions which govern action is neither necessary nor sufficient for understanding the action concerned. It is not necessary insofar as there are many actions, such as waiting, walking, smiling and frowning, which may be understood without uncovering some rule in accordance with which they are performed. These actions are understood through the attribution of appropriate descriptions; and in many cases, the only conventions which are relevant are those which regulate, not the performance of the action, but rather the use of the phrases whereby that action is described. On the other hand, there are situations in which action is clearly part of a ritual or routine. Yet even then, the comprehension of the conventions which constitute the ritual may not be sufficient for understanding the action. For an action may have a significance which transcends the meaning endowed by the conventions of everyday life, and the elucidation of this significance may require a theoretical reconstruction of institutional and structural features which are initially inaccessible to the consciousness of lay actors. The latter possibility, which is raised by the writings of Ricoeur and Habermas, will be pursued at a subsequent stage; here I shall restrict my comments to several points which emerge from the above critique. Winch allows, it should be noted, that the comprehension of conventions may not be sufficient for understanding an action. However, the resulting lacuna cannot be filled by his vague and sporadic allusions to the 'point' of the relevant rule. Moreover, Winch's neglect of institutional and structural considerations makes it difficult for him to cope with the problem of understanding ideology, as Gellner, MacIntyre and others rightly remark.[2] For the interests which ideologies express, as well as the mechanisms which obstruct such expression, cannot be grasped without recourse to an analysis of institutions and social structure. Finally, Winch says very little about how the conventions which govern action are to be disclosed through social analysis. There are passages wherein Winch alludes to the feelings and tastes of those who seek to understand, whereas in other contexts he suggests that the clarificatory process is more of a logical exercise than an empathic or empirical one. The latter suggestion has led some commentators to accuse Winch of advocating a form of a priori sociology, a reproach that Winch indignantly rejects.[3] Whatever the justice of this reproach, it is clear that Winch's analysis of understanding remains abstract, failing to specify the ways in which social conventions may be elucidated through the investigation of particular acts.

Winch returns to the problem of understanding in an essay concerned with various issues in social anthropology.[4] When anthropologists are dealing with a society which is radically different from their own, they cannot simply assume, according to Winch, that their standards of intelligibility or rationality are identical with those which prevail in the alien society. Anthropologists must be careful not to impose their own standards upon the society which they seek to understand; instead, the anthropologist 'must jettison his sophistication'[5] and try to align the two systems of concepts without evaluating either. The points of reference for this feat of conceptual co-ordination are provided by several notions which transcend any particular society, for they are entailed, in Winch's view, by the very idea of social life. Thus Winch proposes that the notions of birth, death and sexual relations 'are inescapably involved in the life of all known human societies in a way which gives us a clue where to look, if we are puzzled about the point of an alien system of institutions'.[6] However, Winch's attempt to establish a neutral framework for understanding an alien society is unsatisfactory in several respects. To begin with, Winch poses his problem in a dubious manner. For even supposing that a clear sense could be given to the notion of a standard of intelligibility or rationality, it is by no means obvious that such standards are peculiar to particular societies, nor is it apparent that one's position could be jettisoned for the sake of understanding another. On the contrary, there may be a form of rationality which is common to all cultures, a possibility which will be considered in the following chapter; and the comprehension of an alien concept may be more akin to a process of projection and modification, as the idea of the hermeneutical circle implies. In the second place, it seems naive to assume that anthropologists could translate the concepts of an alien society into their own categories without evaluating either. For anthropologists' categories are not value-free, as is amply illustrated by the various interpretations of Zande magical rites. Third, even if Winch were right in appealing for transcendental assistance to resolve his anthropological puzzle, it is difficult to see how he could justify this appeal from within the confines of his own position. For Winch's deliberations on the idea of social life demand the same riposte which he loftily levels at MacIntyre: just *whose* idea of social life is at issue? Finally, Winch's claim that the notions of birth, death and sexual relations provide the reference points for understanding an alien society appears quite inadequate in sociological terms, since it makes no allusion to phenomena such as production, legitimation and power. So although Winch may be applauded for his concern with problems related to the understanding of human action, there are good grounds to suppose that he has failed to resolve these problems in ways which are acceptable for the social sciences.

Explanation

In contrast to the concept of understanding, the notion of explanation receives little sympathy in the work of ordinary language philosophers. The distaste for this notion is instilled by the writings of Wittgenstein, who insists from early on that 'the cause or history behind our present behaviour is of no interest to us . . . In our study of symbolism there is no foreground and background.'[7] As a critique of psychologistic theories of meaning, Wittgenstein's exhortation is as salutary as those made by Frege and Husserl a generation before. However, in the literature which appeared after Wittgenstein's death, this exhortation is transformed into an uncompromising attack on the notion of explanation and the concept of cause. Thus Melden, Peters, Dray, Winch, Louch and others draw a sharp contrast between understanding an action in terms of the reasons or motives for which it is performed, and explaining an action by reference to the causes which bring it about; and they claim that such explanations are wholly irrelevant to the task of understanding human action. In the present section, I attempt to undermine this post-Wittgensteinian dogma by examining two of the arguments in which it is espoused. The first argument is to be found in the writings of Winch, who maintains that explanatory techniques have no more than heuristic value in the social sciences. The second argument is concerned with psychoanalysis, which is explored by MacIntyre, Toulmin and Flew from the standpoint of ordinary language philosophy. I suggest that the proponents of these arguments construct an artificial opposition between motive and cause, thereby failing to see that understanding and explanation may be complementary rather than contradictory moments in the methodology of social science.

Winch's attack on the relevance of explanation readily follows from his account of meaningful action and social relations. For if meaningful actions as well as meaningful utterances are governed by rules, and if rules are intersubjective conventions which establish social relations with others, then it would seem to follow that social relations between actors are like logical relations between propositions. Accordingly, Winch submits that 'social interaction can more profitably be compared to the exchange of ideas in a conversation than to the interaction of forces in a physical system',[8] and any attempt to combine a context of governing rules with a network of causal laws is bound to create 'logical difficulties'. To understand human action is neither to apply general theories to particular instances, nor to proffer statistics concerning probable courses of behaviour; rather, it is to trace the 'internal connections' between the concepts which constitute the social relations of everyday life. Generalisations and external descriptions have no methodological role in this account, although they 'may be helpful', Winch occasionally concedes, 'in calling one's attention to features of historical situations which one might otherwise have overlooked'.[9] However, it is not difficult to see that Winch's argument fails to demonstrate the methodological irrelevance of explanation in the social sciences. For as I sought to show in the previous chapter, Winch is mistaken to maintain that social relations exist only in and through ideas, since there are relations which may remain unarticulated by lay concepts; and the clarification of such relations, as well as the structural conditions upon which they depend, may require a form of explanation which is not exhausted by the 'tracing of internal connections'. Moreover, even supposing that Winch's account were adequate for understanding what an action is, it would still say very little about why, on any particular occasion, a certain action was performed. To characterise an incident as an act of war may commit one to saying that various conditions obtain, but it so far says nothing about why this particular incident occurred or how the hostilities will proceed; and the latter are surely legitimate issues for social scientific inquiry.[10] Finally, it may be noted that Winch, together with Melden, Peters and others, tends to presuppose a conception of causality deriving from the writings of Hume. This conception, which is not assumed in the more subtle analyses of Wittgenstein,[11] is thoroughly and competently criticised in the recent Anglo-Saxon literature.[12] Here I shall simply suggest that the rigid opposition between understanding and explanation is anchored in a conception of causality which is itself unsound. It may be concluded, therefore, that Winch's attack on the relevance of explanation is a move which is made without satisfactory support.

The opposition between understanding and explanation permeates the writings of ordinary language philosophers who are concerned with the methodology of psychoanalysis. Moore recalls how Wittgenstein regarded the confusion between reason and cause as the source of the 'abominable mess' into which the disciples of Freud had plunged,[13] and the same 'confusion' provides the basis for MacIntyre's critique of the concept of the unconscious.[14] The details of this alleged confusion between reason and cause are explored in a series of articles by Toulmin, Flew and others.[15] Toulmin distinguishes three types of explanation: those, respectively, in which the explanans gives a stated reason, a reported reason and a cause. He suggests that psychoanalytic explanation falls somewhere between these types, but emphasises that 'the kernel of Freud's discovery is the introduction of a technique in which the psycho-therapist begins by studying the *motives for*, rather than the *causes of* neurotic behaviour'.[16] Flew endorses the latter view, claiming that Freud is led astray as soon as he begins to theorise about his work, for only then does he forget his practical concern with the motives of neurotic behaviour and begin to search for 'something quite different, namely, the alleged *efficient causes* of such behaviour'.[17] However, these criticisms of Freud surely miss their mark, and not simply because the writings of Freud contain testable generalisations about human development, as Peters is anxious to show.[18] For what the criticisms disregard is the possibility that neurotic behaviour lies at the very intersection of intentional action and unconscious compulsion, so that the radical disjunction between reason and cause is neither an illuminating nor an appropriate tool for psychoanalytic inquiry. As Ricoeur rightly insists, the language of psychoanalysis is not accidentally but essentially a mixed discourse, a 'semantics of desire'. Thus, rather than appealing to reasons and motives at the expense of any reference to cause, it may be suggested that what is required by psychoanalysis in particular, and the social sciences in general, is a framework which transcends the motive–cause alternative, integrating the moments of understanding and explanation into a systematic and coherent methodology.

Adequacy and critique
The perspective of ordinary language philosophy generates an approach to the problem of adequacy and the question of critique. The so-called 'problem of adequacy' was raised by Schutz in his reformulation of Weber's interpretative sociology;[19] it concerns the relation between the theoretical constructs elaborated by the social scientist on the one hand, and the everyday concepts employed by lay actors on the other. Ordinary language philosophers approach this problem in a manner deeply indebted to the views of Wittgenstein, who urges his followers to abandon their metaphysical inclinations for the mundane analysis of everyday language, while forbidding them to interfere with linguistic use. Winch, Louch and others apply this precept to the social sphere, arguing that social scientists must anchor their theories in the concepts of lay actors and refrain from external critique. Their argument rightly emphasises the peculiar relation between social science and its subject matter, and justly guards against the premature dismissal of lay actors' ideas. Nevertheless, the argument establishes a connection between social theory and lay concepts which is unduly restrictive. I shall endeavour to defend the latter claim by assessing various passages in the writings of Winch. I shall argue that Winch's stipulations for the adequacy of social scientific

theories are vague and untenable, and that his admonitions against critique are undermined by his own account.

Winch's contribution to the problem of adequacy rests upon the assumption that the social scientist is in a position which is crucially different from that of the natural scientist. Both types of scientist are part of a regulated community of researchers, but the social scientist alone is concerned to investigate a phenomenon which is itself governed by rules; 'and it is these rules, rather than those which govern the sociologist's investigation, which specify what is to count as "doing the same kind of thing" in relation to that kind of activity'.[20] Thus, in Winch's view, the judgements of identity which underpin general statements in the social sciences must be made in accordance with the criteria that are employed in the activity under investigation. It follows that the technical concepts which may appear in such statements must remain 'logically tied' to the notions of ordinary actors. However, it is surely mistaken to maintain that 'judgements of identity' in the social sciences can be made only in accordance with lay criteria. As I argued in the previous chapter, there may be stable relations in the social world which are not recognised by the actors themselves, and which do not satisfy any criteria for the application of everyday concepts. For example, there are relations of production and distribution, hierarchies of power and processes of legitimation, all of which may remain wholly or partially opaque to the actors which they enmesh. Winch declares that he has no desire to preclude a 'more reflective understanding' of social life, insisting only that such understanding 'must necessarily presuppose, if it is to count as genuine understanding at all, the participant's unreflective understanding'.[21] Yet what 'presuppose' means here is far from clear, and hence it is difficult to tell just how much scope Winch allows for theoretical reflection. Moreover, he makes no attempt to elucidate the ways in which the results of such reflection may impinge upon the awareness and activity of lay actors. Winch's idea of social science, like Wittgenstein's conception of philosophy, is infused with the fear of intrusion, so that any concern with the practical implications of social theory is precluded from the very start. So while Winch is right to stress that the relation between social science and its subject matter is particularly complex, his account of this relation leaves something to be desired.

Winch's conception of social life has consequences for the question of critique. The customs and conventions which characterise a culture have, according to Winch, their own criteria of intelligibility and rationality. If one wishes to understand a particular culture one must grasp these criteria, and any attempt to evaluate its conventions from an external standpoint is bound to go astray. A practice can appear rational to someone only in the light of certain standards; and 'if *our* concept of rationality is a different one from his, then it makes no sense to say that anything either does or does not appear rational to *him* in *our* sense'.[22] In addition to presupposing a variable concept of rationality, Winch's argument assumes that one can meaningfully speak of a standpoint which is 'external' to a particular culture. The latter assumption is justly questioned by Gellner, Jarvie and others,[23] who rather cynically suggest that Winch's world is like a fairyland of hermetically sealed tribes. There are passages wherein Winch appears to recognise the unreality of his view, conceding that 'it is impossible to keep a discussion of the rationality of Black Magic or of astrology within the bounds of the concepts peculiar to them; they have an essential reference to something outside themselves'.[24] Yet this concession undermines Winch's original admonition, for it acknowledges an element of transcendence which runs counter to the abstract idea of an external standpoint. The sense in which such an element may provide a foundation for the conduct of critique, and the way in which a critical moment may be integrated into a coherent methodology, are issues which will be considered in due course.

II. Hermeneutic phenomenology

Motive and cause

The methodology of social science is a topic of central concern to authors within the tradition of hermeneutic phenomenology. Such a concern is evident in the writings of Ricoeur, whose contributions to this topic are closely linked to the evolution of his own philosophical approach. In his early work, Ricoeur undertakes an eidetic analysis of the will, contrasting this approach with the reductive orientation of the social sciences. The results of the latter disciplines can be reflectively appropriated only by way of a diagnostic relation, which enables consciousness to recover 'the vestiges of a phenomenology which it discovers there in an objectified and in some way alienated form'.[25] In subsequent writings, the diagnostic relation is eclipsed by the concept of archaeology, attesting to Ricoeur's progressive interrogation of the nature of the subject. Psychoanalysis and similar methods are no longer regarded as quasi-naturalistic sciences pursued at the expense of the subject, but rather as hermeneutic disciplines dedicated to deciphering and extending the realm of subjectivity. In the present section, I focus on one of the issues which reflects this change of emphasis, namely the question of the relation between motive and cause. I try to show that Ricoeur's initial conception of this relation is mistaken, but that his recent writings suggest a provocative view which demands further reflection.

Ricoeur's initial conception of the relation between motive and cause is presented in *Freedom and Nature*, within the context of the first articulation of the will. The intentional correlate of 'I decide' is the project, and motivation provides the involuntary foundation upon which the project rests. To motivate is to legitimate or justify a project, which has nothing to do with causation on the level of objects. For 'it is the nature of a cause to be knowable and understood prior to its effects',[26] whereas the meaning of a motive is inseparable from the decision which it supports. Thus Ricoeur rejects any attempt to situate the basic structures of willing within a general cosmology of physical determinism. However, this conception of the relation between motive and cause is unsatisfactory for several reasons. In the first place, it is implausible to suggest that the sphere of motivation can be differentiated from that of causation in terms of the alleged independence of cause and effect. For the extent to which a cause is semantically and epistemologically independent of its effect depends upon how the relevant events are described;[27] and an event may be described as the cause of some occurrence, just as a feeling may be characterised as the motive for some act. Second, it seems wrong to regard the problem of whether a motive can be a cause as decisive for the question of whether determinism is true, as Ricoeur appears to do. For even if every event that occurs has a cause, it would not follow that the occurrence of every event is strictly determined in advance.[28] Hence one must treat with suspicion that spectre of determinism which haunts Ricoeur's early work, compelling him to juxtapose motive and cause in order to preserve an interstice for human freedom. Finally, the antithesis of motive and cause is attenuated by psychoanalysis, which unveils a realm of affectivity that bypasses the channels of conscious deliberation. In *Freedom and Nature*, Ricoeur eludes this conclusion by regarding psychoanalysis as a quasi-naturalistic science concerned with the primordial matter of human experience as opposed to its intentional form. However, the distinction between matter and form does not do justice to the peculiar character of the psychoanalytic domain; and to regard this discipline as a quasi-naturalistic science may be misleading, as the later Ricoeur would admit. Thus, there are good reasons to suppose that Ricoeur's initial conception of the relation between motive and cause is unsound.

Ricoeur returns to the problem of the relation between motive and cause in his recent writings on psychoanalysis. In *Freud and Philosophy*, he maintains that psychoanalytic statements can be located neither within the causal language of the natural sciences nor within the motive language of phenomenology. Ricoeur agrees with Toulmin, Flew and others that motive in the sense of 'reason for' and cause in the sense of 'dependence on' are radically distinct; but he contends that the distinction between motive and cause does not resolve the problem posed by psychoanalytic discourse. For 'such discourse is governed by a unique type of being, which I shall call the semantics of desire; it is a mixed discourse that falls outside the motive–cause alternative'.[29] The notion of a semantics of desire is an original and intriguing idea, epitomising the dispossession of immediate consciousness which characterises Ricoeur's recent writings as a whole. However, the grounds for contending that such a semantics falls outside of the motive–cause alternative are not altogether clear, and I shall distinguish between a weaker and a stronger thesis. According to the weaker thesis, the motive–cause alternative is inadequate because psychoanalytic discourse includes statements about motives as well as statements about causes, so that it cannot be reduced to either sphere without remainder. Ricoeur appears to endorse this thesis in his comments on the contributions of Toulmin and Flew, for he objects to the latter only insofar as they regard the conjunction of motivational and causal statements as a mistake. However, there are other passages in which Ricoeur seems to defend a much stronger and more interesting thesis. For he sometimes suggests that psychoanalysis discloses a dimension of experience where meaning and force coincide, so that one must 'elaborate an intermediate concept of desire as being at once a motive and a cause'.[30] This suggestion points towards a conceptual inquiry which might avoid the sterile antithesis of motive and cause. Unfortunately, Ricoeur does not pursue such an inquiry in any depth, and at a later stage I shall offer a few remarks which may help to amend this deficiency.

Dialectic of interpretation

The recent writings of Ricoeur propose a way of integrating explanation and understanding into a systematic methodology of social science. In accordance with the hermeneutical discourse on human action, Ricoeur maintains that the possibility of treating action as a text renders each of the two movements in the dialectic of interpretation applicable to the social sphere. The first movement comprises the attempt to guess the meaning of an action as a whole, and this guess is then submitted to a process of validation. In the second movement, a depth interpretation is attained through the mediation of the explanatory methods of structuralist analysis. Ricoeur is surely correct to hold that explanation and understanding do not necessarily exclude one another, and he is right to search for a general hermeneutical theory which would subject all forms of human action to a depth interpretation. I believe nonetheless that the specific details of Ricoeur's account cannot be sustained as they stand. For the arguments which support the extension of the dialectic of interpretation to the field of human action are inconsistent and imprecise, and they disregard some important features of the social world.

The extension of the first movement of the dialectic of interpretation to the field of human action is defended on two levels. The first level concerns the provisional projection of meaning; and Ricoeur maintains that just as texts are characterised by a specific plurivocity, so too the meaning of an action may be construed in several ways. The latter claim is certainly acceptable insofar as it means that an action may be variously described. However, it is difficult to see how the defence of this claim is in any way facilitated by the model of the text. Indeed, Ricoeur appears to contravene this model by appealing to Anscombe's account of how the description of an action invokes a motive or want that presupposes a desirability characterisation;[31] for such an appeal does not accord with the intentional autonomisation of action that follows from the model of the text. A similar discrepancy arises on the second level of Ricoeur's defence. Here he argues that just as the conflicting interpretations of a text may be discursively defended with varying degrees of success, so too we impute actions to agents and defend these imputations by refuting the excuses which would defeat the claim. Once again, however, Ricoeur impugns the model of the text by resting his argument on the writings of Hart; for the latter author emphasises that the relevant excuses may include intentional and circumstantial considerations.[32] Finally, Ricoeur is undoubtedly right to suggest that the question of what can defeat a claim is crucial to both literary criticism and the social sciences. Yet this suggestion is misleading insofar as it implies that there are other disciplines, such as the natural sciences, which do not proceed through argumentation but through some sort of straightforward empirical verification. Moreover, the suggestion is inadequate insofar as it provides no indication of what in fact can defeat a claim in particular cases. It seems evident, therefore, that Ricoeur's attempt to extend the first movement of the dialectic of interpretation to the field of human action lacks consistent and compelling support.

The extension of the second movement of the dialectic of interpretation to the field of human action is also defended on two levels. The first level concerns the role of structuralist analysis, which is applicable to social phenomena insofar as the latter possess a semiological character. Ricoeur observes that such an application confers upon the social sciences a type of explanation distinct from the classical causal model, for it posits relations that are correlative rather than consecutive or sequential. However, Ricoeur does not clearly specify the extent to which social phenomena may be said to have a semiological character, nor does he accurately calculate the price to be paid for this formalisation. He says that the adoption of the semiological approach implies that the symbolic function is no longer 'a mere effect in social life' but rather 'its very foundation'.[33] Yet in contrast to Ricoeur's apparent acceptance of this implication, it must be insisted that communication is more than a reversible exchange of signs, and that communication is not the totality of the social world. The latter point is implicit in Ricoeur's critique of the Lacanian account of psychoanalysis, since this critique is focused on the inability of that account to thematise the bar of repression which separates the spheres of discourse. However, if the explanatory dimension of social science is to be provided by structuralist analysis, then such a science would be ill-equipped to investigate the social equivalent of this psychic bar, namely the social mechanisms of power and ideology. Of course, Ricoeur is aware that structuralist analysis is insufficient on its own, and the second level of his defence is concerned to establish a hermeneutical supplementation to this mode. He maintains that just as language-games are forms of life, so too social structures are 'attempts to cope with existential perplexities, human predicaments and deep-rooted conflicts'.[34] These perplexities and predicaments are the *aporias* of social existence, constituting that referential dimension of social structures which must be appropriated in the final stage of the dialectic of interpretation. However, this analogical argument thrives upon the presence of vague and ambiguous terms. The sense, for example, in which a social structure may be said to have a referential dimension is quite unclear, as is the sense in which such a dimension may be attributed to a language-game as a whole. Moreover, as I shall argue more fully in the final chapter, it is by no means evident how a structuralist analysis is to facilitate the elucidation of the referential dimension, nor is it apparent how this dimension is to be unfolded from the object of investigation. Finally, insofar as the process of validation is an aspect of the first movement in the dialectic of interpretation, it is not clear how the structural explanation and depth interpretation are in turn to be assessed. In the light of these numerous difficulties, it must be concluded that Ricoeur's contribution to the theory of interpretation is in need of some modification.

Hermeneutics and critical theory

Ricoeur employs the dialectic of interpretation to arbitrate in the debate between hermeneutics and critical theory. This arbitration assumes the form of two complementary theses: first, that a hermeneutics of tradition can fulfil its programme only if it introduces a critical distance; and second, that a critique of ideology can achieve its aim only if it incorporates a reinterpretation of cultural tradition. In defending these theses, Ricoeur makes some forceful criticisms of the central positions in the debate. Moreover, he rightly indicates some fundamental points of convergence, revealing that the two positions are not as radically opposed as their principal proponents might suggest. I shall contend, however, that Ricoeur's attempted arbitration is not wholly successful. For on the one hand, his defence of the first thesis dissolves the primordial unity of subject and object which characterises the hermeneutics of Heidegger and Gadamer, thereby reopening without resolving the problem of justification. On the other hand, Ricoeur's defence of the second thesis does not seriously confront the theory of communicative competence, thus eschewing some of the most pressing issues in critical theory.

Ricoeur defends the first thesis by arguing that the consciousness of historical efficacy contains within itself a moment of critical distance. For such consciousness can be realised only through the objectified medium of the text, and the text presupposes the four forms of distanciation which accompany the process of inscription. Ricoeur thereby displaces the primordial bond between subject and object which underlies the writings of Heidegger and Gadamer; the primitive hermeneutical phenomenon is no longer belonging as such, but rather the interplay between participatory belonging and alienating distanciation. However, the displacement of the primordial bond undermines the ontological basis for Heidegger's rejection of the quest for foundation, and for Gadamer's dissociation of method and truth. Problems of justification are thus reinstated to a position of crucial importance. If the text confronts the reader as an object to be interpreted, then questions arise as to how one can adjudicate between competing interpretations, and as to whether a particular interpretation can be independently assessed. Ricoeur is, of course, fully aware of the centrality of these issues, which lie along the path of the '"descending dialectic" from the fundamental towards the derived'.[35]

Nevertheless, as I shall argue in the following chapter, I do not believe that Ricoeur provides satisfactory answers to such questions. Here I wish only to note that the urgency of these issues is highlighted by the manner in which distanciation introduces the moment of critique. Ricoeur maintains that since the referential power released by the depth interpretation of a text is capable of projecting an alternative world, this power carries within itself the possibility of a critical recourse against the real. Moreover, since the final appropriation of the world which the text unfolds may expand the horizons of consciousness, the process of interpretation creates the possibility for a critique of the egoistic illusions and ideological distortions of the subject. However, in neither case does Ricoeur show why the world unfolded by the text should constitute a standpoint for the critique of reality or consciousness, rather than reality or consciousness constituting a standpoint for the critique of the world so disclosed. The consciousness of historical efficacy may carry within itself a critical moment, but so far that moment stands without a substantial foundation.

In defence of the second thesis, Ricoeur argues that critical theory presupposes hermeneutics in a way that vitiates its claim to an independent epistemological status. The first level of the argument is concerned with Habermas's general theoretical views, and Ricoeur contends that these views can be justified only in terms of a hermeneutics such as Heidegger's. This contention has considerable force insofar as the theory of cognitive interests is linked to the distinction between labour and interaction; but the necessity of the link is uncertain, and I have already suggested that the latter distinction should be abandoned altogether. The second level of Ricoeur's argument concerns the claim that critical theory is characterised by a unique integration of explanation and understanding. In opposition to this claim, Ricoeur maintains that the paradigmatic object of all hermeneutical disciplines is the text; and hence it follows from the theory of interpretation that all such disciplines share a methodological structure in which understanding is mediated by explanatory procedures. Ricoeur is surely right to contest the claim to methodological uniqueness which is espoused by some exponents of critical theory, for the process of depth interpretation is not restricted to an object domain of systematically distorted communication. However, I have cast doubt upon Ricoeur's use of the text as a general model for the object of interpretation, and I have suggested that his account of the methodology of depth interpretation must be revised. The third and most profound level of Ricoeur's argument concerns the status of the emancipatory interest. The claim at this level is that critical social science, considered in terms of the object and the content of its knowledge-constitutive interest, is dependent upon the historical-hermeneutic disciplines. For the ideologies which this science seeks to analyse are, after all, distortions of communication; and the goal which it seeks to attain is nothing other than the ideal of communication free from constraint. Ricoeur also maintains that this ideal would be empty and abstract unless it were substantiated through a reinterpretation of the past. In reply to the first aspect of this claim, it must be said that Habermas acknowledges the dependence of critical theory upon both the empirical-analytic sciences and the historical-hermeneutic disciplines. Habermas insists, however, that critical theory cannot be reduced to either of these other types, since to do so would be to collapse this theory into economism on the one hand or idealism on the other. Indeed, Habermas's insistence on the irreducibility of critical theory is reflected in Ricoeur's own view that psychoanalysis is both a hermeneutics and an energetics; but Ricoeur tends to overemphasise the hermeneutic dimension, which curtails the utility of his interpretative theory for investigating the institutional and structural features of the social world. The second aspect of Ricoeur's claim presses to the heart of Habermas's project, calling into question any attempt to justify the critique of ideology in a purely formalistic fashion. However, Ricoeur's attack cannot be sustained as it stands, for it simply asserts that the theory of communicative competence cannot fulfil its task. In the following chapter, I shall argue that this theory does contain a number of serious difficulties; but it also suggests a course of research which is worthy of being pursued. Indeed, the theory of communicative competence is anticipated by certain aspects of Ricoeur's own work, such as the eschatological overtones of his conception of truth and his remarks on the transcendental conditions of discourse. Finally, the unexamined possibility of providing an independent justification for the conduct of critique weakens the fourth level of Ricoeur's argument. For the ideas encapsulated in the ideal speech situation may stem from the tradition of the Enlightenment, but Habermas does not appeal to the authority of that tradition for the justification of this ideal. So while Ricoeur's arbitration in the debate between hermeneutics and critical theory is both penetrating and provocative, it nevertheless leaves some of the most important issues open.

III. Critical social theory

Depth hermeneutics
Authors within the tradition of critical social theory have devoted

considerable attention to the methodology of social science. During the last decade, Habermas has reformulated and developed some of his predecessors' views, crystallising his innovations in a series of important contributions. In the present section, I examine Habermas's contribution to the problem of the relation between explanation and understanding. Unlike Winch and in a manner similar to Ricoeur, Habermas seeks to integrate these elements into a unified theory of interpretation. He finds the key for such an integration in psychoanalysis, a discipline which attempts to decipher behavioural symptoms by recourse to the generalised history of infantile development. In accordance with this model of depth hermeneutics, Habermas correctly contends that a critical social science cannot remain at the level of lay actors' accounts of their own action, as many ethnomethodologists suggest. On the other hand, such a science cannot simply eliminate the interpretative dimension in favour of an exhaustive explanation, as recommended by certain proponents of functionalism, structuralism and systems theory. Rather, Habermas rightly insists that a critical social science must acknowledge the irreducible status of the category of meaning, while at the same time recognising that the elucidation of meaning in particular cases may require the invocation of objectifying concepts. However, I shall attempt to show that Habermas's account of the category of meaning contains some unresolved difficulties, and that the way in which he proposes to invoke objectifying concepts is unclear. So although the general direction of Habermas's hermeneutical programme is as commendable as that of Ricoeur's, the specific details of his proposal are equally in need of revision.

Habermas conceives of the object of depth hermeneutics as a form of communication which has been systematically distorted by the exercise of repression. The exclusion of the relevant experience from the sphere of public language is marked by symptomatic symbols, whose privatised significance remains inaccessible to the subjects concerned. However, I argued in the previous chapter that the concept of systematically distorted communication does not provide a suitable specification of the scope of depth hermeneutics; and I suggested that it is implausible to regard the object of such hermeneutics as an initially incomprehensible symbol. Indeed, it is difficult to see how Habermas could sustain the latter view in the light of his recent writings on the theory of language. Habermas distinguishes between four basic validity claims which, he believes, are necessarily presupposed by every normally functioning language-game. Truth, correctness and sincerity are counterfactual claims which could be redeemed if certain expectations were impugned; but intelligibility, in the sense of grammatical well-formedness, is a factual condition which must already be fulfilled if the language-game is to function at all. Yet if that is the case, then the expressions and actions of the language-game must be in some sense understandable to the participants, and hence cannot be wholly incomprehensible to them. Habermas might reply to this conclusion by arguing that although intelligibility is a factual condition of communication, it is in some way parasitic upon the counterfactual claims which are implicitly raised. Such a reply is intimated in a recent paper, wherein Habermas maintains that we understand the meaning of a text only insofar as 'we know why the author felt himself entitled to put forward (as true) certain assertions, to express (as truthful) certain intentions, to recognize (as valid) certain values and norms'.[36] However, this line of reply is unsatisfactory in several respects. First, it is not clear why understanding should be dependent upon the redemption of these claims, nor is it easy to see how this account could be defended in the absence of a more developed theory of meaning. Second, even if this account were accepted, it would not show that in certain cases these claims are to no extent redeemed. Third, it is not obvious how the revised account is to be reconciled with the programme of depth hermeneutics, which Habermas distinguishes from its orthodox counterpart in terms of the recourse to an explanatory dimension. For if orthodox hermeneutics seeks to understand the meaning of a text, then it too must reconstruct a context which would redeem the relevant validity claims; and such a reconstruction would be in some sense an 'explanation' of the meaningful object, even if, as I shall now try to show, it would not be the only possible sense.

The explanatory dimension of depth hermeneutics provides a tool for the clarification of a symbol whose meaning is initially opaque. This tool functions by way of a theoretical reconstruction of determinant conditions, enabling the interpreter to explain the genesis of the problematic symbol. However, it is not clear just what sense of 'reconstruction' is relevant here, for Habermas employs this concept in several ways. On some occasions, he uses 'reconstruction' to refer to the psychoanalytic projection of an original scene in which an individual experienced and repressed an unbearable conflict (R_1). On other occasions, Habermas describes the systematically generalised history which facilitates this projection as a reconstruction, namely as a reconstruction of the stages of a developmental process (R_2). In a third sense, one may speak of the reconstruction of a context which contributes to the redemption of the validity claims discussed in the previous paragraph (R_3). Habermas also suggests that in certain cases one must go beyond such a contextual reconstruction, and attempt 'to explicate the meaning of a symbolic formation in terms of the rules according to which the author must have brought it forth'[37] (R_4). At a more abstract level still, one may seek to reconstruct, not the rules whereby particular formations are produced, but rather the general competencies which a speaker or actor must possess (R_5). These five types of reconstruction are further distinguishable from the sense in which Habermas's recent book is a reconstruction of historical materialism, that is, a reformulation of the key concepts and basic assumptions of a certain theoretical framework (R_6). Finally, it may be noted that the precise status of these various types of reconstruction, as well as the ways in which they may be capable of generating explanations, are by no means clear.[38] In lieu of a more detailed analysis of such issues, it must be concluded that Habermas's account of the explanatory dimension of depth hermeneutics is regrettably imprecise.

Conduct of critique

Habermas is concerned to establish a social science which incorporates a moment of critique. Rather than viewing the social world as an inviolable given, such a science must seek to disclose the barriers which obstruct the human self-formative process and to eliminate these barriers through a method of systematic self-reflection. In *Knowledge and Human Interests*, the method of self-reflection is modelled on the psychoanalytic dialogue, and the standards which render such reflection possible are said to possess 'theoretical certainty'. 'The human interest in autonomy and responsibility is not mere fancy, for it can be apprehended a priori. What raises us out of nature is the only thing whose nature we can know: *language*.'[39] In his subsequent writings, Habermas attempts to substantiate the suggestion that the theory of language can provide a foundation for critique. His pursuit of this attempt is a highly original and praiseworthy project, raising issues which are of profound importance for the philosophy of social science. I shall suggest, nonetheless, that the present state of the project is somewhat confused and incomplete, so that the task of grounding critical theory remains unfulfilled.

Habermas's recent contributions to the problem of foundation are premissed upon a distinction between reconstruction and critique. The relevant sense of reconstruction is that which was labelled R_5 in the previous section, and which consists in the elucidation of the general competencies of speaking and acting subjects. Critique, on the other hand, is concerned with the subjectively produced illusions that objectively constrain the social actor, constituting part of the particular self-formative process of an individual or group. Unlike the reconstruction of anonymous systems of rules which competent subjects must possess, critique aims to disclose the contents of a false consciousness in a way that has practical consequences. Yet critique invokes a reconstruction insofar as the characterisation of consciousness as false, or of communication as distorted, presupposes some conception of a situation to which these characterisations do not apply. The conception which Habermas proposes for this purpose is that of the ideal speech situation, which may be formulated in terms of the dialogue-constitutive universals that define communicative competence. However, I shall contend in the following chapter that Habermas's argument for the necessary presupposition of an ideal speech situation is unsound, and hence the claim that this situation provides a foundation which is immanent in every act of speech must be held in doubt. Moreover, precisely how the ideal speech situation is supposed to fulfil its foundational role is not entirely clear. Sometimes Habermas suggests that the concept of the ideal speech situation, together with the model of pure communicative action which is somehow contained within it, provides a formal standard for the identification and critique of systematically distorted communication. The ideal speech situation is defined by the thesis of symmetry, whereas systematically distorted communication is characterised by 'the uneven distribution of dialogue constitutive universals'.[40] Yet Habermas proffers no clues as to how one would recognise whether the distribution of dialogue-constitutive universals were symmetrical or not. Moreover, as I shall argue in detail later, such symmetry is an insufficient criterion for the elimination of internal constraints, since forces may operate in modes other than that of restricted access to speech-acts. Finally, it is questionable whether the formal nature of the ideal speech situation could provide a critical standard for historically specific forms of action and communication, a question pointedly posed by Ricoeur. It might be possible to counter the latter objection by appealing to another way in which the ideal speech situation could be employed.

Habermas returns to the problem of foundation in his recent writings on the theory of legitimation. In this context, he proposes a somewhat different type of reconstruction, namely a 'counterfactually projected reconstruction' (R_7), as a tool for the exercise of critique. This type of reconstruction attempts to unmask relations of power by comparing 'normative structures existing at a given time with the hypothetical state of a system of norms formed, *ceteris paribus*, discursively'.[41] The hypothetical system of norms is justified in terms of a reconstruction of general competencies (R_5), insofar as it is projected in accordance with the question of how societal members would have interpreted their needs and established their norms if they had accomplished these tasks under the conditions of an ideal speech situation. Habermas submits that this abstract question could be rendered more concrete for social analysis by imagining cases of conflict in which the relevant parties would be forced to perceive and assert their interests. Such an ascription of interests would retain an hypothetical status; and although it could be supported by empirical indicators, it could be finally confirmed only through a practical discourse among the subjects involved. In this way, Habermas appears to provide a standard for the critique of ideology which is not purely formal, but which acquires its content from the conclusions attained under conditions that are formally defined. Yet Habermas's proposal remains hindered by conceptual and practical difficulties. For while he is right to criticise prescriptivists for their inadequate account of moral argument, it seems doubtful whether he has provided a satisfactory alternative. Habermas maintains that the backing which must be adduced in practical discourse consists of the interpretation of needs; and he claims that the formal properties of discourse require that the latter must be needs that can be communicatively shared, or in other words, generalisable interests. However, not only is the nature of these interests obscure, but the sense in which they must be generalisable is far from clear. If the relevant interests are needs which must be shared by every potential participant of a practical discourse, 'whereby I counterfactually include all of the conversational partners which I could find if my life history were co-extensive with the history of humanity',[42] then it is difficult to imagine any interests which would be generalisable in the requisite sense. Moreover, it is by no means clear just *who* these conversational partners would be, if they were extricated from their real life situations and transposed into a counterfactual realm of self-transparency and idealised discourse.[43] As a final point, it may be added that Habermas's proposal concerning the conduct and justification of critique remains abstract, and his ideas have yet to be implemented in a systematic way. So although Habermas has rightly emphasised the importance of developing a social science which incorporates a moment of grounded critique, it must be said that his attempts to provide the requisite foundation are programmatic at best.

Theory and practice

The search for a unity of theory and practice is one of the central themes of Habermas's work. This theme provides the framework for his inquiry into the history of political thought and for his investigation into the epistemological structure of the various sciences. In the latter investigation, Habermas contends that just as the empirical-analytic sciences eliminate the dimension of human *praxis* by conceiving of theory in a technical sense, so too the historical-hermeneutic disciplines tend to abandon the realm of theory in favour of a practical inquiry into the functions of ordinary language. It is in the model of psychoanalysis that Habermas finds the resources to overcome this unhappy disjunction of theory and practice. However, the unity thereby restored is fragile in crucial respects, as Habermas himself admits. I shall maintain, moreover, that the modifications which he recommends in order to rectify these weaknesses fail to resolve the most important problems.

In *Knowledge and Human Interests*, Habermas portrays psychoanalysis as a discipline which integrates elements of the empirical-analytic sciences and the historical-hermeneutic disciplines into a framework of systematic self-reflection. By predicating the correctness of an interpretation on the successful continuation of a self-formative process, psychoanalysis provides the link between theoretical explanation and practical emancipation once promised by the eighteenth-century concept of committed reason. However, as several commentators observe,[44] this link is attenuated by the ambiguity in the concept of self-reflection, which incorporates aspects of reconstruction and critique. For insofar as rational self-reflection is essentially the reconstruction of the conditions of possible knowledge or speech, then the critical dissolution of distorted communication may be related to reason, but it is no longer the realisation of reason as such. Moreover, the attempt to apply the model of psychoanalysis to the level of society as a whole is laden with difficulties. Many critics justly object that social analysis is not simply psychoanalysis writ large:[45] the social world is torn apart by classes and interest groups whose conflictual relations and political alternatives cannot be adequately conceptualised within the framework of a therapeutic dialogue. On the level of social analysis, there is no single subject who submits himself or herself willingly to be cured, but rather a number of classes or groups whose interrelations of domination and subordination are the object of analysis, and whose susceptibilities to processes of enlightenment are not the same. Furthermore, on the social level, the inducement of enlightenment does not coincide with the attainment of emancipation; for an enlightened subject population is still, for all that, a subject population. Whatever social significance one may give to the Freudian concept of 'working through', it is obvious that political practice is not simply a matter of talking through an interpretation and making it one's own. The acceptance of a particular analysis of the social world is undoubtedly an important part of politics, but with this acceptance the struggle has only just begun. For these and other reasons, it seems clear that Habermas's initial attempt to link theory and practice through the model of psychoanalysis cannot be sustained.

Habermas has replied to some of the difficulties in his approach with a series of distinctions which curtail the role of the psychoanalytic model. In the new introduction to *Theory and Practice*, Habermas differentiates between three levels of validity within the structure of critical theory. There is, first, the level on which scientific hypotheses are formulated and proposed, and where validity is connected with the truth of statements which are defended in theoretical discourse. On a second level, critical theory participates in the organisation of enlightenment, whereby scientific hypotheses initiate processes of reflection which terminate in authentic insights. The third level refers to the selection of strategies and tactics for the conduct of political struggle; here the aim is prudent decisions which can only be redeemed in the practical discourse of the parties concerned. The model of psychoanalysis can be employed only on the second of these levels, that is, 'for normatively structuring the relationship between the Communist Party and the masses who let themselves be enlightened by the Party concerning their own situation'.[46] However, while these distinctions may help to avoid an over-extended use of the psychoanalytic model, they merely exacerbate the original problems which that model was invoked to resolve. By relegating the redemption of truth claims to the realm of theoretical discourse, and by severing the latter from the organisation of enlightenment and the conduct of struggle, the relation between theoretical truth and political practice becomes more remote than ever. Sometimes Habermas attempts to restore this relation by asserting that the therapeutic dialogue which structures the organisation of enlightenment culminates in an insight which redeems both a claim to truth and a claim to authenticity. However, this postulated convergence of truth and authenticity is quite problematic, and it ignores the real possibility of a conflict in the redemption of these claims. Moreover, by separating both of these claims from the level of political struggle, Habermas destroys whatever semblance of unity his postulated convergence may create. How the results of a therapeutic dialogue enter into the practical deliberations of a subject population is nowhere specified in any detail, and hence the way in which theoretical statements provide a basis for political strategies remains unclear. These difficulties are especially evident in the analysis of contemporary capitalism which Habermas offers in *Legitimation Crisis*. For the argument of the book is cast in the form of scientific hypotheses which could be redeemed in theoretical discourse, and little attempt is made to link these hypotheses to the processes of enlightenment and struggle. Moreover, the critical moment of critical theory, which the final part of *Legitimation Crisis* ties to the conclusions of a practical discourse, does not fit neatly into the trichotomy of levels presented in *Theory and Practice*. So even if the distinctions introduced by Habermas serve to mitigate some of the difficulties in his earlier views, they do not succeed in resolving the basic issues which are at stake.

IV. Towards a methodology of social science

Generation and structuration

The critical discussions of the foregoing sections indicate a direction for the development of a more adequate methodology. This constructive task is closely linked to the theory of action, for methodological issues cannot be divorced from the conceptualisation of an object domain. In the previous chapter, I argued that one of the central mistakes in much of the contemporary literature on action is the tendency to generalise from a linguistic model. In opposition to this tendency, I offered an analysis of the concept of action which thematised its relations to the institutional and structural dimensions of the social world. I shall now resume the analysis on a methodological plane, seeking to show how these dimensions may form the basis for an explanatory component in the social sciences. The statement of this aim immediately distances my proposal from the accounts of ordinary language philosophers, who are inclined to expel the concept of explanation from the sphere of social inquiry. The introduction of an explanatory component does not, however, imply a return to a methodology modelled on the natural sciences; for this component is firmly rooted in, and fully respectful of, the peculiar constitution of the social world. I shall therefore proceed by introducing some distinctive methodological concepts, which will in turn provide a means of reformulating the programme of depth interpretation initiated by Ricoeur and Habermas.[47]

The explanatory component of the social sciences must be clarified by reference to the relation between action and structure. I have suggested that action and structure are linked through the medium of institutions, which may be conceived as specific constellations of social relations and material resources. Institutions are characterised by a variety of schemata which define the parameters of permissible action. Such schemata are transmitted through trial and error, imitation and concerted inculcation, enabling the agent to negotiate the routine and novel circumstances of everyday life. Schemata become inscribed in the desires, inclinations, attitudes and beliefs of the subject, constituting that sphere of values which Ricoeur places at the roots of voluntary action. In a similar vein, Bourdieu characterises the habitus as 'systems of durable, transposable *dispositions*',[48] which regulate practice without presupposing a conscious or collective orchestration of action. Moreover, as both Ricoeur and Bourdieu rightly suggest, the form of regulation which is relevant here is peculiarly generative. Institutional schemata do not specify the course of action to be pursued in every foreseeable situation, but merely provide general principles for the creative production of particular acts. Hence I shall speak of the 'schematic generation' of human action. The latter concept may be clarified by locating it within the context of several traditional debates. Rather than appealing to either the motive of an action or its cause, the concept of schematic generation points towards a stable and efficacious inclination which eludes this sharp alternative. For on the one hand, such inclinations cannot be adequately conceptualised as the agent's recognisable grounds for performing the action; nor, on the other hand, can they be simply conceived as the antecedent conditions which compel the agent to act. The concept of schematic generation avoids the hypostatisations and reifications of role theory, insofar as it eliminates the need to posit a package of detailed instructions for every institutionalised act. The concept equally eludes the reductionism of some interpretative sociologies, for it emphasises that social interaction is always more than the sum of its individual and ephemeral aspects. Schematic generation indicates the locus of the agent's historicity, marking the point at which the accumulated conventions of the past impinge upon the actor and govern the creative production of the future. Finally, in a manner reminiscent of the early Ricoeur, the concept of schematic generation offers an avenue for transcending the dilemma of freedom and necessity. For schemata generate action in a way which is not deterministic, establishing flexible boundaries for the negotiation of unanticipated situations; and one must not preclude the possibility that under certain circumstances, subjects may reflect upon and transform such schemata in accordance with their collective interests.

The level of social structure provides a further foothold for an explanatory component in the social sciences. I have proposed that social structure may be conceived as a series of elements and their interrelations, which conjointly define the conditions for the persistence of a social formation and the limits for the variation of its constituent institutions. Among these elements are those which are necessary conditions for the continuation of a particular type of social formation, and which specify the limits for the alteration of a certain kind of institution. It is these elements which endow institutions with their peculiar structural features, predetermining their degree of stability and infusing their schemata with the colours of social class. To investigate these elements is to study what I shall call the 'social structuration' of institutions.[49] The concept of social structuration may be clarified by contrasting it with the notion of structural causality, which Ricoeur employs as a basis for the explanatory dimension in his theory of interpretation. The notion of structural causality is introduced by Althusser to account for the way in which the parts of a structure are determined by the whole, such that the whole is present in each of its parts.[50] Althusser is surely right to insist that the aetiological role of social structure cannot be analysed in terms of the classical conception of causality, since the ideas of temporal priority and constant conjunction do not necessarily apply. It seems clear, however, that Althusser's notion of structural causality does not facilitate the requisite analysis, for it remains restricted by both his abstraction from the 'real-concrete' and his disregard of human agency. Althusser maintains that in attempting to think through the effectivity of a structure on its elements, 'never for an instant do we set foot beyond the absolutely impassable frontier which separates the "development" or specification of the concept from the development and particularity of things'.[51] By means of this contention, which amounts to a veritable sophism, Althusser precludes an inquiry into the ways in which social structure impinges upon the institutions and actions which constitute the social world. Indeed, it is the relation between structure and action which confers upon the concept of social structuration its most peculiar characteristics, one of which was crystallised by Habermas in his early allusion to the 'causality of fate'. For not only is action circumscribed by structure through the medium of social institutions, but structure is reproduced by action through the process of schematic generation; and yet action may also replace a particular structure, in which case the social structuration of institutions gives way to the active transformation of social structure.

Depth interpretation

The concepts of schematic generation and social structuration provide a means of reformulating the methodology of depth interpretation. This methodology is oriented towards a specification of the meaning of action; and while it recognises that such specifications are practically accomplished by lay actors in everyday life, it nevertheless assumes that the meaning of action is neither exhausted nor determined by lay actors' accounts of what they are doing. In the present section, I attempt to show how the elucidation of meaning may be facilitated by the reconstruction of the schemata which generate action, and by the clarification of the elements which structurate institutions. In thus proposing a systematic interrelation between the understanding of human action and the explanation of its social genesis, I shall be defending a particular version of the hermeneutical programme propounded by Ricoeur and Habermas. The version is characterised by two principal movements, although the latter will differ in detail from the movements distinguished by Ricoeur. In developing this programme, I do not wish to suggest that it incorporates all of the interesting questions which may be asked of action and the social world, or that it constitutes in some sense a comprehensive methodology of social science. My claim is merely that this programme presents an important way of connecting the understanding of action to a distinctively social level of explanation.[52]

The first movement in the depth interpretation of action involves the reconstruction of institutional schemata. The relevant sense of reconstruction is similar to that which was labelled R_4 above, and which Habermas links to the 'rules' in accordance with which particular symbolic formations are produced. In the present context, the object of reconstruction is the schemata which generate the action in question. Such schemata may be elucidated through a process of comparison and abstraction, whereby one elicits a general formula for the production of multifarious acts. As a practically effective principle, this formula is part of the interactive competence of lay actors, although it may seldom attain a state of discursive awareness. The explicit articulation of such a formula enables the investigator to explain the performance of an action in terms of the application of institutional schemata to particular circumstances.

Moreover, this mode of explanation may permit the action to be re-described, and thereby re-understood, in the light of its schematic genesis. An excellent example of such an approach may be found in the work of Bourdieu, who substantiates his theoretical reflections with extracts from fieldwork in Kabylia. The exchange of gifts is a common feature in Kabyle life, often instigating reciprocal gestures which may continue indefinitely. Yet behind the appearance of material beneficence, Bourdieu unfolds a principle of action which is centred on the 'sense of honour', and which 'enables each agent to engender all the practices consistent with the logic of challenge and riposte, and only such practices, by means of countless inventions'.[53] From the standpoint of this principle, the act of exchanging gifts may be understood as part of a continuous process of defending and defeating the honour of the parties concerned. In a similar way, it may be suggested that the action of agents in industrialised societies may be interpreted in the light of the schemata which characterise the constituent institutions, and which form generative principles for the production of particular acts. The reconstruction of institutional schemata may thereby provide an explanatory mediation for the depth interpretation of human action.

The second movement in the methodology of depth interpretation involves the reconstruction of structural elements. The sense of reconstruction which is relevant here resembles that which was labelled R_2 in the discussion of Habermas. For the reconstruction of structural elements presupposes a theory of social development, and the developmental stages specify the conditions which must be satisfied by institutions of a particular type. Such a reconstruction enables one to grasp various aspects of institutions which would otherwise remain concealed, including the limits to the exercise of power and the efficacy of ideology, as well as the dynamics of institutional persistence and collapse. A structural analysis may facilitate the depth interpretation of action by situating agents within a context of conditions of which they are ignorant or only dimly aware. An intriguing example of this method may be found in a recent study of working-class culture by Willis.[54] The author correctly contends that one cannot remain at the level of the actors' discursive awareness of what they are doing, but must 'plunge beneath the surface of ethnography in a more interpretative mode'.[55] Accordingly, Willis argues that the 'lads'' evasion of authority in the workplace may be interpreted as a 'cultural penetration' of the fact that labour-power is a variable resource in capitalist society; and he maintains that their failure to differentiate between various types of work is a penetration into the nature of general abstract labour. Willis does not confront the question of the justification of interpretations which arises from his account, nor does he attempt to defend the applicability of the structural elements which his interpretations presuppose. I shall return to these issues in the following chapter, although here it may be noted that the pursuit of the latter task allows an important role for statistics. Whatever the merits of the attack on statistical analysis which is made by sociologists preoccupied with the problem of meaning,[56] that attack does not demonstrate that such analysis is irrelevant to the process of interpretation; and one way in which it may be relevant is by clarifying the extent to which the institutions of a social formation satisfy the conditions of a structural type.[57] Finally, it should be clear that the two movements in the methodology of depth interpretation are closely interrelated. For just as the understanding of action is enhanced by an account of its schematic generation, so too the comprehension of institutions is enriched by an analysis of their social structuration. The appeal to the explanatory dimension of social structure may therefore provide a depth interpretation of human action which is mediated by a profounder grasp of social institutions.

Critique and self-reflection

The methodology of depth interpretation establishes a framework for the conduct of critique. The development of a critical social science is one of the concerns which unites the work of Ricoeur and Habermas, despite the many differences that separate their accounts. The possibility of such a science also receives some support from writers within the tradition of analytical philosophy. Searle, Anscombe and Foot cast doubt upon the view that statements of value are radically distinct from statements of fact,[58] thereby countering a common defence of the thesis that social science must be value-free. Kovesi and Connolly maintain that phenomena are necessarily described from particular standpoints, and that the descriptions which are relevant to the social sciences are proffered from a standpoint which is essentially moral.[59] Hesse argues that since theories in the natural and social sciences are always underdetermined by the facts, the selection of competing theories requires the invocation of criteria which may incorporate considerations of value.[60] In the following paragraphs, I assume that such arguments, together with those of Ricoeur and Habermas, give some plausibility to the idea of a critical social science. I thus proceed to distinguish several potential objects of critique, and to link the critical moment of social science to the self-reflection of acting subjects.

The role of critique in the social sciences may be clarified by distinguishing two categories of potential objects. The first category is concerned with the sphere of consciousness and ideology, which is a focal point of critical analysis in the writings of Ricoeur and Habermas. In accordance with the methodology of depth interpretation outlined above, the analysis of the awareness of an agent or of the contents of a system of signification may proceed by recourse to the reconstruction of institutional schemata and structural conditions. If the reconstruction produces descriptions of action which differ from the accounts of lay actors, or interpretations of social interests and societal arrangements which diverge from the prevailing views, then the way is prepared for a critique of consciousness and ideology. The conduct of such critique may have important practical consequences, insofar as it may help to illuminate the social conditions of action for the actors themselves. However, the role of critique in the social sciences cannot be restricted to the dissolution of a false consciousness concerning the institutional and structural arrangements of a particular social formation. For critical analysis may also be directed at a second category of potential objects, namely at the institutional and structural arrangements concerned. In undertaking this type of analysis, one must consider not only what possibilities are precluded from realisation by the existing arrangements, but also what value those possibilities might possess. One cannot subject an institution or social structure to critique unless one can show that the possibilities which they preclude are in some sense preferable to those which they permit; and this cannot be shown in the absence of an argument which fuses factual and normative elements, as Habermas rightly maintains. I shall return to the problem of justification in the final chapter, where an attempt will be made to overcome some of the difficulties in Habermas's account. At this point it may be said that by endorsing his general approach, I disavow the strategy of immanent critique defended by Ricoeur, as well as the scientistic structuralism propounded by Godelier and others.[61] For the conduct of critique requires a foundation from which it proceeds, and such a foundation is not provided by an appeal to the inevitable march of economic and scientific progress.

The link between critique and self-reflection is a pivotal point in the philosophy of social science. In the hermeneutical theory elaborated by Ricoeur, the process of interpretation involves a progressive expansion of the horizons of consciousness, whereby the subject apprehends that effort to exist and desire to be which is crystallised in the world of the text. Habermas's social theory similarly reserves a central position for the subject, since it premisses the conduct of critique on the contents of a will which would be formed under the conditions of ideal speech. The critical programme sketched in the previous paragraph may be connected to a notion of self-reflection which lies in between the conceptions espoused by Ricoeur and Habermas. For the reconstruction of institutions and social structure may induce subjects to reflect upon the circumstances in which they act; and such reflection may enable subjects to grasp, not so much the effort to exist, but rather those conditions of their existence which had hitherto remained opaque. The notion of self-reflection thus proposed must be detached from the model of psychoanalysis, which is prejudiced by the peculiarity of the analytic situation. Self-reflection must be freed of contemplative connotations, and conjoined instead to the idea of the active appropriation of an alternative state of affairs. It may be suggested, moreover, that the factual underdetermination of scientific theory elevates the self-reflection of the subject to a crucial epistemological role. At a later stage I shall argue that the truth of theoretical reconstructions is dependent upon the appropriation of derived interpretations under conditions that can be formally defined, and that such conditions establish a framework in which the institutional and structural arrangements of a society may be rationally assessed. Here it will suffice to note that the above suggestion marks the re-appearance of practice in the very constitution of social scientific theory. This primordial unity of theory and practice is a central theme of Habermas's early work, which in this respect must be upheld against his subsequent views. For to regard scientific truth claims as redeemable in a theoretical discourse divorced from its practical counterpart, in the manner of the later Habermas, is to obscure the role of practice in the selection of social scientific theory and to sacrifice the selective procedure to an implicit principle of prediction and control.

In this chapter, I attempt to show that the writings of Ricoeur and Habermas make some valuable contributions to the methodology of social science, overcoming many of the limitations of the ordinary language approach. I argue nonetheless that these contributions contain a number of difficulties, the elimination of which requires a thorough reconsideration of the issues involved. In an effort to meet this demand, I introduce several explanatory concepts, anchoring these in the thematisation of the relation between action and structure. I then employ these concepts as a means of reformulating the methodology of depth interpretation. Finally, I seek to integrate this methodology with the conduct of critique, suggesting that the pursuit of self-reflection has profound implications for the status of social scientific theory. This final suggestion raises crucial and complex questions of epistemology, which form the subject matter of the following chapter.

6. Problems in the theory of reference and truth

The problems of reference and truth form a common focal point in the traditions of ordinary language philosophy, hermeneutic phenomenology and critical social theory. Wittgenstein, Strawson and others explicate the referential relation by means of the applicability of identifying descriptions and criticise the conception of truth which posits a correspondence between language and the world. The recent work of Ricoeur proffers the intriguing idea of split reference, coupling this idea with a notion of truth which terminates the dialectic of interpretation. One of Habermas's most original proposals is the formulation of a consensus theory of truth, which specifies the conditions for the rational redemption of truth claims in terms of the necessary presuppositions of speech. In the present chapter, I conclude my critical discussion of the three traditions by undertaking an assessment of these contributions. Among other things I attempt to show, first, that the link between reference and description is less secure than ordinary language philosophers suggest, and that these philosophers fail to furnish a theory of truth; second, that Ricoeur's remarks on the problems of reference and truth are incomplete, often relying upon authors whose views are at variance with his own; and third, that Habermas's argument for the necessary presupposition of an ideal speech situation is problematic, so that his conjunction of rational consensus and truth must be held in doubt. In the final part of the chapter, I seek to sketch a framework for a more satisfactory solution to the problems of reference and truth, with the aim of elaborating an epistemology which would be appropriate for the depth interpretation of human action.

I. Ordinary language philosophy

Reference and constitution
Ordinary language philosophy generates a distinctive approach to the problem of reference. Against the backcloth of theses concerning the

autonomy of grammar and the constitution of objects, Wittgenstein suggests that an expression refers in virtue of the descriptive phrases which
may be substituted for it. This suggestion is elaborated in the writings of
Strawson, Searle and others, who regard referring as an activity dependent upon the applicability of an indeterminate range of identifying
descriptions. The so-called 'cluster theory of reference' thereby establishes a flexible relation between word and object, providing general
guidelines for the specification of particular referents. I shall argue
nonetheless that the cluster theory cannot be sustained. For the applicability of identifying descriptions is neither a necessary nor a sufficient
condition of successful reference, and the link between identifying description and speakers' cognition is one which is open to question. I shall
conclude this section with the claim that the problem of reference is
deceptively dissolved by Winch, who absorbs the referential function
into an over-extended theory of constitution.

The cluster theory maintains that successful reference occurs if and
only if there exists an object to which the speaker's expression uniquely
applies. An expression applies to an object if and only if the object
satisfies the description which the speaker uses, or most of the descriptions which are commonly associated with the name that is used. However, it has been forcefully argued by Kripke, Donnellan and others that
even if most of the descriptions commonly associated with a name are
satisfied by one unique object, that object is not necessarily the referent of
the name; and even if there is no object of which most of the descriptions
are true, it does not necessarily follow that the name fails to refer.[1] For one
can imagine cases in which there are mistaken beliefs about the object
which is referred to by name, and yet the speaker may succeed in
referring to that object all the same. The possibility of mistaken beliefs
points to a further difficulty in the cluster theory which Kripke and
Donnellan do not pursue. In an attempt to elucidate the conditions of
unique reference, both Strawson and Searle submit that the speaker's
awareness or intention is a crucial consideration. Thus Strawson proposes that for a speaker to be referring to one particular, 'there must be *at
most* one such particular *which he has in mind*';[2] and Searle proclaims that
the function of the definite article 'is to indicate the speaker's intention to
refer uniquely'.[3] Yet it is by no means clear that unique reference may be
secured by appealing to the awareness or intention of the speaker. For
there are cases in which the speaker may be referring to more than one
object, even though the speaker may think that he or she is referring to
only one. Innumerable examples of such cases may be found in Freud's

analyses of recounted dreams.[4] For instance, the interpretation of the dream entitled 'Irma's injection' reveals that 'Irma' is a condensed symbol representing a series of figures, irrespective of the individual which Freud may have had in mind when recounting the dream. Similarly, there are cases in which the speaker may be referring to an object quite different from the particular which the speaker thinks he or she is referring to, as is amply illustrated by Freud's study of displacement in dreams and parapraxes. I hope to show in a subsequent section how the possibility of displacement may generate an objection to the alternative theory of reference proposed by Kripke and Donnellan. At this stage, I shall simply endorse Ricoeur's suggestion that the referential relation can be dissociated from the agent's intentions, without accepting his view that such dissociation is a peculiar feature of writing. For in spoken as well as written discourse, the awareness or intention of the speaker or writer is merely a provisional indication, rather than a decisive criterion, of the particular to which he or she is referring.

In the writings of Wittgenstein, the problem of reference is discussed against the backcloth of a thesis concerning the constitution of object domains. This thesis contends that the world is articulated within particular language-games, so that the rules which govern the use of an expression constitute a specific organisation of phenomena. The emphasis on constitution is more evident in Winch's work, wherein the thesis is formulated in the following terms: 'reality is not what gives language sense. What is real and what is unreal shows itself *in* the sense that language has.'[5] Winch attempts to defend this formulation by imagining a tribe in which the language-games of measurement are not played. 'We might say of such a people', Winch reflects, '"For them height has no reality"; and *this* would be a comment on the kinds of language game they play.'[6] Similarly, the Westerner who does not participate in the language-game of Zande magic might say that 'witches have no reality'. In both cases, to say that '*x* is not real' or 'there is no *x*' is not to report the outcome of an empirical investigation, but rather to confess that one can see no sense in the entire complex of activities. I believe, however, that Winch's defence of the constitutive thesis is unsound, and that his formulation results in an obliteration of the problem of reference. For as Jarvie rightly points out, the analogy between height and witches is misleading.[7] A witch is a purported entity whose existence may be asserted or denied, whereas height is a measurable property which an object may or may not possess. Moreover, when one says 'there are no witches', one does not ordinarily mean 'there is no sense in that complex of occult activities', but rather 'there is no entity that "witch" refers to'. Such discrepancies indicate that Winch has overstepped the legitimate boundaries of the constitutive thesis, thus reducing the problem of reference to the question of whether the language-game as a whole has sense. This reduction is consistent with the conceptual idealism of his approach, which identifies the reality of social phenomena with the ideas embodied therein. Yet however consistent Winch's account may be, it seems clear that it fails to establish a satisfactory relation between the thesis of constitution and the theory of reference.

Truth and validity

The concept of truth is analysed by a number of ordinary language philosophers. The later Wittgenstein expresses occasional but acute misgivings about the analysis of 'true' in terms of 'tallying with the facts', as 'the very thing that is in question is what "tallying" is here'.[8] Similar misgivings are apparent in Strawson's critique of Austin's attempt to resurrect a correspondence theory of truth on the basis of the theory of speech-acts. The critique of the correspondence theory marks one of the important points at which ordinary language philosophy converges with the hermeneutics of Heidegger and Ricoeur, as well as with the critical theory of Habermas. This point of convergence defines, moreover, a philosophical standpoint which deserves to be defended against the current revival of Tarski's work. However, in this section I restrict my remarks to a consideration of the contributions which ordinary language philosophers have made to the problem of truth and related issues. I argue that the constructive comments offered by Strawson in the wake of his critique do not amount to a theory of truth. I also suggest that the critical reflections of Wittgenstein and others on the question of validity in psychoanalysis are premissed upon an unexamined notion of scientificity.

Strawson contends that the central mistake of Austin's thesis is that it confuses the issue of how the word 'true' is used with the question of the conditions which must obtain when a statement is true. Strawson allows that Austin's account of these conditions may be correct; but he denies that in using the word 'true', one is asserting that such conditions obtain. For when one studies the actual functioning of expressions like 'that's true', one sees that this word is employed simply as an abbreviatory device to express agreement or accord. Strawson is surely right to emphasise the connection between the concepts of truth and agreement, an emphasis which is reflected in the recent writings of Habermas. I shall try to show, however, that the specific way in which Strawson draws and defends this connection is less than satisfactory. In the first place, it is questionable whether Strawson's inquiry into the uses of 'true' provides an adequate analysis of the meaning of this word. For as Searle and others observe,[9] to know that expressions like 'good' or 'kind' are used to commend or compliment someone is not necessarily to know what such expressions mean. Second, while there may be a close connection between the concepts of truth and agreement, it seems obvious that this connection cannot be an unqualified one. A doctrine or belief may command a widespread consensus within a society, and yet its proclamations may be false nonetheless. Third, the concept of truth has what may be called an 'evidential dimension' which remains unexplicated by Strawson's analysis of the expression 'that's true'. There is, in most cases, something in the world that makes a difference to whether a statement is true or false; and while this 'something' may not be a 'fact' to which the statement does or does not 'correspond', it may at least be a source of evidence which could count for or against the statement in question. As a fourth and final point, one must query Strawson's claim that 'is true' is not used to make a statement about a statement. For it is this claim which predetermines the narrowness of his approach, justifying his rejection of the question of the conditions under which a statement is true. Indeed, it may not be entirely clear what an adequate theory of truth would comprise; 'but it is sufficiently clear', as Warnock aptly remarks, 'that Strawson has not constructed one'.[10]

Ordinary language philosophers offer some pertinent reflections on the question of validity in psychoanalysis. Wittgenstein notes with apparent approval that Freud provides a completely new account of 'correct explanation': 'not one agreeing with experience, but one accepted'.[11] Yet rather than pursuing the positive implications of this account, Wittgenstein tends to stress the extent to which it falls short of a scientific ideal. 'Freud is constantly claiming to be scientific', he chides, 'but what he gives is *speculation*.'[12] The contention that psychoanalysis does not satisfy the criteria of scientificity may be construed in two alternative ways. On the one hand, one may accept the contention as a demonstration that psychoanalysis is a skill akin to that practised by the artist or the novelist, and susceptible to the same sort of aesthetic evaluation.[13] On the other hand, one may employ the discrepancy to castigate psychoanalysis as 'the most sophisticated form of metaphysics ever to enjoy support as a scientific theory'.[14] The assumption that underlies both of these alternatives is that psychoanalysis is not a science, whatever else it may be; and it is precisely this assumption which must be placed in doubt. For the conception of science that supports such an assumption has been radically questioned by recent work in the philosophy of science, which reveals that the model of science as an hypothetical-deductive system of testable laws must be thoroughly reassessed.[15] Moreover, as Habermas and Ricoeur rightly insist, it is misleading to assess psychoanalysis against the epistemological exemplar of the natural sciences. Such an assessment overlooks the differences in objects and aims which characterise these disciplines, and underplays the role of self-reflection in the analytic situation. The latter role, which is hesitatingly acknowledged in the remarks of Wittgenstein, is utterly eliminated in the positivistic critique levelled by Nagel and others. However difficult it may be to resolve the problem of validity in psychoanalysis and the social sciences, one would be well advised to guard against the implicit importation of a scientific ideal which is itself misconceived.

Rationality

The nature and scope of rationality is a theme which receives some attention in the writings of ordinary language philosophers. The later Wittgenstein holds that the provision of reasons is possible only within particular systems of belief, so that rational argumentation is circumscribed by persuasion. A similar view is espoused by Winch, who underlines the cultural relativity of rational standards. Yet there are passages in Winch's work which suggest that the concept of rationality may have features that are common to all cultures. In the present section, I conduct a critical analysis of this suggestion, with the aim of showing that Winch's view is inadequate in several respects. I also argue that some of the limitations of Winch's approach are shared by the account of moral reasoning outlined by Hare, as well as that propounded by his neo-Wittgensteinian critics. In the end it will be proposed that these limitations can be overcome only by elaborating a concept of rationality which is not restricted to the internal consistency of a system of beliefs, but which incorporates instead a consideration of the conditions under which the defence of such beliefs may be achieved.

Winch encounters the problem of rationality in his discussion of the issues involved in understanding a primitive society. In opposition to the alleged ethnocentrism of Evans-Pritchard, Winch maintains that the criteria of rationality and intelligibility may vary from one society to the next. It is therefore quite misleading, in Winch's view, for anthropologists to impose their own criteria upon the society which they seek to understand, as if these criteria were the standards of rationality as such. Winch allows nonetheless that there are considerations which enable anthropologists to grasp the criteria of rationality that prevail in a society other than their own. The most general consideration is concerned with the demand for consistency, which ensures that a society with a language is also a society with some concept of rationality. 'Rationality is not *just* a concept *in* a language like any other', writes Winch; 'it is a concept necessary to the existence of any language: to say of a society that it has a language is also to say that it has a concept of rationality.'[16] Yet while the general concept of rationality is common to all cultures, the specific criteria of rationality are not; and the clarification of the latter requires a contextual investigation which is guided by the limiting notions of birth, sexuality and death. I have already argued that these limiting notions do not provide a satisfactory framework for the type of investigation that Winch recommends. Here I shall attempt to show that the trans-cultural concept of rationality proposed by Winch must also be regarded as inadequate. For although Winch may be right to maintain that the concept of rationality is linked to the conditions of possible communication, it seems mistaken to suppose that the only condition which is relevant is the consistency of what is said. The status of non-contradiction is itself a contentious issue, and there may well be other conditions which are necessary presuppositions of communication. Winch appears to acknowledge the latter possibility in an essay entitled 'Nature and convention', where he maintains that there could not be a linguistic community in which speaking truthfully were not the norm. 'The notion of a society in which there is a language but in which truth-telling is not regarded as the norm is', Winch insists, 'a self-contradictory one.'[17] Whether there are other such conditions which may be necessary presuppositions of communication, and whether rationality can be conceived as a crystallisation of these conditions, are questions which will be confronted in due course.

The accounts of moral reasoning offered by ordinary language philosophers generally share a restricted conception of rationality. Within the framework elaborated by Hare, moral reasoning conforms to a syllogistic pattern in which a singular imperative is deduced from the conjunction of a universal imperative and a factual statement. The universal imperative is a principle which one must decide to accept; and if one chooses to accept some other principle, then no rational argument can be adduced to demonstrate that one is wrong. For reason in moral argument is, in Hare's view, relegated to the role of examining the consistency between the principles which one has decided to accept and the singular imperatives that one is prepared to endorse. The decisionism of Hare's account has been justly criticised from a Wittgensteinian standpoint, on the grounds that a moral reason cannot be specified in terms of its consistency with a personally chosen ideal. 'Certain things count as reasons for me not', Beardsmore contends, 'because they are the sort of things to which I consistently appeal, but because they are the sort of things which I and others have been brought up to appeal to and accept within some social context.'[18] This objection rightly emphasises the social conditions of moral debate, which place conventional limits on what can count as a reason for a particular judgement. However, by insisting upon the fundamental diversity of social standards and the ineradicable possibility of moral disagreement, the Wittgensteinian critics do not wholly overcome the limitations of Hare's account. For the authority of personal ideals is merely supplanted by the sovereignty of social standards, and a rational justification of the latter is precluded from the start. The possibility of formulating a wider framework for rational argumentation, in moral as well as other spheres, is an issue which will be considered in the sections that follow.

II. Hermeneutic phenomenology

Objectivity and the unconscious

Problems of epistemology form a central theme within the tradition of hermeneutic phenomenology. Ricoeur's contributions to this theme vary in the course of his career, in accordance with the transition from his earlier to his later work. In his early writings, the status of social scientific constructs is prejudged by the emphasis on a philosophy of the subject which preserves a niche for human freedom. With the gradual modification of Ricoeur's conception of the subject and with his growing awareness of the importance of interpretation, specific questions of epistemology become increasingly interlocked with the general problem of hermeneutics. In the present section, I attempt to trace this transformation through an analysis of Ricoeur's views on the status of the unconscious. I hope to show that his early remarks on this issue are problematic, but that his later writings offer a provocative account which is in need of further development.

In *Freedom and Nature*, Ricoeur encounters psychoanalysis within the context of the third cycle of the will. The phenomenon of willing is completed by an act of consent, whereby the subject acquiesces to the involuntary dimensions of character, the unconscious and life. The establishment of a relation between the necessity of the unconscious and the freedom of the subject requires, in Ricoeur's view, an account which avoids two extremes. On the one hand, the account must avoid the type of realism which attributes thought to the unconscious; on the other hand, it must eschew the form of idealism which assigns to consciousness a transparence that it does not possess. 'We must first of all reject this apparent dilemma', maintains Ricoeur, 'in order to pose correctly the new paradox of an *indefinite matter* of signification and an *infinite capacity* of thought.'[19] The formulation of this paradox enables Ricoeur to recognise the primordial affectivity which sustains an act of consciousness, without infringing the phenomenological thesis that restricts meaning to the conscious realm. The affective matter may be called 'unconscious' when it is dissociated from the intentional form which gives it meaning; and thus dissociated, it constitutes a quasi-causal domain which is accessible to the naturalistic methods of psychoanalysis. Yet the dissociation is purely abstract, and it cannot justify the view that the unconscious is an animate being which lurks beneath the surface of conscious life. As Ricoeur insists, 'the consequence of the past is never more than a potentiality of thought and meaning in the actual form of *my* thought'.[20] I wish to suggest, however, that this novel analysis is problematic in several respects. In the first place, the distinction between affective matter and intentional form seems suspect, since the memorial matter of the unconscious is already pre-formed both by particular circumstances of the past and by psychological mechanisms which lie beyond conscious control. Second, the phenomenological restriction of meaning to the conscious realm cannot be readily reconciled with the psychoanalytic approach, which assumes that certain experiences may be repressed because of the significance which they possess. Third, the conception of the unconscious as an abstraction which constitutes a quasi-causal domain does not reflect the peculiar nature of psychoanalysis, which is characterised by a discourse that is essentially mixed. The latter point is subsequently and forcefully stated by Ricoeur, whose further reflections on the unconscious proceed less from the demands of a phenomenology of freedom than from a hermeneutical meditation on Freud.

In *Freud and Philosophy*, the status of the unconscious is a problem which is approached from an altered philosophical perspective. In contrast to the earlier emphasis on the centrality of the subject, Ricoeur introduces a concept of archaeology which attests to the progressive displacement of the conscious sphere. The subject is no longer regarded as the sole source of signification, for 'by this displacement, immediate consciousness finds itself dispossessed to the advantage of another agency of meaning – the transcendence of speech or the emergence of desire'.[21] The displacement of the subject is closely linked to a second shift in Ricoeur's views, a shift which concedes that the emergence of desire can be grasped only through the interpretation of the signs wherein that desire is expressed. It follows that the status of the unconscious cannot be considered independently of the specific procedures of psychoanalytic interpretation. Thus, Ricoeur argues that the unconscious is relative to a hermeneutic constellation which comprises, first, the rules for deciphering the signs and symptoms displayed in the analytic situation; second, the consciousness of the analyst to whom such symbols are expressed; and third, the language of transference, within which the analytic dialogue unfolds. By relativising the unconscious to this hermeneutic constellation, Ricoeur attempts to provide a Kantian critique of psychoanalytic concepts, that is, a critique which 'justifies them by their power of regulating a new domain of objectivity and intelligibility'.[22] Whatever difficulties there may be in the details of this attempt, it seems to pose the problem of the unconscious in a particularly penetrating light. Moreover, this approach may provide an illuminating perspective for exploring the status of social structure, as well as the relation between the agent and those dimensions of the social world upon which agency depends. It is unfortunate that Ricoeur does not pursue this line of inquiry in any depth, allowing his contributions to the social sciences to remain regrettably incomplete. In the final part of the chapter, I shall suggest a few ways in which this theoretical lacuna might be filled.

Reference

The notion of reference occupies a key position in the theory of language elaborated by Ricoeur. The referential relation is one of the crucial characteristics which differentiate the semantics of discourse from a semiotics of the sign. 'What is *intended* by discourse [*l'intenté*]', observes Ricoeur, 'is irreducible to what semiotics calls the signified [*le signifié*], which is nothing but the counterpart of the signifier of a sign within the language code.'[23] Ricoeur further maintains that the inscription of discourse in writing does not dissolve the referential relation, but rather reinstates it in a manner which distinguishes hermeneutics from the structuralist analysis of the text. However, although Ricoeur is right to emphasise the importance of the referential relation, his analysis remains deficient in certain respects. For he does not satisfactorily explain how one succeeds or fails to refer, under what conditions a successful reference occurs, and what counts as the referent on any particular occasion. When Ricoeur's writings are interrogated along such lines, it becomes clear that his intriguing idea of split reference must be submitted to further thought.

Ricoeur contends that the semantics of discourse must acknowledge a distinction between the sense of an expression and its reference. Pursuing this Fregean distinction in a Strawsonian direction, Ricoeur proposes that an expression has reference only in its use. So whether an expression succeeds or fails to refer depends upon the particular circumstances in which the act of discourse is performed, and not upon some aspect of the propositional content alone. Yet Ricoeur does not clarify the nature of this contextual dependence, nor does he specify the sort of circumstances that are to be regarded as relevant in assessing the success or failure of a referential claim. If someone utters a referring expression on a particular occasion, then it is by no means clear how, on Ricoeur's account, one is to determine which object or state of affairs the speaker has referred to, or whether the speaker has succeeded in referring to anything at all. There are passages wherein Ricoeur appears to endorse the cluster theory of reference; for he cites Strawson and Searle with approval, and he notes that one may unfold new referents 'only by describing them as precisely as possible'.[24] However, it has already been suggested that the cluster theory is unsound, since the applicability of identifying descriptions is neither a necessary nor a sufficient condition of successful reference. Thus, on the semantic level, Ricoeur's analysis of the referential relation would seem to be less than adequate.

The core of Ricoeur's contribution to the problem of reference is to be found at the level of the text. The forms of distanciation which characterise the process of inscription entail the suspension of all connections to the dialogical situation. Yet Ricoeur maintains that this suspension does not eliminate the referential relation as such; rather, it constitutes the condition for the realisation of a second order reference 'whose explication is the task of interpretation'.[25] In a manner analogous to the power of redescription exercised by models and metaphors, the literary work as a whole is capable of projecting a new way of being, of disclosing a possible world. Ricoeur may well be right to suppose that the referential relation can obtain in more ways than one, and that the disclosure of ulterior referents can be linked to the process of interpretation. However, it must be said that the account proffered by Ricoeur leaves some important issues open. It is not obvious, for instance, that a text as such may be said to refer, as distinct from the particular expressions within it; and this obscurity is especially acute in the case of human action, which Ricoeur conceptualises on the model of the text. Moreover, Ricoeur's account fails once again to specify the conditions of successful reference. How a text may 'disclose a possible world' is quite unclear, and how one may determine just which world it does disclose remains uncertain. It seems unlikely that these difficulties could be overcome by appealing to the works of those authors whom Ricoeur cites in support of his views. Hesse does indeed raise the problem of metaphorical reference, but she does not resolve it in a manner exploitable by Ricoeur. She maintains that the referent of a model or metaphor is, in the last analysis, the 'primary system', or the literally describable domain of the explanandum.[26] Yet the whole thrust of Ricoeur's account transcends such restrictions to a pre-conceived object domain, demanding an alternative formulation of being which is freed from the hegemony of scientific thought. This demand similarly precludes any assistance from the writings of Black, whose view of metaphor as an interaction of associated commonplaces retains the principal subject as the referent of the metaphorical expression.[27] It is the philosophy of Heidegger which offers the most suitable support for Ricoeur's movement towards an alternative formulation of being. The closing pages of *The Rule of Metaphor* are undoubtedly Heideggerian in tone, and indeed Ricoeur regards the latter's work as 'an inescapable attempt and temptation'.[28] Nonetheless, it is difficult to see how a re-course to Heidegger could resolve the epistemological problems posed above. For a radical return to the disclosure of being leaves little room for a debate about which being is thereby disclosed. I shall consider Heidegger's views at greater length in the following section; here I shall simply suggest that however tempting these views may appear, it seems unlikely that they could generate a theory of reference which would mitigate the deficiencies in Ricoeur's account.

Validity and truth

The concepts of validity and truth are essential elements in the theory of interpretation elaborated by Ricoeur. The possibility of validating inter-pretations prevents hermeneutics from collapsing into scepticism, and the recognition of a claim to truth distinguishes this discipline from structuralism. Ricoeur attempts to unite these two elements in the double movement of the dialectic of interpretation, whereby an initial under-standing is submitted to a process of validation and a structural explana-tion is complemented by a quest for truth. Ricoeur is surely right to raise the problems of validity and truth within the context of interpretative theory; and in view of the epistemological difficulties which have always plagued hermeneutics,[29] this in itself is an exemplary contribution. Nevertheless, it seems to me that the solutions which Ricoeur proposes are less than satisfactory. For the criteria of validation which support an interpretation are far from clear, and the notion of truth which terminates the hermeneutic process is quite opaque. In the end I shall cast further doubt upon Ricoeur's dialectic of interpretation, which forges a hasty and unhappy union of Hirschian validity and Heideggerian truth.

The problem of validity is encountered in the first movement of the dialectic of interpretation. Ricoeur allows that the meaning of a text may be construed in a variety of ways, but he maintains that this possibility does not lead to arbitrariness. For although there are no rules for the production of readings, there are methods for their subsequent validation. 'There are', Ricoeur submits, 'criteria of relative superiority which may easily be derived from the logic of subjective probability.'[30] However, Ricoeur does not undertake a systematic derivation of such criteria, nor do the writings referred to by Ricoeur provide much assistance in this respect. The allusion to Popper which precedes the above quotation merely confuses the issue in question. For so far from supporting a 'logic of subjective probability', Popper attacks all 'subjective' accounts of logic and favours the concept of falsifiability over that of probability.[31] The reference to Hirsch is more promising, since this author similarly maintains that one of the tasks of interpretation is to show that a given reading is more probable than another.[32] Hirsch proposes several criteria which govern the probability of a reading, but he recognises that these criteria alone are incapable of adjudicating between competing and equally coherent accounts. To forestall such a stalemate, Hirsch insists that what the author meant must be taken as the normative horizon for the meaning of the text. Ricoeur does not explicitly endorse the criteria proposed by Hirsch, and he unequivocally rejects the return to authorial meaning as the decisive instance; but Ricoeur provides mere clues as to where alternative criteria may be found. One such clue is contained in a recent paper on the question of proof in psychoanalysis.[33] Ricoeur argues that a good psychoanalytic interpretation must be coherent with the basic tenets of Freudian theory, must satisfy the rules for decoding the text of the unconscious, must be therapeutically effective, and must form an intelligible narrative. These four criteria are capable of complementing and reinforcing one another, thereby rendering a particular interpretation 'plausible and, in the best cases, probable and even convincing'.[34] Yet Ricoeur does not explain why the basic tenets of Freudian theory are themselves to be accepted, nor does he specify what kind of evidence would be suitable for their support. Moreover, Ricoeur does not clarify the relation which obtains between a validated interpretation and the reality to which it may refer, a relation which is attenuated by Ricoeur's emphasis on the phenomenon of phantasy. Finally, the self-reflection of the patient plays an uncertain role in Ricoeur's account, since he tends to conjoin the concept of reflection to a distinct problematic of truth. One may justly infer, therefore, that Ricoeur's remarks on the question of validity are in need of amplification.

The problem of truth is posed in the context of the second movement in the dialectic of interpretation. Ricoeur maintains that to pass from the sense of a statement to its reference is to inquire into its claim to truth; and the hermeneutic equivalent of this semantic transition consists in passing from the structure of the text to the world which it unfolds. Just as the text establishes a referential relation which transcends the dialogical situation, so too it raises a claim to truth whose redemption may reveal a primordial realm of being. Ricoeur is thus drawn towards the ontological conception of truth espoused by Heidegger and his followers, while criticising their tendency to dissociate truth from the interpretative procedures whereby it is disclosed. I wish to suggest, however, that this tentative rapprochement is standing on unsteady ground. In the first place, it is by no means apparent that truth can be predicated of a text or an analogue of a text, as opposed to a sentence or a statement. Heidegger defends such a view by arguing that the truth of a statement presupposes the openness of being;[35] but why the essence of truth should be identified with what the truth of a statement presupposes is not entirely clear. Moreover, to conceive truth as the disclosure of being, as the 'revelatory "letting-be" of what-is',[36] is to obscure the extent to which what-is must be made manifest through discourse. There are passages in which Ricoeur acknowledges the latter point, recoiling from Heidegger's route with the query, 'Is it not once again *within language* itself that we must seek the indication that understanding is a mode of being?'[37] Yet Ricoeur regards the truth of a text as the world which it unfolds, and thus tends to elude the type of epistemological confrontation which he explicitly strives to induce. How one is to arbitrate between conflicting truth claims is unclear on Ricoeur's account, just as Heidegger does not deign to say how he would defend his interpretation of being. Finally, it may be noted that the dialectic of interpretation posits a problematic relation between validity and truth. For depth-interpretative procedures cannot be severed from the question of validity; and there are potential objects of interpretation, such as human actions, for which it seems implausible to suppose that they may have a truth-value which is distinct from the validity of their interpretation. In lieu of a more sustained discussion of these and other difficulties, it must be concluded that Ricoeur's encounter with the problem of truth leaves a number of weighty issues open.

III. Critical social theory

Reference and object domains
The epistemological problems of the social sciences are a topic of central concern to authors within the tradition of critical social theory. Such concern is evident in the writings of Habermas, whose contributions to these problems are of profound importance. In *Knowledge and Human Interests*, Habermas argues that the object domains and validity claims of the various sciences are predetermined by a structure of interests which is anchored in the natural history of the human species. Subsequent publications differentiate the realm of action from that of discourse, so that object domains of action-related experience remain predetermined by interests while validity claims are discursively redeemed. Within this reformulated framework, the theory of constitution is concerned to establish that there are two basic dimensions for the objectification of possible experience. There is the dimension of sensory experience, in which things are perceived and events reported in a physicalistic language; and there is the dimension of communicative experience, in which persons are encountered and utterances expressed in an intentional language. Both physicalistic and intentional languages contain denotative expressions which identify a range of possible objects, and which thereby specify a class of permissible referents. In this section, I hope to show that Habermas's fragmentary comments on the problem of reference leave something to be desired. I also suggest that his argument for the differentiation of object domains is unsound, and that it does little to secure the autonomy of the 'critical social sciences'.

The languages in which sensory and communicative experiences are expressed contain terms which enable a speaker to identify particular objects. Such terms include proper names, but these in turn must embrace or entail predicative expressions. For in Habermas's view, 'a properly functioning system of reference has to have a certain propositional content',[38] since reference presupposes some characterisation of the object concerned. Why reference presupposes such a characterisation, and in what sense the latter is presupposed, are questions which are not directly confronted by Habermas. However, a sympathetic footnote to Searle suggests that Habermas, like Ricoeur, endorses the cluster theory of reference. I have already indicated that this theory is open to a number of serious objections. Here I shall simply add that such objections are not mitigated by Habermas's interpretation of the minimal propositional content in terms of quasi-Kantian categories for the objectification of experience. For the content required by the cluster theory is concerned with a series of describable characteristics which a speaker must know about an object if he or she is to succeed in referring to it; and the question of whether a speaker must know these characteristics in order to succeed in referring is not answered by appealing to the categories which the recognition of such characteristics might presuppose. Clarifying the conditions of possible description might illuminate the conditions of successful reference if it could be shown that reference was dependent upon description, but it is precisely this dependency which is in doubt. So whatever the merits of Habermas's discussion, it seems to shed little additional light on the problem of reference.

Habermas maintains that the application of a common categorial framework to the spheres of sensory and communicative experience results in a differentiated object domain. The denotative terms of the physicalistic language identify things and events, whereas similar terms in the intentional language identify persons and utterances, thereby distinguishing two classes of permissible referents. This argument appears to establish the differential constitution of object domains by assuming the distinction between two spheres of experience, which are already defined in terms of their respective constituents. Yet the appearance of circularity is dispelled by the introduction of a further dichotomy, namely that between instrumental and communicative action. 'We create the two fundamental object domains by rendering schematic the same set of categories (or cognitive schemata) in the realms of instrumental or communicative action',[39] and there is a 'transcendental link' between these two realms of action and the respective spheres of sensory and communicative experience. Habermas thus shifts the weight of his constitutive argument onto the distinction between two types of action; that this is a distinction which cannot bear any such burden is a claim which I have defended above. Here it will suffice to note that the two object domains provide the reservoirs of action-related experience which are thematised by the empirical-analytic sciences and the historical-hermeneutic disciplines. The genesis of the object domain of the sciences with which Habermas is particularly concerned, viz. the critical social sciences, is not incorporated into the theory of constitution. This attests, no doubt, to the derivative status of the interest in emancipation, a status which Habermas does not disguise. However, it also means that the nature of the 'object domain' engendered by systematically distorted communication is left unclear. This conclusion concurs with the previous critique of the concept of systematically distorted communication, in which I argued that this concept does not provide a suitable specification of the scope of depth hermeneutics. Such criticisms may not undermine Habermas's recent efforts, but they do, it seems to me, point to serious complications in the theory of constitution which he outlines.

Truth

Since the publication of *Knowledge and Human Interests*, Habermas has devoted considerable attention to the formulation of a theory of truth. In contrast to his earlier position, Habermas no longer specifies the meaning of truth in terms of the structure of interests, but rather in terms of the conditions which guarantee the discursive redemption of validity claims. For truth, according to Habermas, is itself a validity claim, and the justification of this claim is secured by the consensus of participants in a situation of idealised speech. In the course of formulating this account, Habermas compellingly criticises many traditional theories of truth, and rightly emphasises the link between truth and justification. Nevertheless, when the argument which underlies his 'consensus theory of truth' is analysed in detail, it becomes clear that this theory rests upon a number of dubious contentions. Moreover, the argument as a whole establishes a gulf between realms of discourse and contexts of action-related experience which is detrimental to the development of an adequate epistemology.

The consensus theory of truth rests upon an argument which may be summarised in the following four steps:

(1) It is statements, and not sentences or utterances, which are true or false.

(2) Truth is a validity claim which is connected with constative speech-acts: to say that a statement is true is to say that the assertion of the statement is justified.

(3) The assertion of a statement is justified if and only if that statement would command a rational consensus among all who could enter into a discussion with the speaker.

(4) A rational consensus is a consensus that is argumentatively attained under the conditions of an ideal speech situation.

The crucial point of the argument is expressed by step (2); and this point is at the same time the most problematic. For it is by no means obvious that to say that a statement is true is to say that the assertion of the statement is justified. Habermas appears to treat this thesis as analytic, since he defends it with the observation that 'truth means "warranted assert-ability"'.[40] If this were indeed what 'truth' meant, then it would be meaningless to say that the assertion of a statement is justified when the statement itself is false. Yet it is possible to imagine cases in which this would not be meaningless. For example, if a person is jumping up and down and holding his or her foot with care, then one may be justified in asserting that the person is in pain, even though that may be false. The discrepancy between justified assertion and truth is especially clear in the case of statements which are made about events that may or may not transpire in the future. One may have very good grounds for maintaining that it will rain tomorrow, but the truth of this statement is dependent upon what happens tomorrow, and not upon the grounds that one has today. The difficulties in step (2) call into question the third stage of the argument. Habermas holds that the justification for the assertion of a statement consists in the capacity of the latter to command a rational consensus among the potential participants of a discourse. However, if truth cannot be equated with the justified assertion of a statement, then whatever this third thesis does establish, it does not amount to a theory of truth. Whether the concept of rational consensus can be clarified within the framework of an ideal speech situation, and whether the latter in turn can be endowed with a status that is not merely contingent, are issues which will be discussed in the following section. Yet if the preceding remarks are correct, then the implications of that discussion for the elaboration of a theory of truth will be otherwise than Habermas may have thought.[41]

Habermas's analysis of the concept of truth does not adequately eluci-date what I have called its 'evidential dimension'. By distinguishing the conditions for the discursive redemption of validity claims from the conditions for the objectivity of experience, and by regarding truth as a particular type of validity claim, Habermas both attenuates and obscures the relation between truth and the contexts of action-related experience. Habermas concurs with Strawson that a fact is what a true statement asserts; but he adds that even a state of affairs is nothing other than the 'propositional content' of a statement that has survived discursive argu-mentation. 'When we *say* that facts are states of affairs which exist, we *mean* not the *existence* of objects, but the truth of propositional contents.'[42] Indeed, a fact is not an object, and Habermas is right to chide Austin and others for conceiving of facts on the model of things. However, it seems equally implausible to maintain, as Habermas does, that an existing state of affairs is merely the content of a proposition which is true. There are moments when Habermas relaxes this uncomfortable legislation, conceding that 'in the case of elementary empirical propositions such as "this ball is red" a close affinity exists between the objectivity of experience and the truth of a proposition as expressed in a corresponding statement'.[43] Yet Habermas does not explain why this special condition should hold for 'elementary empirical propositions' alone, nor does he clarify wherein this 'close affinity' between experience and 'corresponding statements' consists. Similar obscurities arise in the characterisation of the role of experimental data in the redemption of scientific claims to truth. Although Habermas contends that in stating a fact one is not asserting that some experience exists, he nevertheless allows that one can 'draw upon structurally analogous experiences as data in an attempt to legitimate the truth claim embodied in [a] statement'.[44] Habermas does not specify what kind of 'structurally analogous experiences' would be relevant here, nor how they could be 'drawn upon' to legitimate a truth claim; but he does suggest that questions such as these could be answered by a 'non-objectivistic philosophy of science'. The development of such a philosophy is a task which he has yet to pursue, but it may be noted that the direction which Habermas indicates is not wholly compatible with his initial approach. For if the participants of a discourse may adduce certain kinds of experience, 'structurally analogous' though it may be; and if the discursive realm includes certain kinds of action, even though it may be 'experimental' in nature; then it is quite unclear what remains of the distinction between contexts of action-related experience and realms of discourse, a distinction which is fundamental to the whole of Habermas's recent work. Without a more explicit and consistent explanation of the relations between the conditions of truth and the objectivity of experience, Habermas's analysis of these issues must be regarded as crucially incomplete.

Ideal speech situation

The concept of the ideal speech situation plays a central role in Habermas's reformulation of the foundations of critical theory. For the ideal speech situation defines the conditions under which a factually attained consensus would hold as rational, thereby specifying the sense in which Habermas conjoins agreement and truth. The ideal speech situation also forms a framework for the rational redemption of normative claims, and hence purports to provide a basis for the critique of ideology. Some of the difficulties which surround these functions have been discussed in previous sections. Here I shall attempt to elucidate and assess the thesis which underpins the employment of this concept, namely the thesis that the ideal speech situation is a necessary presupposition of communication. In propounding this thesis, Habermas develops a highly original and attractive position. Moreover, in spite of what some unsympathetic and uncomprehending critics suggest,[45] Habermas does offer a coherent argument for the thesis. I shall contend nonetheless that Habermas's argument is unsound in certain respects, so that the use which he wishes to make of the ideal speech situation must be placed in doubt.

Habermas maintains that the ideal speech situation is a necessary presupposition of linguistic communication. The argument in support of this thesis may be reconstructed in seven steps:

(1) The process of communication implies that it is possible for at least two subjects to come to an agreement about a state of affairs.

(2) To come to an agreement implies that it is possible to distinguish between a genuine and a deceptive agreement.

(3) A genuine agreement is an agreement induced by the force of better argument alone.

(4) The force of better argument prevails if and only if communication is not hindered through external and internal constraints.

(5) Communication is not hindered through internal constraints if and only if for all potential participants there is a symmetrical distribution of chances to select and employ speech-acts.

(6) A situation in which there is a symmetrical distribution of chances to select and employ communicative, constative, representative and regulative speech-acts is an ideal speech situation.

(7) Therefore, the process of communication implies the possibility of an ideal speech situation.

The first step of this argument makes a bold and sweeping claim; but the terms of this claim are unclear, and the grounds for its defence seem inadequate. Habermas explains that the requisite agreement rests upon the recognition of the four basic validity claims, thus terminating 'in the intersubjective mutuality of reciprocal understanding, shared knowledge, mutual trust, and accord with one another'.[46] Yet why all communication must presuppose the possibility of agreement along these particular lines is far from clear. Habermas sustains this thesis by assuming that the four validity claims are implicitly and necessarily raised with the utterance of *every* speech-act; but this, it seems to me, is a highly questionable assumption. In what sense does reading a poem, telling a joke or greeting a friend presuppose the truth of what is said? Is not sincerity characteristically suspended rather than presupposed by the participants in a process of collective bargaining, or by friends engaged in the light-hearted activity of 'taking the mickey'? In what sense, precisely, does the utterance of a sentence like 'The sky is blue this morning' raise a claim to correctness which is clearly distinguishable from its intelligibility or its truth? No doubt Habermas would deny that the above instances constitute counter-examples to his thesis, insisting instead that they must be treated as subsidiary forms of communication, as mere 'derivatives of action oriented to reaching an understanding/agreement (*verständigungs-orientierten Handelns*)'.[47] Yet such a reply would simply assume what must be shown, namely that orientation to reaching an understanding/ agreement is the basic aim of communication; and this demonstration is provided neither by restricting the analysis to speech-acts in the 'standard form',[48] nor by exploiting the ambiguity in the word '*Verständigung*'. Thus, in the absence of a more adequate defence of this thesis, it must be said that Habermas's argument begins on a step that is by no means secure.

The remaining stages of the argument contain difficulties which are equally grave. For although the concept of agreement may presuppose the possibility of distinguishing between genuine and illusory cases, it does not seem to follow that a genuine agreement is one induced by the force of better argument alone. If one were suspicious about whether an agreement was genuine or not, it would indeed be relevant to point out that the final decision bore little resemblance to the quality of the arguments adduced. Yet it would also be relevant to observe that the participants were using certain concepts in vague and ambiguous ways; or that they did not grasp the full implications of the conclusions they appeared to endorse; or that while they expressed their agreement in word, they did not concur with their expressions in deed. Moreover, it is difficult to see why subjects could not be said genuinely to agree about something unless their agreement were induced by the force of better argument, as opposed, for example, to the feeling of compassion or the commitment to a common goal. Let us suppose, nonetheless, that Habermas has identified one of several modes whereby genuine and deceptive agreements may be distinguished. The question then arises as to whether this mode is adequately explicated by the fourth and fifth steps in the argument. Habermas maintains that the force of better argument prevails if and only if communication is not hindered by external and internal constraints, and that internal constraints are excluded if and only if for all potential participants there is a symmetrical distribution of chances to select and employ speech-acts. What it means to speak of 'a symmetrical distribution of chances to select and employ speech-acts' is not altogether clear; and how one is to characterise the exclusion of external constraints, which seem to have been swept under the fifth step of the argument, remains uncertain. More importantly, it seems doubtful whether the elimination of internal constraints could be guaranteed by a symmetrical distribution of chances to select and employ speech-acts, however the latter stipulation may be construed. For one can imagine a debate in which all potential participants have an equal opportunity to deploy communicative, constative, representative and regulative speech-acts; and yet in spite of this formal equality, the final decision is merely an expression of the prevailing status quo, reflecting something other than the force of better argument. What Habermas's assumption of symmetry seems to neglect, and what his occasional allusions to the model of 'pure communicative action' do nothing to mitigate,[49] is that the constraints which affect social life may operate in modes other than the restriction of access to speech-acts, for example by restricting access to weapons, wealth or esteem. The neglect of these considerations is closely connected to the distinction between labour and interaction, as well as to the use of psychoanalysis as a model for critical theory.[50] I have developed my objections to the latter issues in previous chapters; here it will suffice to say that if the criticisms made in this section are sound, then Habermas has failed to provide a satisfactory defence of the view that the ideal speech situation is a necessary presupposition of communication and a sufficient condition for the attainment of a rational consensus. Whether an alternative formulation can overcome the difficulties of Habermas's account, and what status such a formulation may have in a coherent epistemology, are questions which remain to be answered.

IV. Towards a theory of reference and truth

Reference and objectivity

The foregoing critique prepares the way for a constructive contribution to the theory of reference and truth. This contribution will build upon the positive remarks of previous chapters concerning the conceptualisation of action and the methodology of interpretation. An attempt will be made to outline an epistemology which is apposite to the project of providing depth interpretations of human action. In the present section, I begin this task by reconsidering the problems of reference and objectivity. These problems are particularly complex in the context of social science, as there are referring expressions both in the ordinary language of lay actors and in the theoretical discourse of investigators. Here I focus on the former and try to establish a connection with the latter by arguing that the referential relation in everyday speech cannot be divorced from a theory of the social-psychological conditions of action. The specification of particular referents must therefore be linked to a process of interpretation. This process is facilitated by theoretical constructs which, in order to mark their peculiar status, may be ascribed a certain objectivity. I shall briefly apply this account to the case of ideology, suggesting that the analysis of the ideological phenomenon must invoke a theory which discloses a systematic split in the referential object. So while the referent of an expression may be one or more objects external to a system of signification, nevertheless the determination of the referent presupposes some form of theoretical mediation. Thus, in the end, the problem of referential determination can only be resolved within the framework of a theory of truth.

The referential relation must be explored in conjunction with the social-psychological conditions of action. A defence of this approach can be elicited from an analysis of the theory which Kripke and Donnellan propose as an alternative to the cluster account. The so-called 'causal' or 'historical explanation' theory maintains that if a speaker uses a name intending to refer to an individual and predicate something of it, then successful reference will occur 'when there is an individual that enters into the historically correct explanation of who it is that the speaker intended to predicate something of'.[51] The individual will then be the referent and the statement will be true or false depending on whether the individual has the property designated by the predicate. It should be noted, to begin with, that this account does not eliminate the role of theory in the specification of particular referents, although Donnellan tends to obscure this role with his simplifying assumption of 'an omniscient observer of history'. I wish to suggest, however, that even supposing a 'correct explanation' could be given of how a speaker acquired a name which he or she now employs, such an explanation would not necessarily identify the referent of that name. For one can imagine a case in which a name refers to an object or individual which the speaker's use of the name serves not to reveal, but rather to conceal. Suppose, for example, that a speaker S says 'last night I dreamt that I was murdered by Isabelle'. An historical investigation may establish that S acquired this name while reading a novel on the previous day. Yet it seems by no means certain that in recounting the dream, S is necessarily referring, if referring at all, to the fictional character which terminates the explanatory chain. For it appears quite conceivable that in calling the assassin 'Isabelle', S is in fact concealing from himself or herself an individual who is highly significant, and whose identity could be disclosed only through a process of interpretation. If this is so, then Donnellan is surely mistaken to invoke the notion of a block in order to account for referential failure. For the explanation of S's acquisition of 'Isabelle' terminates in a 'block' in Donnellan's sense, and yet S's use of this name may well refer nonetheless. The above example also suggests that any attempt to employ the intentions of the speaker as a reference-preserving link, as Kripke appears to do,[52] is unlikely to succeed. For the example indicates that what the speaker intends to refer to may be no guide to what the referent is, since the referent itself may be blocked or fragmented by the mechanism of repression. Indeed, so far from the speaker's intentions serving as an unproblematic guarantee of referential continuity, it is rather the interpretative unfolding of ulterior referents which may serve to unmask the speaker's intentions; and if this process encounters a 'splitting' of the referential object, to borrow a provocative expression from Ricoeur, then it merely attests to the complex constitution of the speaking and acting subject.

The disruption of the referential relation by the social-psychological conditions of action is a crucial characteristic of ideology. The ideological phenomenon frequently functions by means of a systematic split in the referential object, so that a symbol or expression explicitly refers to one particular but implicitly denotes another. Innumerable examples of this *modus operandi* may be found in the writings of Barthes, and in the intriguing analysis of advertising recently conducted by Williamson.[53] The Barthean image of the saluting Negro in uniform on the cover of *Paris-Match* functions as an ideology only insofar as it signifies not merely a particular individual, but also the general context of French imperialism. However, Barthes's analysis of the ideological phenomenon leaves the referential relation unexplored, a deficiency which follows directly from the limitations of the structuralist approach. By assuming with Saussure that the signified is identical with the concept, Barthes simply bypasses the problem of the relation between language and the extra-linguistic reality to which it refers. There are passages wherein he appears to perceive this problem, recognising that 'the concept is in no way abstract: it is filled with a situation. Through the concept, it is a whole new history which is implanted in the myth.'[54] Yet Barthes does not say just how the concept is 'filled with a situation' and by what means history is 'implanted in the myth'. Moreover, it is difficult to see how such questions could be answered in the absence of a more adequate social theory. For as the above examples suggest, the relation between a symbol and the object to which it refers is mediated by a complex of social-psychological conditions; and hence the clarification of that relation, as well as the specification of particular referents, requires a theory which is capable of explicating these conditions. Such a theory includes constructs which, by virtue of their revelatory role, may be ascribed a certain objectivity. In this regard, Ricoeur's justification of the concept of the unconscious provides an instructive approach to the problem of the status of social structure.[55] Just as the concept of the unconscious is relative to a hermeneutic constellation constituted in the analytic situation, so too the notion of social structure is bound to an interpretative process which is undertaken in particular social and political circumstances. Just as the concept of the unconscious can be justified in terms of its capacity to disclose a domain of experience, so too the justification of the notion of social structure consists in its ability to articulate a realm of being which lies at the base of social and political consciousness. Finally, it may be noted that if the specification of particular referents is dependent upon a theory which explicates the social-psychological conditions of action, then the question of referential determination cannot be answered in isolation from an account of truth. Accordingly, it is to the clarification of the latter notion that the subsequent section will turn.

Truth and justification

The depth interpretation of human action raises the perennial problem of truth. The centrality of this problem is recognised by both Ricoeur and Habermas, whose proposed solutions have been criticised above. I shall now attempt to sketch an alternative account which may help to overcome some of the weaknesses in their proposals. Concurring with the critique of the correspondence theory developed by Strawson, Habermas and others, I proceed to defend a particular version of the view that truth is concerned with justification. I try to apply this account to the methodology of depth interpretation, with the aim of showing that theoretical reconstructions and derived interpretations are susceptible of some defence. However, since it seems plausible to suppose that reconstructions may be underdetermined by empirical evidence, it may appear that their truth value is intrinsically indeterminate. I conclude this section with the suggestion that such an appearance may be dispelled by invoking a principle of self-reflection, which provides a non-empirical criterion for the redemption of claims to truth.

The concept of truth may be analysed in terms of the notion of justification. The specific way in which I shall elaborate this analysis may be summarised by the following thesis: it is statements which are true or false, and to say that a statement is true is to say that adequate evidence can be adduced in its support. In linking the concept of truth to the provision of evidence, this thesis bears some resemblance to the account of truth in terms of 'warranted assertability'. However, the view which I shall defend differs from the latter account, and hence from Habermas's proposal, in two important respects. In the first place, I wish to distinguish between the justification for the assertion of a statement, and the justification for the assertion that a statement is true. There may well be cases in which these two types of justification overlap or even coincide, but it seems mistaken to assume that this must necessarily be so. One may assert, for example, that a person P is in pain, and one may justify this assertion on the basis of what P does; but the justification of the assertion that it is true that P is in pain may require an appeal to additional evidence, such as how P feels at the time in question. This distinction thus implies the rejection of any redundancy theory of truth, according to which 'x' and 'x is true' are to be regarded as logically equivalent. By emphasising that the conditions of justification for the assertion of these statements may differ, it might be possible to meet the first objection which I levelled at Habermas's proposal, and to counter the general argument which Martin, Putnam and others have directed against the justificatory approach.[56] The second major difficulty in Habermas's account may be overcome by allowing a more central role for the notion of evidence. The latter notion, which is a key element in Toulmin's original analysis of the pattern of argument,[57] tends to disappear in the wake of Habermas's dichotomy between the discursive redemption of validity claims and the objectivity of experience. The question of what kind of evidence could be adduced in support of a particular claim, and of when such evidence would count as adequate for its defence, are issues which I shall briefly consider below. Here it will suffice to suggest that only by stressing the notion of evidence can one offer an analysis of truth which will avoid both a relativisation of theories and an hypostatisation of facts, without retreating into an hermetically sealed realm of unadulterated discourse.

The analysis of truth in terms of justification may be applied to the methodology of depth interpretation. The statements which express theoretical reconstructions of institutions and social structures can be defended by recourse to a variety of empirical data. Explicit statements of protocol and implicit connotations of proverbs, formal relations of authority and informal patterns of association, are but a few of the many sources of data for defending the reconstruction of institutional schemata.[58] A theory of social structures and their succession may receive some support from the results of historical and anthropological research. Statistical analysis may yield a justification for the claim that a particular social formation is characterised by a certain social structure.[59] Yet in spite of the considerable range of relevant data, there are good grounds to suppose that theoretical reconstructions may remain underdetermined by empirical evidence. The thesis of the underdetermination of scientific theories has been widely defended in the recent philosophical literature, including the writings of Hesse.[60] One of the implications which Hesse draws from this thesis is that the adjudication of underdetermined theories may require the invocation of 'non-empirical criteria'. In the natural sciences, such criteria have been reduced to the principle of prediction and control; but there is no *prima facie* reason for holding that the same principle must be adopted in the social sciences. On the contrary, I wish to propose, and shall briefly defend below, the view that the crucial non-empirical criterion for the selection of theoretical reconstructions is provided by a principle of self-reflection. The interpretations derived from a reconstruction of institutions and social structure may be initially disavowed by the actors, who may not recognise themselves under the descriptions thereby produced. Nevertheless, the decisive condition for the acceptance of the interpretation, and hence for the defence of the reconstruction from which it is derived, is the ultimate appropriation of the interpretation by the subjects concerned. The principle of self-reflection thus asserts that the redemption of the truth claim expressed by theoretical reconstructions is dependent, in the last analysis, upon the ability of such reconstructions to generate interpretations which clarify the conditions of action for the actors themselves, and which thereby provide the actors with the means to free themselves from the circumstances in which they are enmeshed. The implications of this account for the problem of the relation between theory and practice have been noted elsewhere. The principal task which remains is to give some sense to the notion of 'the last analysis', which elevates the subject to a crucial epistemological role without capitulating to the prevailing attitudes of everyday life.

Rationality

The conditions for the redemption of claims to truth may be linked to the concept of rationality. As writers within the tradition of critical social theory have always maintained, the concept of rationality cannot be restricted to a characterisation of the means which are appropriate for attaining a predetermined goal. For there is an important sense in which the goal may also be assessed as rational, not simply as a means to a further end but as an end in itself. In this final section of the chapter, I suggest that the circumstances where a goal may be assessed as rational are identical with the conditions under which a truth claim may ultimately be redeemed; and I propose, following Habermas, that these conditions may be specified in terms of the necessary presuppositions of speech. If the proposal is correct, then it will vindicate Winch's view that the concept of rationality is in some way concerned with the foundations of communication. However, the account which I offer of these foundations, and the implications which I draw from this account, will differ greatly from anything that can be found in the writings of Winch.

The ability to participate in a discussion presupposes a grasp of the conditions which crystallise the concept of rationality. I shall not attempt to defend this sweeping thesis with the rigour and the detail that it demands. I shall, instead, merely sketch an argument which will highlight the similarities with and differences from Habermas's account, and which will enable me to offer a few remarks in support. The argument may be summarised in the following way:

(1) The ability to participate in a discussion presupposes being able to understand the statements of another speaker.

(2) Being able to understand the statements of another speaker requires a knowledge of the conditions that would justify one both in asserting the statement, and in asserting that the statement is true.

(3) To know the conditions that would justify one in asserting that a statement is true is to know what would count as adequate evidence for its defence.

(4) What counts as adequate rests upon a consensus which may be called into question, and the restoration of a consensus requires a situation in which participants can express their opinions and draw their conclusions in the absence of constraint.

(5) The absence of constraint presupposes the exclusion of one-sided power relations, in whatever mode these relations may obtain.

(6) The situation so defined establishes a framework for action and speech

wherein an agreement attained concerning what counts as adequate may be characterised as a rational consensus.

(7) Therefore, the ability to participate in a discussion presupposes a grasp of the conditions which crystallise the concept of rationality.

The first step of the argument forms a basis which is considerably broader than that from which Habermas begins, since it appeals to the general requirements of understanding.[61] Step (2) suggests that these requirements could be unfolded, at least partially, in terms of a criterial semantics which is supplemented by a theory of truth. For while the writings of Wittgenstein rightly emphasise the concept of criterion, they do not sufficiently distinguish between the criteria which justify the assertion of a statement and the conditions under which it is true; and if anything has been attained by recent work in the philosophy of language, then it is the recognition that the latter conditions, as well as the former criteria, are relevant to the explication of meaning.[62] Step (3) simply reiterates a point which I defended above, namely that the conditions of truth cannot be abstracted from the context of justified assertion. The fourth step is, I candidly concede, the most problematic part of the argument. The step submits that the normative aspect of the concept of truth can be elucidated in terms of a discursive situation which is free from constraint. It seems plausible to suppose that someone may question what counts as adequate evidence for the assertion that a statement is true. The inquirer may demand, not merely a clarification of what the level of adequacy is, but rather a consideration of what the level should be; and such a demand, it seems to me, would propel the participants towards a situation in which opinions could be expressed and conclusions drawn in the absence of any constraint. For we do assume, I think, that the demand of the persistent inquirer could be legitimately met; and we do seem to discount the possibility of legitimately meeting this demand by appealing only to the authority of traditional or established standards. The fifth step emphasises that the situation which we appear to presuppose cannot be defined simply in terms of an equal opportunity to select and employ speech-acts, since domination may be actualised in other ways. The definition of the presupposed situation would require a theory of action which thematised the various modes in which one-sided power relations can obtain. Assuming that such a theory could be provided, the presupposed situation would specify the conditions under which an agreement attained concerning the level of adequacy, and hence concerning the meaning and the truth of what may be said, could be characterised as a rational consensus. It is in this sense that the ability to participate in a discussion seems to presuppose an apprehension of the conditions which crystallise the concept of rationality.

The rational framework presupposed by speech may be ascribed a distinctive status and assigned a crucial role within the epistemology of interpretative theory. The argument for the presupposition of such a framework differs in at least two respects from the defences which may be provided for theoretical reconstructions in the social sciences. First, the argument is not concerned with the contingent conditions of particular actions or institutions, but rather with the necessary presuppositions for the intelligibility of speech. Insofar as intelligibility is an essential aspect of any language, the reconstruction of its presuppositions would seem to possess a peculiar universality, similar perhaps to the universality possessed by the reconstruction of the structural conditions of any society. The second respect in which the argument differs from those proffered in the social sciences is concerned with the relation that it bears to itself. For if the argument is correct, then the rational framework of action and speech would be a presupposition of the argument's own intelligibility. Habermas may thus be right to suggest that the reconstruction of the conditions of possible speech constitutes a form of knowledge which 'has always claimed a special status: that of "pure" knowledge'.[63] The implications of this suggestion for the theory of knowledge-constitutive interests, which allows too little scope for this form of knowledge, cannot be explored in the present context.[64] Instead I shall restrict the following remarks to a consideration of three functions which the rational framework might fulfil. First, the framework may specify the conditions for the ultimate redemption of the truth claims associated with theoretical reconstructions. For the redemption of such claims depends, in the last analysis, upon the acceptance of theoretically derived interpretations of action by the actors themselves; and 'the last analysis' is, I propose, precisely the circumstance in which the relations of domination which characterise the existing state of affairs have been suspended or dissolved. This proposal raises fundamental problems concerning the extent to which the suspension of asymmetrical power relations can be counterfactually conceived, and concerning the sense in which subjects placed in such counterfactual conditions would remain the same. Moreover, the proposal leaves open the question of whether the conditions presupposed by communication would be sufficient to secure the agreement or acceptance which is necessary for the redemption of claims to truth. Here I can do no more than express the belief that however deep and intractable such problems may be, they do not destroy the fruitfulness of the proposal submitted above. The second function which the presupposed framework might fulfil concerns the determination of reference and the ascription of interests. The possibilities of split reference and false consciousness demand an account of referential determinacy and real interests which does not endow the actor with a premature authority. Accordingly, it may be suggested that as with other interpretations, the truth value of those which identify referents or ascribe interests is ultimately dependent upon their acceptability to the subjects concerned under the rational conditions of action and speech. Ricoeur is thus right to insist that consciousness, like truth, is not a given but a task, namely 'the task of becoming-consciousness'.[65] For it is only through the process of interpretation that subjects can come to know the conditions and the complexities of their own existence. The third and final function that I wish to note pertains to the very principle of self-reflection. If the framework of rationality is a necessary presupposition of speech, then the invocation of the principle of self-reflection is neither arbitrary nor vacuous. It is not arbitrary because the proponents of a theoretical reconstruction may be pressed to secure a rational consensus concerning the adequacy of the evidence which could be, or which has been, adduced in its support; and if this consensus is rational, then it must in principle elicit the agreement of anyone who would participate in the domination-free discussion, including the subjects whose actions are the topic of theoretically derived interpretations. Moreover, the principle of self-reflection is not vacuous insofar as a subject which is capable of speech must, if the foregoing account is correct, have some grasp of the conditions under which a discursively attained agreement would count as a rational consensus. The presupposition of a rational framework is thus of crucial significance for a theory of interpretation which is concerned with critique. Indeed, it would not be irrelevant to recall a brief but penetrating remark from the writings of Habermas: 'on this unavoidable fiction rests the humanity of relations among men who are still men'.[66]

It would be appropriate to conclude this chapter by drawing together some of its central themes. An attempt is made to assess the contributions of ordinary language philosophy, hermeneutic phenomenology and critical social theory to certain epistemological issues. I try to show that these contributions are deficient in various respects, but that the writings of Ricoeur and Habermas contain a number of insights which are worthy of being pursued. In the final section of the chapter, I endeavour to develop these insights in the direction of an epistemology which would be appropriate for the depth interpretation of human action. I maintain that the referential relation cannot be abstracted from the social-psychological conditions of action, and hence that the specification of particular referents must proceed under the auspices of hermeneutics. The concept of truth is analysed in terms of justification and an attempt is made to integrate this analysis with the methodology of interpretation. Finally, the conditions for the redemption of claims to truth are linked to a framework of rationality, which is characterised as a necessary presupposition of speech. I am fully aware that the constructive remarks which I offer are all too cursory and incomplete, and that the supporting arguments which I propose are in need of additional defence. Nevertheless, if these positive suggestions indicate a promising course for further research, then they have fulfilled their principal aim.

Conclusion

In the preceding chapters, I have explored the contributions to the philosophy of social science which may be found in the writings of authors belonging to different intellectual traditions. This comparative analysis is invited and facilitated by a remarkable feature of twentieth-century thought: its convergence on the phenomenon of language. Like philosophers in the Anglo-Saxon world, both Ricoeur and Habermas emphasise the centrality and importance of language. Yet unlike many of their Anglo-Saxon counterparts, neither Ricoeur nor Habermas regards the analysis of this phenomenon as an activity divorced from broader philosophical and theoretical concerns. Thus Ricoeur views language as a medium of objectification and assigns hermeneutics the task of unfolding the dimensions of being which are expressed in, and disclosed by, the semantic structure of symbols and texts. Habermas conceives of language as the locus of ideology, suggesting that the distortions effected by the exercise of power can be criticised through a reconstruction of the presuppositions of speech. So for authors within widely differing traditions, language has become a common field of analysis, a common intersection for divergent aims. However, whereas ordinary language philosophers tend to treat this field as the ultimate ground of inquiry, both Ricoeur and Habermas view it as a region through which interpretation must proceed, but which in the end it must surpass.

The conceptions of language espoused by Ricoeur and Habermas are interwoven with their approach to the social sciences. As with post-Wittgensteinian philosophers, these Continental thinkers are opposed to the wholesale importation of naturalistic methods into the social sphere. For such an importation, they rightly argue, does violence to the peculiar constitution of the social world. However, in contrast to ordinary language philosophers, both Ricoeur and Habermas recognise that this peculiar constitution demands a methodology which incorporates objectifying concepts. The distanciations involved in the production of texts and their analogues, or the distortions effected by the exercise of power, can be elucidated only by means of an explanatory technique. This primordial appeal to a form of explanation establishes the possibility of an intimate and reciprocal relation between philosophy and social science. For on the one hand, the recovery of a being which is disguised and disclosed requires the mediation of an objective analysis; and hence, as Ricoeur insists, a philosophy that strives towards ontology must pass through the methods and results of disciplines which study the objectifications of the human world. On the other hand, the critique of ideological distortions stands in need of rational justification; and so, as Habermas contends, a social science which seeks to be critical must clarify the conditions under which its claims to truth can be redeemed. Like post-Wittgensteinian philosophers, both Ricoeur and Habermas thus propose a close connection between philosophy and social science. However, whereas followers of Wittgenstein tend to treat social science as a mere branch of philosophy, both Ricoeur and Habermas offer an account which respects the autonomy of these two domains.

The common ground of language, and the common concern with philosophy and social science, provide the backcloth for the critical analyses of this study. The analyses are focused around three themes, which pertain in turn to the conceptualisation of action, the methodology of interpretation, and the theory of reference and truth. With regard to the first of these themes, I argue that ordinary language philosophers have dealt inadequately with problems of expression and repression, of history and social change, and of meaningful action and social relations. The writings of Ricoeur contain some penetrating insights into the connection between language and experience, and into the ways in which action is dependent upon aspects of the social world. Yet I criticise, among other things, Ricoeur's proposal to conceptualise action as a text; for this proposal rests upon an illegitimate extrapolation from language and results in an undesirable reification of action. The work of Habermas rightly links the analysis of action to considerations of power and ideology, conjoining this account to a general theory of social change. I argue, however, that Habermas's typology of action is unsound. I also question his conceptualisation of ideology and suggest that his account of the relation between action and structure leaves many questions unanswered.

In turning to problems of methodology, I begin by examining Winch's recommendations for the interpretation of action. I try to show that these recommendations are for the most part unacceptable. I oppose the tendency of Winch and others to concentrate on understanding at the expense of explanation, and I argue that Winch fails to give an adequate account of the role of theory and critique in the social sciences. Many of these weaknesses are avoided in the writings of Ricoeur and Habermas, who both seek to elaborate a theory of interpretation which incorporates explanatory and critical elements. I argue nonetheless that the methodology proposed by Ricoeur is unsatisfactory in certain respects. As a consequence of its derivation from the theory of the text, Ricoeur's methodology does not provide a suitable framework for investigating the social conditions of action; and while this methodology aspires to be critical, it does not offer a firm basis for the conduct of critique. The work of Habermas suggests a more promising approach to such issues. When probed in more detail, however, Habermas's remarks on methodology appear imprecise and incomplete. Moreover, while Habermas rightly aims to establish a link between theory and practice, it seems clear that so far he has failed to secure this bond.

The final theme which I explore is concerned with problems of epistemology. I criticise the accounts of reference and truth which predominate in the literature of ordinary language philosophy. I also suggest that ordinary language philosophers tend to adhere to an overly narrow conception of rationality. The writings of Ricoeur offer some intriguing ideas on reference and objectivity, and rightly raise the questions of truth and justification within the context of hermeneutics. I contend, however, that there are important shortcomings in Ricoeur's contributions to these issues. For Ricoeur never explains precisely how one is to determine the referent in particular cases, nor does he specify criteria which would be adequate for the adjudication of conflicting interpretations. Habermas provides a clue which may be helpful in these respects, insofar as he links the concept of truth to the idea of a rational consensus attained through discourse. I try to show, however, that the details of Habermas's account are open to serious objections, so that his proposal is in need of further thought.

The critical and comparative analyses prepare the way for my constructive contribution to these themes. This contribution seeks to sketch the contours of a critical and rationally justified theory for the interpretation of action, a project which I have provisionally called 'critical hermeneutics'. I begin this sketch by repudiating the tendency to conceptualise action in accordance with a linguistic exemplar, whether the latter be a rule-governed use or an objectified text. I focus instead on the general category of human action, concerning which I submit several theses. Action is conceived as an event which may be described in various ways, such that the meaning of an action is specified by the manner in which it is described. Although action presupposes a subject, the meaning of an action is not decided by the subject's intentions; for what the subject does may be quite different from what he or she intended to do. I then try to situate action within a wider context of institutions and social structure. Institutions are regarded as specific constellations of social relations and material resources; and social structure is conceived as a series of elements and their interrelations, which conjointly define the conditions for the persistence of a social formation and the limits for the variation of its component institutions. I seek to show how this account of the relation between action and structure could be developed to incorporate considerations of power, ideology and history.

My proposals on the level of methodology are closely linked to the conceptualisation of the social domain. I begin by introducing the concepts of schematic generation and social structuration, linking each to a particular dimension of the social world. These concepts are then employed to reformulate the programme of depth interpretation. I suggest that action may be redescribed, and thereby re-understood, by recourse to the explanatory reconstruction of the schemata which generate acts and the elements which structurate institutions. The elaboration of such a programme could provide a framework for the conduct of critique. For the reconstruction of institutional and structural conditions would prepare the way for a redescription of action which diverges from lay actors' accounts, as well as a reconsideration of the possibilities which the conditions in question preclude. By linking these redescriptions and reconsiderations to a principle of self-reflection, I point towards a methodology in which practice would be essential to the very constitution of social scientific theory.

In the final chapter, I indicate a direction for the development of an epistemology which would be apposite to the methodology of depth interpretation. I argue that the referential relation must be analysed in conjunction with a theory of the social-psychological conditions of action, and maintain that such an analysis must incorporate a notion of split reference similar to Ricoeur's. Since the determination of particular referents requires the mediation of theoretical constructs, this complex of issues must be linked to an account of truth. I defend a version of the justificatory analysis of truth, formulated in a way which hopefully avoids the objections that may be levelled at such an approach. The analysis is then applied to the methodology of depth interpretation, with the aim of showing that theoretical reconstructions are susceptible of some defence. I suggest, nonetheless, that the redemption of theoretical claims to truth is ultimately dependent upon a principle of self-reflection. Following Habermas, an attempt is made to clarify the conditions under which this principle may be invoked through a re-examination of the concept of rationality, which is analysed in terms of the necessary presuppositions of communication.

My attempt to outline a critical theory for the interpretation of action leaves many issues open. I have often stressed that my constructive remarks are of a tentative character, merely pointing towards a position which has yet to be developed in detail. Precisely what such detail would look like is a question which can be answered only in the course of further research. In drawing this study to a close, I should like to identify a few of the areas which, in my opinion, are especially in need of attention. On a theoretical level, the analysis of action must be developed in a way which unfolds the connections with the constitution of the subject on the one hand, and the constitution of the social world on the other. My proposals concerning institutions and social structure must be substantiated by reference to specific examples of social analysis. Similarly, the methodological concepts which I introduce must be rendered more precise. The status of the explanations which these concepts permit, and the nature of the evidence which these explanations require, must be examined in greater detail. The suggestions which I offer with regard to epistemology are undoubtedly the most provisional. My constructive remarks on reference, objectivity and truth are all in need of elaboration and defence. If the concept of rationality can indeed be linked to the presuppositions of communication, then continued work on the theory of language may shed some light on these difficult issues.

The development of a critical theory of interpretation may have important implications for substantive social inquiry. It seems to me that one of the most promising areas for the application of an interpretative theory is the area of ideology. This central and notoriously complex feature of social life still awaits a satisfactory analysis. Such an analysis would benefit from the ideas discussed in this study – one need only think of the use of symbols and metaphors in political discourse, the ways in which one-sided power relations restrict the articulation of experience and interests, the modes by which ideologies may be interpreted and conflicts of interpretation resolved. To pursue these issues in a substantive inquiry would help to illuminate and reformulate the theoretical problems. It would help, for example, to clarify the character of social interests and the form of social explanations. In thus advocating a depth-hermeneutical approach to the analysis of ideology, I take Ricoeur and Habermas as guides. For both of these thinkers firmly situate language and action in the social world, and both forcefully affirm the deep and ineluctable link between philosophy and social science.

Notes

Abbreviations

The following abbreviations are used for works which are frequently cited in the notes:

PI   Ludwig Wittgenstein, *Philosophical Investigations*, third edition, trans. G. E. M. Anscombe (Oxford: Basil Blackwell, 1968)

ISS   Peter Winch, *The Idea of a Social Science and its Relation to Philosophy* (London: Routledge & Kegan Paul, 1958)

FN   Paul Ricoeur, *Freedom and Nature: The Voluntary and the Involuntary*, trans. Erazim V. Kohák (Evanston: Northwestern University Press, 1966)

FP   Paul Ricoeur, *Freud and Philosophy: An Essay on Interpretation*, trans. Denis Savage (New Haven: Yale University Press, 1970)

CI   Paul Ricoeur, *The Conflict of Interpretations: Essays in Hermeneutics*, edited by Don Ihde (Evanston: Northwestern University Press, 1974)

RM   Paul Ricoeur, *The Rule of Metaphor: Multi-Disciplinary Studies of the Creation of Meaning in Language*, trans. Robert Czerny with Kathleen McLaughlin and John Costello, SJ (London: Routledge & Kegan Paul, 1978)

HHS   Paul Ricoeur, *Hermeneutics and the Human Sciences: Essays on Language, Action and Interpretation*, edited and translated by John B. Thompson (Cambridge: Cambridge University Press, 1981)

TP   Jürgen Habermas, *Theory and Practice*, trans. John Viertel (London: Heinemann, 1974)

TRS   Jürgen Habermas, *Toward a Rational Society: Student Protest, Science, and Politics*, trans. Jeremy J. Shapiro (London: Heinemann, 1971)

KHI   Jürgen Habermas, *Knowledge and Human Interests*, trans. Jeremy J. Shapiro (London: Heinemann, 1972)

LC   Jürgen Habermas, *Legitimation Crisis*, trans. Thomas McCarthy (London: Heinemann, 1976)

CES   Jürgen Habermas, *Communication and the Evolution of Society*, trans. Thomas McCarthy (London: Heinemann, 1979)

1. Ordinary language philosophy

1 Bertrand Russell, 'The philosophy of logical atomism', in *Russell's Logical Atomism*, edited by David Pears (London: Fontana/Collins, 1972), pp. 31–2.

2 Cf. Bertrand Russell, 'On denoting', in *Contemporary Readings in Logical*

Theory, edited by Irving M. Copi and James A. Gould (New York: Macmillan, 1967), pp. 93–105.

3 Bertrand Russell, 'The philosophy of logical atomism', p. 129.

4 Ludwig Wittgenstein, *Tractatus Logico-Philosophicus*, trans. D. F. Pears and B. F. McGuinness (London: Routledge & Kegan Paul, 1961), secs. 4.031–4.0311.

5 Ludwig Wittgenstein, *Tractatus Logico-Philosophicus*, trans. C. K. Ogden (London: Routledge & Kegan Paul, 1922), sec. 7.

6 Rudolf Carnap, *The Logical Structure of the World*, trans. Rolf A. George (London: Routledge & Kegan Paul, 1967), p. v.

7 Otto Neurath, 'Sociology and physicalism', trans. Morton Magnus and Ralph Raico, in *Logical Positivism*, edited by A. J. Ayer (New York: The Free Press, 1959), p. 295.

8 Cf. Rudolf Carnap, 'Pseudoproblems in philosophy: the heteropsychological and the realism controversy', in *The Logical Structure of the World*, pp. 301–43.

9 A. J. Ayer, *Language, Truth and Logic*, second edition (London: Victor Gollancz, 1967), p. 34.

10 Cf. John Wisdom, *Logical Constructions* (New York: Random House, 1969).

11 Cf. Ludwig Wittgenstein, 'Some remarks on logical form', in *Essays on Wittgenstein's 'Tractatus'*, edited by Irving M. Copi and Robert W. Beard (London: Routledge & Kegan Paul, 1966), pp. 31–7.

12 Ludwig Wittgenstein, *Philosophical Remarks*, edited by Rush Rhees, trans. Raymond Hargreaves and Roger White (Oxford: Basil Blackwell, 1975), p. 110.

13 Otto Neurath, 'Protocol sentences', trans. George Schlick, in *Logical Positivism*, p. 201 (italics removed). See also Ayer's critique of ostensive propositions in *Language, Truth and Logic*, chapter v.

14 Ludwig Wittgenstein, *Philosophical Grammar*, edited by Rush Rhees, trans. Anthony Kenny (Oxford: Basil Blackwell, 1974), p. 210.

15 *PI*, sec. 63.

16 Cf. Gilbert Ryle, 'Systematically misleading expressions', in his *Collected Papers*, vol. II (London: Hutchinson, 1971), pp. 39–62; and John Wisdom, 'Philosophical perplexity', in his *Philosophy and Psychoanalysis* (New York: Philosophical Library, 1953), pp. 36–50.

17 Cf. J. L. Austin, *Sense and Sensibilia*, edited by G. J. Warnock (Oxford: Oxford University Press, 1962); and G. A. Paul, 'Is there a problem about sense-data?', in *Logic and Language*, first series, edited by Antony Flew (Oxford: Basil Blackwell, 1951), pp. 101–16.

18 Cf. P. F. Strawson, 'On referring', in his *Logico-Linguistic Papers* (London: Methuen, 1971), pp. 1–27.

19 P. F. Strawson, 'Construction and analysis', in A. J. Ayer et al., *The Revolution in Philosophy* (London: Macmillan, 1956), pp. 103–4.

20 *PI*, sec. 65.

21 Cf. John Wisdom, 'Metaphysics and verification', in *Philosophy and Psychoanalysis*, pp. 51–101.

22 J. L. Austin, 'Are there a priori concepts?', in his *Philosophical Papers*, edited by J. O. Urmson and G. J. Warnock (Oxford: Oxford University Press, 1970), p. 38.

23 *PI*, sec. 40.

24 Cf. J. L. Austin, 'The meaning of a word' and 'Other minds', in *Philosophical Papers*, pp. 55–75 and 76–116.

25 Cf. P. F. Strawson, 'On referring'.

26 Gilbert Ryle, 'The theory of meaning', in *Collected Papers*, vol. II, p. 365.

27 *PI*, sec. 43.

28 Ibid., p. 220.

29 Cf. P. F. Strawson, 'On referring'.

30 Cf. Gilbert Ryle, 'Ordinary language' and 'Use, usage and meaning', in *Collected Papers*, vol. II, pp. 301–18 and 407–14.

31 J. L. Austin, *How to do Things with Words*, second edition, edited by J. O. Urmson and Marina Sbisà (Oxford: Oxford University Press, 1976), p. 100.

32 Cf. Ludwig Wittgenstein, *Preliminary Studies for the 'Philosophical Investigations', Generally Known as the Blue and Brown Books* (Oxford: Basil Blackwell, 1969), p. 17.

33 *PI*, sec. 23.

34 John R. Searle, *Speech Acts: An Essay in the Philosophy of Language* (Cambridge: Cambridge University Press, 1970), p. 16.

35 *PI*, secs. 85, 87.

36 Cf. J. L. Austin, 'How to talk – some simple ways', in *Philosophical Papers*, pp. 134–53.

37 John R. Searle, *Speech Acts*, p. 37.

38 Cf. J. L. Austin, *How to do Things with Words*, lecture IX.

39 Cf. P. F. Strawson, 'Intention and convention in speech acts', in *Logico-Linguistic Papers*, pp. 149–69; and H. P. Grice, 'Meaning', in *Philosophical Logic*, edited by P. F. Strawson (Oxford: Oxford University Press, 1967), pp. 39–48.

40 For an illuminating discussion of Wittgenstein's 'criterial semantics', see P. M. S. Hacker, *Insight and Illusion: Wittgenstein on Philosophy and the Metaphysics of Experience* (Oxford: Oxford University Press, 1972), chapter x.

41 *PI*, sec. 142.

42 Cf. J. L. Austin, 'Other minds'.

43 P. F. Strawson, *Individuals: An Essay in Descriptive Metaphysics* (London: Methuen, 1959), p. 105.

44 *PI*, sec. 126.

45 Ibid., sec. 124.

46 J. L. Austin, 'A plea for excuses', in *Philosophical Papers*, p. 185.

47 P. F. Strawson, *Individuals*, p. 10.

48 Ludwig Wittgenstein, *Philosophical Grammar*, p. 184.

49 *PI*, sec. 373.

50 Cf. J. L. Austin, *Sense and Sensibilia*, chapter VII.

51 J. L. Austin, 'A plea for excuses', p. 182.

52 Cf. P. F. Strawson, *Individuals*, p. 15.

53 Cf. Peter Winch, 'Understanding a primitive society', in *Rationality*, edited by Bryan R. Wilson (Oxford: Basil Blackwell, 1970), pp. 78–111.

54 *PI*, sec. 79.

55 Ibid., sec. 309.

56 P. F. Strawson, *Individuals*, p. 20.

57 John R. Searle, *Speech Acts*, p. 88.

58 Ludwig Wittgenstein, *On Certainty*, edited by G. E. M. Anscombe and

G. H. von Wright, trans. Denis Paul and G. E. M. Anscombe (Oxford: Basil Blackwell, 1974), sec. 97.

59 Ibid., sec. 612.

60 P. F. Strawson, 'Truth', in *Logico-Linguistic Papers*, p. 196.

61 Cf. R. M. Hare, *The Language of Morals* (Oxford: Oxford University Press, 1952).

62 *PI*, sec. 621.

63 Ludwig Wittgenstein, *The Blue and Brown Books*, p. 143.

64 Cf. A. I. Melden, *Free Action* (London: Routledge & Kegan Paul, 1961), chapter 5.

65 Cf. Gilbert Ryle, *The Concept of Mind* (Harmondsworth: Penguin, 1949), chapter 3.

66 Ibid., p. 67.

67 Cf. J. L. Austin, 'A plea for excuses'.

68 *PI*, sec. 646.

69 Cf. J. L. Austin, 'Three ways of spilling ink', in *Philosophical Papers*, pp. 272–87.

70 G. E. M. Anscombe, *Intention* (Oxford: Basil Blackwell, 1972), p. 29.

71 *PI*, sec. 693.

72 Cf. Ludwig Wittgenstein, *Zettel*, edited by G. E. M. Anscombe and G. H. von Wright, trans. G. E. M. Anscombe (Oxford: Basil Blackwell, 1967), secs. 227, 238.

73 *PI*, sec. 584.

74 R. S. Peters, *The Concept of Motivation* (London: Routledge & Kegan Paul, 1958), p. 7.

75 Cf. A. I. Melden, *Free Action*, chapter 9.

76 *ISS*, pp. 51–2.

77 See H. Stuart Hughes, *Consciousness and Society: The Reorientation of European Social Thought 1890–1930* (St. Albans: Paladin, 1974); and William Outhwaite, *Understanding Social Life: The Method Called 'Verstehen'* (London: George Allen & Unwin, 1975).

78 *PI*, sec. 154.

79 Cf. Ludwig Wittgenstein, 'Remarks on Frazer's *Golden Bough*', trans. A. C. Miles and Rush Rhees, *The Human World* (1971), pp. 28–41.

80 *PI*, sec. 206.

81 *ISS*, p. 108.

82 Peter Winch, 'Understanding a primitive society', p. 107.

83 Ludwig Wittgenstein, *Zettel*, sec. 437.

84 R. S. Peters, *The Concept of Motivation*, p. 14.

85 Cf. A. I. Melden, *Free Action*, chapter 9.

86 *ISS*, p. 133. See also A. R. Louch's critique of the nomological model in *Explanation and Human Action* (Oxford: Basil Blackwell, 1966).

87 *PI*, p. 232.

88 Ludwig Wittgenstein, *Lectures and Conversations on Aesthetics, Psychology and Religious Belief*, edited by Cyril Barrett (Oxford: Basil Blackwell, 1966), p. 24.

89 *PI*, sec. 124.

90 Cf. R. S. Peters, *The Concept of Motivation*, chapter 1.

91 *ISS*, p. 3.

92 A. R. Louch, *Explanation and Human Action*, p. 191.

2. Hermeneutic phenomenology

1 Cf. Wilhelm Dilthey, 'The development of hermeneutics', in his *Selected Writings*, edited and translated by H. P. Rickman (Cambridge: Cambridge University Press, 1976), pp. 247–63.
2 F. Schleiermacher, quoted in Richard E. Palmer, *Hermeneutics: Interpretation Theory in Schleiermacher, Dilthey, Heidegger, and Gadamer* (Evanston: Northwestern University Press, 1969), p. 88.
3 F. Schleiermacher, quoted in Paul Ricoeur, 'The task of hermeneutics', in *HHS*, p. 46.
4 Wilhelm Dilthey, 'The development of hermeneutics', p. 260.
5 Wilhelm Dilthey, 'The construction of the historical world in the human studies', in *Selected Writings*, p. 176.
6 The corpus of Dilthey's work is itself the object of conflicting interpretations, and I make no attempt to broach the current controversies here. For a new and substantial contribution to these controversies, see Michael Ermarth, *Wilhelm Dilthey: The Critique of Historical Reason* (Chicago: University of Chicago Press, 1978).
7 Edmund Husserl, *Ideas: General Introduction to Pure Phenomenology*, trans. W. R. Boyce Gibson (London: George Allen & Unwin, 1931), p. 110 (italics removed).
8 Ibid., p. 153 (italics removed).
9 Edmund Husserl, *Cartesian Meditations: An Introduction to Phenomenology*, trans. Dorion Cairns (The Hague: Martinus Nijhoff, 1960), p. 30.
10 Edmund Husserl, *The Crisis of European Sciences and Transcendental Phenomenology: An Introduction to Phenomenological Philosophy*, trans. David Carr (Evanston: Northwestern University Press, 1970), p. 186.
11 Martin Heidegger, *Being and Time*, trans. John Macquarrie and Edmund Robinson (Oxford: Basil Blackwell, 1967), p. 32.
12 Ibid., p. 183.
13 Hans-Georg Gadamer, *Truth and Method* (London: Sheed & Ward, 1975), pp. 273–4.
14 Ibid., p. 432.
15 Paul Ricoeur, 'Methods and tasks of a phenomenology of the will', in his *Husserl: An Analysis of His Phenomenology*, trans. E. G. Ballard and L. E. Embree (Evanston: Northwestern University Press, 1967), p. 215.
16 *FN*, p. 5.
17 Paul Ricoeur, 'The unity of the voluntary and the involuntary as a limiting idea', trans. Daniel O'Connor, in *Readings in Existential Phenomenology*, edited by Nathaniel Lawrence and Daniel O'Connor (New Jersey: Prentice-Hall, 1967), p. 96.
18 *FN*, p. 486.
19 Paul Ricoeur, 'The antinomy of human reality and the problem of philosophical anthropology', trans. Daniel O'Connor, in *Readings in Existential Phenomenology*, p. 390.
20 Paul Ricoeur, *Fallible Man*, trans. Charles Kelbley (Chicago: Henry Regnery, 1965), p. 11.
21 Ibid., p. 70.
22 Ibid., p. 219.

23 Paul Ricoeur, *The Symbolism of Evil*, trans. Emerson Buchanan (New York: Harper & Row, 1967), p. 349.
24 Paul Ricoeur, 'The hermeneutics of symbols and philosophical reflection: I', trans. Denis Savage, in *CI*, p. 290.
25 Paul Ricoeur, *The Symbolism of Evil*, p. 152.
26 Paul Ricoeur, 'The hermeneutics of symbols and philosophical reflection: I', p. 299.
27 Paul Ricoeur, 'The hermeneutics of symbols and philosophical reflection: II', trans. Charles Freilich, in *CI*, p. 317.
28 *FP*, p. 34.
29 Paul Ricoeur, 'The question of the subject: the challenge of semiology', trans. Kathleen McLaughlin, in *CI*, p. 263.
30 Paul Ricoeur, 'A philosophical interpretation of Freud', trans. Willis Domingo, in *CI*, pp. 171–2.
31 Paul Ricoeur, 'New developments in phenomenology in France: the phenomenology of language', trans. P. G. Goodman, *Social Research*, 34 (1967), p. 14.
32 Cf. Louis Hjelmslev, *Prolegomena to a Theory of Language*, trans. Francis J. Whitfield (Madison: University of Wisconsin Press, 1966).
33 Paul Ricoeur, 'The question of the subject', p. 250.
34 Paul Ricoeur, 'Structure, word, event', trans. Robert Sweeney, in *CI*, p. 84.
35 Paul Ricoeur, 'New developments in phenomenology in France', p. 23.
36 Cf. Emile Benveniste, *Problems in General Linguistics*, trans. Mary Elizabeth Meek (Florida: University of Miami Press, 1971); and 'La forme et le sens dans le langage', in *Le Langage*, II: *actes du XIIIᵉ congrès des sociétés de philosophie de langue française* (Neuchâtel: Editions de la Baconnière, 1967), pp. 29–40.
37 Paul Ricoeur, 'Structure, word, event', p. 86.
38 Ibid., p. 92.
39 Paul Ricoeur, *Cours sur l'herméneutique* (unpublished manuscript, delivered as a series of lectures at the Institut Supérieur de Philosophie, Louvain, 1971–2), p. 16 (my translation).
40 *RM*, p. 217 (translation modified).
41 Ibid., pp. 156–7.
42 Paul Ricoeur, 'Creativity in language', trans. David Pellauer, in *The Philosophy of Paul Ricoeur: An Anthology of His Work*, edited by Charles E. Reagan and David Stewart (Boston: Beacon Press, 1978), p. 133.
43 Paul Ricoeur, *Interpretation Theory: Discourse and the Surplus of Meaning* (Fort Worth: Texas Christian University Press, 1976), p. 59.
44 Paul Ricoeur, 'The problem of double meaning as hermeneutic problem and as semantic problem', trans. Kathleen McLaughlin, in *CI*, p. 66.
45 Paul Ricoeur, 'The hermeneutical function of distanciation', trans. David Pellauer, *Philosophy Today*, 17 (1973), p. 136.
46 Paul Ricoeur, 'The hermeneutical function of distanciation', in *HHS*, p. 136. This is a modified and retranslated version of the essay cited in the previous note.
47 Paul Ricoeur, 'The model of the text: meaningful action considered as a text', in *HHS*, p. 201.
48 Ibid., p. 202.
49 Ibid., p. 211.

50 Paul Ricoeur, *Interpretation Theory*, p. 79.

51 Ibid., p. 87.

52 Ibid.

53 Cf. Jean Nabert, *Elements for an Ethic*, trans. William J. Petrek (Evanston: Northwestern University Press, 1969).

54 *FP*, p. 46.

55 Paul Ricoeur, 'The question of the subject', p. 243.

56 Paul Ricoeur, 'Foreword', in Don Ihde, *Hermeneutic Phenomenology: The Philosophy of Paul Ricoeur* (Evanston: Northwestern University Press, 1971), p. xv.

57 Paul Ricoeur, in Claude Lévi-Strauss, 'Réponses à quelques questions', *Esprit*, 31 (1963), p. 636 (my translation).

58 Cf. Martin Heidegger, *On the Way to Language*, trans. Peter D. Hertz (New York: Harper & Row, 1971), and *Poetry, Language, Thought*, trans. Albert Hofstadter (New York: Harper & Row, 1971); Mikel Dufrenne, *Language and Philosophy*, trans. Henry B. Veatch (New York: Greenwood Press, 1968).

59 Paul Ricoeur, 'Husserl and Wittgenstein on language', in *Phenomenology and Existentialism*, edited by E. N. Lee and M. Mandelbaum (Baltimore: Johns Hopkins University Press, 1967), p. 209.

60 Paul Ricoeur, 'The question of the subject', p. 261.

61 Paul Ricoeur, 'Existence and hermeneutics', trans. Kathleen McLaughlin, in *CI*, p. 19.

62 Ibid., p. 24.

63 Paul Ricoeur, 'New developments in phenomenology in France', pp. 20–1.

64 Paul Ricoeur, 'Structure, word, event', p. 88.

65 *RM*, p. 221 (translation modified).

66 Paul Ricoeur, *Interpretation Theory*, p. 37.

67 Cf. E. D. Hirsch, *Validity in Interpretation* (New Haven: Yale University Press, 1967).

68 Paul Ricoeur, 'The model of the text', p. 213.

69 *FP*, p. 374.

70 Cf. Paul Ricoeur, 'The history of philosophy and the unity of truth', and 'Truth and falsehood', in his *History and Truth*, trans. Charles A. Kelbley (Evanston: Northwestern University Press, 1965), pp. 41–56 and 165–91.

71 Paul Ricoeur, 'Existence and hermeneutics', p. 11.

72 Paul Ricoeur, 'The history of philosophy and the unity of truth', p. 55.

73 Paul Ricoeur, 'The problem of the will and philosophical discourse', trans. Peter McCormick, in *Patterns of the Life-World: Essays in Honor of John Wild*, edited by James M. Edie et al. (Evanston: Northwestern University Press, 1970), p. 273.

74 Further evidence for the suggestion that Ricoeur's work generates three types of discourse on human action may be found on pages 11–19 of Paul Ricoeur, 'Le discours de l'action', in Paul Ricoeur et al., *La Sémantique de l'action* (Paris: Editions du Centre National de la Recherche Scientifique, 1977), pp. 1–137.

75 Paul Ricoeur, 'Le discours de l'action', p. 113 (my translation).

76 Paul Ricoeur, 'Phenomenology of freedom', in *Phenomenology and Philosophical Understanding*, edited by Edo Pivčević (Cambridge: Cambridge University Press, 1975), pp. 183–4.

77 Paul Ricoeur, 'Le discours de l'action', pp. 131–2 (my translation).

78 Paul Ricoeur, *Fallible Man*, pp. 170–1.
79 Paul Ricoeur, 'What does humanism mean?', trans. David Stewart, in Ricoeur's *Political and Social Essays*, edited by David Stewart and Joseph Bien (Athens, Ohio: Ohio University Press, 1974), p. 87.
80 Paul Ricoeur, 'The political paradox', in *History and Truth*, pp. 255–6.
81 Paul Ricoeur, 'The tasks of the political educator', trans. David Stewart, in *Political and Social Essays*, p. 293.
82 Paul Ricoeur, 'The problem of the will and philosophical discourse', p. 288.
83 Cf. Anthony Kenny, *Action, Emotion and Will* (London: Routledge & Kegan Paul, 1963).
84 Paul Ricoeur, 'The model of the text', p. 205.
85 Ibid., p. 208–9.
86 Ibid., p. 208.
87 Ibid., p. 209.
88 Ibid., p. 215.
89 Ibid., p. 220.
90 Ibid., p. 221.
91 The debate was initiated in 1967 with the publication of Jürgen Habermas's *Zur Logik der Sozialwissenschaften*, which contains an incisive critique of Gadamer's *Truth and Method*. Gadamer replied to Habermas and a lively exchange ensued, each protagonist seeking to curtail the universalistic claims raised by the other. Some of the most important essays are collected in *Hermeneutik und Ideologiekritik*, edited by Jürgen Habermas et al. (Frankfurt: Suhrkamp, 1971).
92 Paul Ricoeur, 'Ethics and culture: Habermas and Gadamer in dialogue', trans. David Pellauer, in *Political and Social Essays*, p. 257.
93 Paul Ricoeur, 'Hermeneutics and the critique of ideology', in *HHS*, p. 93.
94 Ibid., p. 97.
95 Ibid., p. 100.
96 *FP*, p. 46.
97 Paul Ricoeur, 'The question of the subject', p. 266.
98 Paul Ricoeur, 'Existence and hermeneutics', p. 15.
99 Cf. Jean Ladrière, *Language and Belief*, trans. Garrett Barden (Dublin: Gill & Macmillan, 1972).
100 Quoted in *History and Truth*, p. 14.

3. Critical social theory

1 G. W. F. Hegel, *The Phenomenology of Mind*, trans. J. B. Baillie (New York: Harper & Row, 1967), pp. 81–2.
2 Ibid., p. 93.
3 The nature of Marx's intellectual debt to Hegel is an issue of considerable complexity, and in these few lines the matter is greatly simplified. For two very different contributions to the current debate, see Herbert Marcuse, *Reason and Revolution* (London: Routledge & Kegan Paul, 1955); and Louis Althusser, *For Marx*, trans. Ben Brewster (Harmondsworth: Penguin, 1969).
4 Karl Marx, *The Economic and Philosophic Manuscripts of 1844*, trans. Martin Milligan (New York: International Publishers, 1964), p. 177.

5 Karl Marx and Frederick Engels, *The German Ideology* (London: Lawrence & Wishart, 1970), p. 50.

6 Cf. Karl Marx, *Capital: A Critique of Political Economy*, trans. Samuel Moore and Edward Aveling (London: Lawrence & Wishart, 1974), especially vol. I, part 1.

7 Frederick Engels, *Herr Eugen Dührings Revolution in Science (Anti-Dühring)*, trans. Emile Burns (London: Martin Lawrence, n.d.), p. 16.

8 Nikolai Bukharin, *Historical Materialism: A System of Sociology* (Ann Arbor: University of Michigan Press, 1969), p. 196 (italics removed).

9 Frederick Engels, 'Introduction to Karl Marx's work *The Class Struggles in France, 1848–1850*', in Karl Marx and Frederick Engels, *Selected Works* (London: Lawrence & Wishart, 1968), pp. 644–5.

10 Cf. Karl Kautsky, *The Class Struggle (Erfurt Program)*, trans. William E. Bohn (New York: W. W. Norton, 1971), pp. 188 ff.

11 Eduard Bernstein, *Evolutionary Socialism: A Criticism and Affirmation*, trans. Edith C. Harvey (New York: Schocken, 1961), p. 197.

12 For an historical sketch of the formation and development of the Frankfurt School, see Martin Jay, *The Dialectical Imagination: A History of the Frankfurt School and the Institute of Social Research 1923–50* (London: Heinemann, 1973). A thorough analysis of the central themes of critical theory may be found in David Held, *Introduction to Critical Theory: Horkheimer to Habermas* (London: Hutchinson, 1980).

13 Theodor Adorno, 'Introduction', in Theodor Adorno et al., *The Positivist Dispute in German Sociology*, trans. Glyn Adey and David Frisby (London: Heinemann, 1976), pp. 9–10.

14 Max Horkheimer, 'Postscript', trans. Matthew J. O'Connell, in Horkheimer's *Critical Theory: Selected Essays* (New York: Herder & Herder, 1972), p. 251.

15 Cf. Max Horkheimer, *Eclipse of Reason* (New York: Oxford University Press, 1947).

16 Max Horkheimer and Theodor Adorno, *Dialectic of Enlightenment*, trans. John Cumming (London: Allen Lane, 1973), pp. 26–7.

17 Cf. Herbert Marcuse, *One Dimensional Man* (London: Sphere, 1972).

18 Walter Benjamin, quoted in Herbert Marcuse, *One Dimensional Man*, p. 200.

19 *TP*, p. 46.

20 Ibid., p. 74.

21 Ibid., p. 258.

22 *KHI*, p. 5.

23 Ibid., p. 133.

24 Ibid., p. 135.

25 Cf. Karl-Otto Apel, 'Communication and the foundations of the humanities', *Acta Sociologica*, 15–16 (1972–3), pp. 7–26.

26 *KHI*, p. 137.

27 Jürgen Habermas, 'The analytical theory of science and dialectics', in *The Positivist Dispute in German Sociology*, p. 152.

28 *KHI*, p. 176.

29 Ibid.

30 Cf. Karl-Otto Apel, *Analytic Philosophy of Language and the Geisteswissenschaften*, trans. H. Holstelilie (Dordrecht: D. Reidel, 1967), and *Towards a Transformation of Philosophy*, trans. Glyn Adey and David Frisby (London:

Routledge & Kegan Paul, 1980); Albrecht Wellmer, *Critical Theory of Society*, trans. John Cumming (New York: Seabury Press, 1974).

31 Jürgen Habermas, *Zur Logik der Sozialwissenschaften* (Frankfurt: Suhrkamp, 1970), p. 259 (my translation).

32 Ibid., p. 287 (my translation).

33 *KHI*, p. 28.

34 Cf. Albrecht Wellmer, *Critical Theory of Society*, chapter 2.

35 *KHI*, p. 42.

36 Cf. Alfred Lorenzer, 'Symbols and stereotypes', trans. Thomas Hall, in *Critical Sociology*, edited by Paul Connerton (Harmondsworth: Penguin, 1976), pp. 134–52. This is a short extract from Lorenzer's *Sprachzerstörung und Rekonstruktion* (Frankfurt: Suhrkamp, 1970).

37 *KHI*, p. 260.

38 *TP*, p. 9.

39 Jürgen Habermas, 'Toward a reconstruction of historical materialism', in *CES*, p. 148.

40 See Jean Piaget, *The Moral Judgement of the Child* (London: Routledge & Kegan Paul, 1932); and *Six Psychological Studies* (London: University of London Press, 1968). See also Lawrence Kohlberg, 'Stage and sequence: the cognitive-developmental approach to socialization', in *Handbook of Socialization Theory and Research*, edited by David A. Goslin (Chicago: Rand McNally, 1969), pp. 347–480; and 'From is to ought: how to commit the naturalistic fallacy and get away with it in the study of moral development', in *Cognitive Development and Epistemology*, edited by Theodore Mischel (New York: Academic Press, 1971), pp. 151–235.

41 Jürgen Habermas, 'Historical materialism and the development of normative structures', in *CES*, p. 97.

42 *LC*, p. 40.

43 Cf. Claus Offe, 'The abolition of market control and the problem of legitimacy, I and II', *Kapitalistate*, 1 and 2 (1973), pp. 109–16 and 73–5; 'Political authority and class structures', in *Critical Sociology* , pp. 388–421; and 'The theory of the capitalist state and the problem of policy formation' (unpublished paper presented at a conference in Florence, 1975).

44 *LC*, p. 95.

45 Jürgen Habermas, 'Wahrheitstheorien', in *Wirklichkeit und Reflexion: Walter Schulz zum 60. Geburtstag*, edited by Helmut Fahrenbach (Pfullingen: Neske, 1973), p. 220 (my translation).

46 *TP*, p. 18.

47 Jürgen Habermas, 'Wahrheitstheorien', p. 214 (my translation).

48 See ibid., p. 254.

49 Ibid., p. 229 (my translation).

50 Ibid., p. 241 (my translation).

51 Cf. Stephen Toulmin, *The Uses of Argument* (Cambridge: Cambridge University Press, 1958), chapter III.

52 See Jürgen Habermas, 'Wahrheitstheorien', p. 243.

53 Ibid., p. 244 (my translation).

54 Ibid., p. 245 (my translation).

55 Ibid., p. 250 (my translation).

56 See Jürgen Habermas, 'Toward a theory of communicative competence', in

Recent Sociology, no. 2, edited by Hans Peter Dreitzel (New York: Macmillan, 1970), p. 134.

57 Ibid., p. 138.
58 Jürgen Habermas, 'What is universal pragmatics?', in *CES*, p. 32 (translation modified).
59 Ibid., p. 36 (translation modified).
60 Jürgen Habermas, 'Vorbereitende Bemerkungen zu einer Theorie der kommunikativen Kompetenz', in Jürgen Habermas and Niklas Luhmann, *Theorie der Gesellschaft oder Sozialtechnologie – Was leistet die Systemforschung?* (Frankfurt: Suhrkamp, 1971), p. 110 (my translation).
61 Ibid., p. 137 (my translation).
62 Jürgen Habermas, 'Wahrheitstheorien', pp. 255–6 (my translation).
63 Jürgen Habermas, 'Vorbereitende Bemerkungen', p. 139 (my translation).
64 Jürgen Habermas, 'Wahrheitstheorien', p. 258 (my translation).
65 Jürgen Habermas, 'Toward a theory of communicative competence', p. 146.
66 Jürgen Habermas, 'Vorbereitende Bemerkungen', p. 120 (my translation).
67 *LC*, p. 113.
68 Jürgen Habermas, 'Vorbereitende Bemerkungen', p. 120 (my translation).
69 Cf. Edmund Husserl, *The Crisis of European Sciences and Transcendental Phenomenology: An Introduction to Phenomenological Philosophy*, trans. David Carr (Evanston: Northwestern University Press, 1970).
70 *KHI*, pp. 195–6.
71 Jürgen Habermas, 'Appendix', in *KHI*, pp. 316–17.
72 Jürgen Habermas, 'Vorbereitende Bemerkungen', p. 117 (my translation).
73 Jürgen Habermas, 'Wahrheitstheorien', p. 233 (my translation).
74 Jürgen Habermas, 'A postscript to *Knowledge and Human Interests*', trans. Christian Lenhardt, *Philosophy of the Social Sciences*, 3 (1973), p. 173.
75 Ibid., pp. 173–4.
76 *TP*, p. 20.
77 Jürgen Habermas, 'Postscript', p. 176.
78 Cf. P. F. Strawson, 'Truth', in his *Logico-Linguistic Papers* (London: Methuen, 1971), pp. 190–213.
79 Jürgen Habermas, 'Wahrheitstheorien', p. 219 (my translation).
80 Jürgen Habermas, 'Vorbereitende Bemerkungen', p. 136 (my translation).
81 *LC*, p. 110. Habermas's argument here is close to that developed by Apel in 'The *a priori* of the communication community and the foundations of ethics: the problem of a rational foundation of ethics in the scientific age', in his *Towards a Transformation of Philosophy*, pp. 225–300. However, Habermas criticises the 'residual decisionistic problematic' of Apel's account, a problematic which derives, according to Habermas, from Apel's concern with the presuppositions of argumentation rather than of communicative action (see *LC*, p. 159).
82 *TP*, p. 37.
83 Ibid., p. 159.
84 Ibid., p. 169.
85 Cf. Herbert Marcuse, 'Industrialization and capitalism in the work of Max Weber', in his *Negations*, trans. Jeremy J. Shapiro (Harmondsworth: Penguin, 1968), pp. 201–26.
86 Cf. Herbert Marcuse, *One Dimensional Man*, chapters 6 and 9.

87 Jürgen Habermas, 'Technology and science as "ideology"', in *TRS*, p. 88.
88 Ibid., p. 119.
89 Ibid., p. 92.
90 Ibid.
91 Jürgen Habermas, 'Toward a reconstruction of historical materialism', p. 132.
92 Jürgen Habermas, 'Historical materialism and the development of normative structures', p. 118.
93 Ibid. (translation modified).
94 Ibid., p. 119.
95 Ibid. (translation modified).
96 Ibid., pp. 119–20.
97 See Jürgen Habermas, 'Technology and science as "ideology"', p. 93.
98 Jürgen Habermas, 'Toward a theory of communicative competence', p. 120.
99 *KHI*, p. 272.
100 Jürgen Habermas, *Zur Logik der Sozialwissenschaften*, p. 294 (my translation).
101 Jürgen Habermas, *Theorie der Gesellschaft oder Sozialtechnologie?*, p. 194 (my translation).
102 *KHI*, p. 19.
103 Ibid., p. 272.
104 Jürgen Habermas, 'Postscript', p. 183.
105 Jürgen Habermas, 'Summation and response', trans. Martha Matesich, *Continuum*, 8 (1970), pp. 128–9.
106 *KHI*, p. 4.
107 Jürgen Habermas, *Zur Rekonstruktion des Historischen Materialismus* (Frankfurt: Suhrkamp, 1976), p. 57 (my translation).
108 Ibid., pp. 56–7 (my translation).
109 Jürgen Habermas, *Zur Logik der Sozialwissenschaften*, p. 308 (my translation).

4. Analysis of action

1 *PI*, sec. 244.
2 Cf. Ludwig Wittgenstein, *Zettel*, edited by G. E. M. Anscombe and G. H. von Wright, trans. G. E. M. Anscombe (Oxford: Basil Blackwell, 1967), secs. 540ff.; and Norman Malcolm, 'Knowledge of other minds', in *Wittgenstein: The 'Philosophical Investigations'*, edited by George Pitcher (London: Macmillan, 1966), pp. 371–83.
3 Cf. Norman Malcolm, 'Wittgenstein's *Philosophical Investigations*', in *Wittgenstein*, pp. 65–103.
4 For a discussion of this and other difficulties with the doctrine of avowals, see P. M. S. Hacker, *Insight and Illusion: Wittgenstein on Philosophy and the Metaphysics of Experience* (Oxford: Oxford University Press, 1972), chapter IX.
5 *PI*, p. 189.
6 G. E. Moore, 'Wittgenstein's lectures in 1930–33', in his *Philosophical Papers* (London: George Allen & Unwin, 1959), p. 316.
7 Cf. Alasdair MacIntyre, *The Unconscious: A Conceptual Analysis* (London: Routledge & Kegan Paul, 1958).
8 *PI*, sec. 108.
9 For example, see Ernst Konrad Specht, *The Foundations of Wittgenstein's Late*

Philosophy, trans. D. E. Walford (Manchester: Manchester University Press, 1969); and Stanley Cavell, *Must We Mean What We Say? A Book of Essays* (Cambridge: Cambridge University Press, 1976).

10 *PI*, sec. 217.

11 Ibid., sec. 415.

12 Cf. Ernest Gellner, 'The new idealism – cause and meaning in the social sciences', in *Positivism and Sociology*, edited by Anthony Giddens (London: Heinemann, 1974), pp. 129–56; I. C. Jarvie, 'Understanding and explanation in sociology and social anthropology', in *Explanation in the Behavioural Sciences*, edited by Robert Borger and Frank Cioffi (Cambridge: Cambridge University Press, 1970), pp. 231–48; and Karl-Otto Apel, *Analytic Philosophy of Language and the Geisteswissenschaften*, trans. H. Holstelilie (Dordrecht: D. Reidel, 1967).

13 *ISS*, pp. 64–5.

14 *PI*, sec. 199.

15 Ibid., secs. 54 and 82.

16 *ISS*, p. 32.

17 Cf. Alasdair MacIntyre, 'The idea of a social science', in *Rationality*, edited by Bryan R. Wilson (Oxford: Basil Blackwell, 1970), pp. 112–30.

18 *ISS*, p. 50.

19 Ibid., p. 121.

20 Ibid., p. 123.

21 Ibid., p. 129.

22 For a discussion of this point, see Don Ihde, *Hermeneutic Phenomenology: The Philosophy of Paul Ricoeur* (Evanston: Northwestern University Press, 1971), chapter 2.

23 Paul Ricoeur, 'Phenomenology and hermeneutics', in *HHS*, p. 120.

24 Cf. Anthony Kenny, *Action, Emotion and Will* (London: Routledge & Kegan Paul, 1963).

25 Paul Ricoeur, 'The model of the text: meaningful action considered as a text', in *HHS*, p. 205.

26 Ibid., p. 207.

27 Ibid., p. 208.

28 It is questionable, moreover, whether the interpretation of a text can be wholly abstracted from the socio-historical conditions of its production. Ricoeur clearly advocates such an abstraction (see, for example, his critique of 'historicism' in the essay entitled 'Appropriation', in *HHS*, pp. 182–93); however, his own interpretation of the work of Dilthey, for instance, firmly situates that work in a particular historical context (see 'The task of hermeneutics', in *HHS*, pp. 43–62).

29 Paul Ricoeur, 'The model of the text', p. 209.

30 Paul Ricoeur, 'Phenomenology of freedom', in *Phenomenology and Philosophical Understanding*, edited by Edo Pivčević (Cambridge: Cambridge University Press, 1975), p. 193.

31 *FN*, p. 123.

32 Ibid., p. 292.

33 Paul Ricoeur, 'The model of the text', p. 207.

34 Paul Ricoeur, 'The hermeneutical function of distanciation', trans. David Pellauer, *Philosophy Today*, 17 (1973), p. 135.

35 Jürgen Habermas, 'A postscript to *Knowledge and Human Interests*', trans. Christian Lenhardt, *Philosophy of the Social Sciences*, 3 (1973), p. 186.

36 See Thomas McCarthy, *The Critical Theory of Jürgen Habermas* (London: Hutchinson, 1978), chapter 1, section 2. Unfortunately, McCarthy does not pursue this observation in a critical direction, tending instead to endorse Habermas's distinction on an analytical level.

37 Jürgen Habermas, 'Der Universalitätsanspruche der Hermeneutik', in his *Kultur und Kritik* (Frankfurt: Suhrkamp, 1973), p. 278 (my translation).

38 Jürgen Habermas, 'Toward a theory of communicative competence', in *Recent Sociology*, no. 2, edited by Hans Peter Dreitzel (New York: Macmillan, 1970), p. 146.

39 Ibid.

40 Jürgen Habermas, 'Historical materialism and the development of normative structures', in *CES*, p. 99.

41 Cf. Michael Schmid, 'Habermas's theory of social evolution', trans. Nicholas Saul, in *Habermas: Critical Debates*, edited by John B. Thompson and David Held (London: Macmillan, forthcoming).

42 For a summary of the critical literature, see Sohan and Celia Modgil, *Piagetian Research: Compilation and Commentary* (Windsor: NFER, 1976); and Ved P. Varma and Philip Williams, editors, *Piaget, Psychology and Education* (London: Hodder & Stoughton, 1976). Some of the implications for Habermas's work of recent criticisms of Piaget's approach are discussed by Thomas McCarthy in 'Rationality and relativism: on Habermas's "overcoming" of hermeneutics', in *Habermas: Critical Debates*.

43 Cf. E. James Anthony, 'Emotions and intelligence', in *Piaget, Psychology and Education*, pp. 43–54.

44 Cf. Jean Piaget, *Structuralism*, trans. Chaninah Maschler (London: Routledge & Kegan Paul, 1971).

45 Giddens similarly argues that Habermas's theory of action and his emphasis on the normative components of interaction result in 'an "absent core" in Habermas's writings: an adequate conceptual scheme for grasping the production and reproduction of society'. See Anthony Giddens, 'Labour and interaction', in *Habermas: Critical Debates*.

46 Cf. Donald Davidson, 'The logical form of action sentences', in *The Logic of Decision and Action*, edited by Nicholas Rescher (Pittsburgh: University of Pittsburgh Press, 1966), pp. 81–95; and 'Agency', in *Agent, Action, and Reason*, edited by Robert Binkley et al. (Oxford: Basil Blackwell, 1971), pp. 3–25.

47 For a similar objection, see Don Locke, 'Action, movement, and neurophysiology', *Inquiry*, 17 (1974), pp. 23–42.

48 For example, see Quentin Skinner, ' "Social meaning" and the explanation of social action', in *Philosophy, Politics and Society*, fourth series, edited by Peter Laslett et al. (Oxford: Basil Blackwell, 1972), pp. 136–57.

49 Paul Ricoeur, 'The model of the text', p. 219.

50 Cf. Roland Barthes, *Elements of Semiology*, trans. Annette Lavers and Colin Smith (London: Jonathan Cape, 1967).

51 For example, see Roland Barthes, *Mythologies*, trans. Annette Lavers (St Albans: Paladin, 1973).

52 Cf. Anthony Giddens, *New Rules of Sociological Method: A Positive Critique of Interpretative Sociologies* (London: Hutchinson, 1976), pp. 118–29; 'Notes on

the theory of structuration', in his *Studies in Social and Political Theory* (London: Hutchinson, 1977), pp. 129–34; and *Central Problems in Social Theory: Action, Structure and Contradiction in Social Analysis* (London: Macmillan, 1979), chapters 2 and 3.

53 In his more recent work, Giddens relies increasingly upon notions like 'institutional form', 'mode of system reproduction' and 'structural principle' (see, for example, *Central Problems in Social Theory*, pp. 107, 110, 141ff.). This indicates, it seems to me, a move away from the conception of social structure as rules and resources; and indeed, it is by no means clear how this conception is to be reconciled with the notion of 'structural principle'.

54 Cf. Maurice Godelier, 'Structure and contradiction in *Capital*', in *Ideology in Social Science: Readings in Critical Social Theory*, edited by Robin Blackburn (London: Fontana/Collins, 1972), pp. 334–68; and *Rationality and Irrationality in Economics*, trans. Brian Pearce (London: New Left Books, 1972).

55 Pierre Bourdieu, *Outline of a Theory of Practice*, trans. Richard Nice (Cambridge: Cambridge University Press, 1977), p. 78.

56 See Roderick Bell et al., editors, *Political Power: A Reader in Theory and Research* (New York: The Free Press, 1969). For discussions of a more philosophical nature, see Hanna Fenichel Pitkin, *Wittgenstein and Justice: On the Significance of Ludwig Wittgenstein for Social and Political Thought* (Berkeley: University of California Press, 1972); Steven Lukes, *Power: A Radical View* (London: Macmillan, 1974); and William E. Connolly, *The Terms of Political Discourse* (Lexington, Mass.: D. C. Heath, 1974).

57 See Karl Mannheim, *Ideology and Utopia: An Introduction to the Sociology of Knowledge*, trans. Louis Wirth and Edward Shils (London: Routledge & Kegan Paul, 1936); and George Lichtheim, *The Concept of Ideology and Other Essays* (New York: Random House, 1967). For a recent discussion of a similar distinction, see Martin Seliger, *Ideology and Politics* (London: George Allen & Unwin, 1976).

58 Cf. Claus Mueller, 'Notes on the repression of communicative behavior', in *Recent Sociology*, no. 2, pp. 101–13; and *The Politics of Communication: A Study in the Political Sociology of Language, Socialization, and Legitimation* (New York: Oxford University Press, 1973).

59 Paul Ricoeur, 'Science and ideology', in *HHS*, pp. 222–46.

60 The current writings of Ricoeur reveal a fresh interest in problems of history and historicity. See, for example, 'History and hermeneutics', trans. David Pellauer, *Journal of Philosophy*, 73 (1976), pp. 683–95; and 'The narrative function', in *HHS*, pp. 274–96.

61 Cf. E. J. Lemmon, 'Comments on D. Davidson's "The logical form of action sentences"', in *The Logic of Decision and Action*, pp. 96–103.

62 Cf. Jacques Derrida, *Speech and Phenomena and Other Essays on Husserl's Theory of Signs*, trans. D. B. Allison (Evanston: Northwestern University Press, 1973).

63 Cf. Maurice Godelier, 'Foreword: functionalism, structuralism and Marxism', in his *Rationality and Irrationality in Economics*, pp. vii–xlii.

5. Methodology of social science

1 *ISS*, p. 82.

2 Cf. Ernest Gellner, 'Concepts and society', in *Rationality*, edited by Bryan R. Wilson (Oxford: Basil Blackwell, 1970), pp. 18–49; and Alasdair MacIntyre, 'Is understanding religion compatible with believing?', in *Rationality*, pp. 62–77.

3 Cf. A. R. Louch, 'The very idea of a social science', *Inquiry*, 6 (1963), pp. 273–86; and Peter Winch, 'Mr. Louch's idea of a social science', *Inquiry*, 7 (1964), pp. 202–8.

4 Peter Winch, 'Understanding a primitive society', in *Rationality*, pp. 78–111.

5 Ibid., p. 102.

6 Ibid., p. 107.

7 Ludwig Wittgenstein, *Philosophical Grammar*, edited by Rush Rhees, trans. Anthony Kenny (Oxford: Basil Blackwell, 1974), p. 13.

8 *ISS*, p. 128.

9 Ibid., p. 135; see also pp. 118–19.

10 For a wholly inadequate reply to a similar objection, see Peter Winch, 'Mr. Louch's idea of a social science'.

11 Cf. Ludwig Wittgenstein, *Lectures and Conversations on Aesthetics, Psychology and Religious Belief*, edited by Cyril Barrett (Oxford: Basil Blackwell, 1966), pp. 13ff.

12 Cf. J. L. Mackie, *The Cement of the Universe: A Study of Causation* (Oxford: Oxford University Press, 1975); and Ernest Sosa, editor, *Causation and Conditionals* (Oxford: Oxford University Press, 1975).

13 Cf. G. E. Moore, 'Wittgenstein's lectures in 1930–33', in his *Philosophical Papers* (London: George Allen & Unwin, 1959), pp. 252–324.

14 Cf. Alasdair MacIntyre, *The Unconscious: A Conceptual Analysis* (London: Routledge & Kegan Paul, 1958).

15 Cf. Margaret MacDonald, editor, *Philosophy and Analysis* (Oxford: Basil Blackwell, 1954).

16 Stephen Toulmin, 'The logical status of psychoanalysis', in *Philosophy and Analysis*, p. 138.

17 Antony Flew, 'Psycho-analytic explanation', in *Philosophy and Analysis*, p. 140.

18 Cf. Richard Peters, 'Cause, cure and motive', in *Philosophy and Analysis*, pp. 148–54.

19 Cf. Alfred Schutz, 'Common-sense and scientific interpretation of human action' and 'Concept and theory formation in the social sciences', in his *Collected Papers*, vol. I, edited by Maurice Natanson (The Hague: Martinus Nijhoff, 1962), pp. 3–47 and 48–66.

20 *ISS*, p. 87.

21 Ibid., p. 89.

22 Peter Winch, 'Understanding a primitive society', p. 97.

23 Cf. Ernest Gellner, 'The new idealism – cause and meaning in the social sciences', in *Positivism and Sociology*, edited by Anthony Giddens (London: Heinemann, 1974), pp. 129–56; and I. C. Jarvie, 'Understanding and explanation in sociology and social anthropology', in *Explanation in the Behavioural Sciences*, edited by Robert Borger and Frank Cioffi (Cambridge: Cambridge University Press, 1970), pp. 231–48.

24 Peter Winch, 'Understanding a primitive society', p. 84.

25 *FN*, p. 13.

26 Ibid., p. 67.

27 For a discussion of this point, see Donald Davidson, 'Action, reasons, and causes', in *The Philosophy of Action*, edited by Alan R. White (Oxford: Oxford University Press, 1968), pp. 79–94; and 'Causal relations', in *Causation and Conditionals*, pp. 82–94.

28 Cf. G. E. M. Anscombe, 'Causality and determination', in *Causation and Conditionals*, pp. 63–81.

29 *FP*, p. 363.

30 Paul Ricoeur, 'Le discours de l'action', in Paul Ricoeur et al., *La Sémantique de l'action* (Paris: Editions du Centre National de la Recherche Scientifique, 1977), p. 92 (my translation).

31 Cf. G. E. M. Anscombe, *Intention* (Oxford: Basil Blackwell, 1972).

32 Cf. H. L. A. Hart, 'The ascription of responsibility and rights', *Proceedings of the Aristotelian Society*, 49 (1948–9), pp. 171–94.

33 Paul Ricoeur, 'The model of the text: meaningful action considered as a text', in *HHS*, p. 219.

34 Ibid., p. 220.

35 Paul Ricoeur, 'Hermeneutics and the critique of ideology', in *HHS*, p. 89.

36 Jürgen Habermas, 'On communicative action' (unpublished paper).

37 Jürgen Habermas, 'What is universal pragmatics', in *CES*, p. 12.

38 For a critical discussion of Habermas's idea of a 'reconstructive science', see Mary Hesse, 'Science and objectivity', in *Habermas: Critical Debates*, edited by John B. Thompson and David Held (London: Macmillan, forthcoming).

39 *KHI*, p. 314.

40 Jürgen Habermas, 'Toward a theory of communicative competence', in *Recent Sociology*, no. 2, edited by Hans Peter Dreitzel (New York: Macmillan, 1970), p. 144.

41 *LC*, p. 113.

42 Jürgen Habermas, 'Wahrheitstheorien', in *Wirklichkeit und Reflexion: Walter Schulz zum 60. Geburtstag*, edited by Helmut Fahrenbach (Pfullingen: Neske, 1973), p. 219 (my translation).

43 I owe this point concerning personal identity to Steven Lukes, who develops it in an essay entitled 'Of gods and demons: Habermas and practical reason', in *Habermas: Critical Debates*.

44 Cf. Thomas McCarthy, *The Critical Theory of Jürgen Habermas* (London: Hutchinson, 1978), chapter 2, section 5.

45 See the objections of Gadamer and Giegel, quoted by Habermas in the new introduction to *Theory and Practice*. For a competent discussion of these and other objections, see Anthony Giddens, 'Habermas's critique of hermeneutics', in *Studies in Social and Political Theory* (London: Hutchinson, 1977), pp. 135–64.

46 *TP*, p. 30.

47 I leave open the question of the extent to which the concepts introduced here could be aligned with recent Anglo-Saxon analyses of causality (see notes 12 and 27), since these analyses are themselves in a state of considerable disarray. An intriguing approach to these issues may be found in the work of Roy Bhaskar, who interprets causal laws as tendencies of generative mechanisms and structures; see *A Realist Theory of Science* (Hassocks, Sussex: Harvester, 1978), and *The Possibility of Naturalism: A Philosophical Critique of the Contemporary Human Sciences* (Hassocks, Sussex: Harvester, 1979).

48 Pierre Bourdieu, *Outline of a Theory of Practice*, trans. Richard Nice (Cambridge: Cambridge University Press, 1977), p. 72.

49 The concept of structuration is developed by Anthony Giddens in, for instance, *New Rules of Sociological Method: A Positive Critique of Interpretative Sociologies* (London: Hutchinson, 1976). My use of this concept differs from Giddens's, in accordance with my criticism of his account of the relation between action and structure.

50 Cf. Louis Althusser and Étienne Balibar, *Reading Capital*, trans. Ben Brewster (London: New Left Books, 1972).

51 Louis Althusser, *Reading Capital*, p. 190.

52 The idea of a complementarity between explanation and understanding receives some sympathy in recent Anglo-Saxon philosophy, but the authors concerned have failed to connect this idea to institutional and structural considerations. See Charles Taylor, *The Explanation of Behaviour* (London: Routledge & Kegan Paul, 1964); and Georg Henrik von Wright, *Explanation and Understanding* (London: Routledge & Kegan Paul, 1971).

53 Pierre Bourdieu, *Outline of a Theory of Practice*, p. 15.

54 Cf. Paul Willis, *Learning to Labour: How Working Class Kids Get Working Class Jobs* (Farnborough, Hants.: Saxon House, 1977).

55 Ibid., p. 119.

56 See Aaron V. Cicourel, *Method and Measurement in Sociology* (New York: The Free Press, 1964), and *The Social Organization of Juvenile Justice* (New York: John Wiley & Sons, 1968); see also Jack D. Douglas, *The Social Meanings of Suicide* (Princeton: Princeton University Press, 1967). For a perceptive discussion of this literature, see Barry Hindess, *The Use of Official Statistics in Sociology: A Critique of Positivism and Ethnomethodology* (London: Macmillan, 1973).

57 For a classic example of this use of statistics, see V. I. Lenin, *The Development of Capitalism in Russia* (Moscow: Progress Publishers, 1972).

58 See the contributions of John R. Searle, G. E. M. Anscombe and Philippa Foot in *The Is/Ought Question*, edited by W. D. Hudson (London: Macmillan, 1969).

59 Cf. Julius Kovesi, *Moral Notions* (London: Routledge & Kegan Paul, 1967); and William E. Connolly, *The Terms of Political Discourse* (Lexington, Mass.: D. C. Heath, 1974).

60 Cf. Mary Hesse, 'Theory and value in the social sciences', in *Action and Interpretation: Studies in the Philosophy of the Social Sciences*, edited by Christopher Hookway and Philip Pettit (Cambridge: Cambridge University Press, 1978), pp. 1–16.

61 Cf. Maurice Godelier, *Rationality and Irrationality in Economics*, trans. Brian Pearce (London: New Left Books, 1972).

6. Theory of reference and truth

1 Cf. Saul Kripke, 'Naming and necessity', in *Semantics of Natural Languages*, edited by Donald Davidson and Gilbert Harman (Dordrecht: D. Reidel, 1972), pp. 253–355; and Keith Donnellan, 'Proper names and identifying descriptions', in *Semantics of Natural Languages*, pp. 356–79.

2 P. F. Strawson, *Individuals: An Essay in Descriptive Metaphysics* (London: Methuen, 1959), p. 182.

3 John R. Searle, *Speech Acts: An Essay in the Philosophy of Language* (Cambridge: Cambridge University Press, 1970), p. 84.

4 Cf. Sigmund Freud, *The Interpretation of Dreams*, trans. James Strachey (Harmondsworth: Penguin, 1976).

5 Peter Winch, 'Understanding a primitive society', in *Rationality*, edited by Bryan R. Wilson (Oxford: Basil Blackwell, 1970), p. 82.

6 Peter Winch, 'Comment', in *Explanation in the Behavioural Sciences*, edited by Robert Borger and Frank Cioffi (Cambridge: Cambridge University Press, 1970), p. 256.

7 Cf. I. C. Jarvie, 'Understanding and explanation in sociology and social anthropology', in *Explanation in the Behavioural Sciences*, pp. 231–48.

8 Ludwig Wittgenstein, *On Certainty*, edited by G. E. M. Anscombe and G. H. von Wright, trans. Denis Paul and G. E. M. Anscombe (Oxford: Basil Blackwell, 1974), sec. 199.

9 Cf. John R. Searle, *Speech Acts*, pp. 136–41.

10 G. J. Warnock, 'A problem about truth', in *Truth*, edited by George Pitcher (New Jersey: Prentice-Hall, 1964), p. 57.

11 Ludwig Wittgenstein, *Lectures and Conversations on Aesthetics, Psychology and Religious Belief*, edited by Cyril Barrett (Oxford: Basil Blackwell, 1966), p. 18.

12 Ibid., p. 44.

13 See certain passages in Alasdair MacIntyre, *The Unconscious: A Conceptual Analysis* (London: Routledge & Kegan Paul, 1958).

14 Michael Scriven, 'The experimental investigation of psychoanalysis', in *Psychoanalysis, Scientific Method, and Philosophy*, edited by Sidney Hook (New York: New York University Press, 1959), p. 227. See also Ernest Nagel, 'Methodological issues in psychoanalytic theory', in the same volume.

15 See Thomas S. Kuhn, *The Structure of Scientific Revolutions* (Chicago: University of Chicago Press, 1970); Imre Lakatos and Alan Musgrave, editors, *Criticism and the Growth of Knowledge* (Cambridge: Cambridge University Press, 1970); and Paul Feyerabend, *Against Method: Outline of an Anarchistic Theory of Knowledge* (London: New Left Books, 1975). For an illuminating discussion of this material, see Mary Hesse, 'In defence of objectivity', *Proceedings of the British Academy*, 58 (1972), pp. 275–92.

16 Peter Winch, 'Understanding a primitive society', p. 99.

17 Peter Winch, 'Nature and convention', in his *Ethics and Action* (London: Routledge & Kegan Paul, 1972), p. 61.

18 R. M. Beardsmore, *Moral Reasoning* (London: Routledge & Kegan Paul, 1969), p. 34. See also D. Z. Phillips and H. O. Mounce, 'On morality's having a point', in *The Is/Ought Question*, edited by W. D. Hudson (London: Macmillan, 1969), pp. 228–39.

19 *FN*, p. 375.

20 Ibid., p. 392.

21 *FP*, p. 422.

22 Ibid., p. 432.

23 *RM*, p. 216.

24 Ibid., p. 298.

25 Ibid., p. 229.

26 Cf. Mary Hesse, *Models and Analogies in Science* (Notre Dame, Indiana: University of Notre Dame Press, 1966).

27 Cf. Max Black, *Models and Metaphors: Studies in Language and Philosophy* (New York: Cornell University Press, 1962).
28 *RM*, p. 309.
29 Cf. Charles Taylor, 'Interpretation and the sciences of man', *Review of Metaphysics*, 25 (1971), pp. 3–51.
30 Paul Ricoeur, 'The model of the text: meaningful action considered as a text', in *HHS*, p. 213.
31 Cf. Karl Popper, *The Logic of Scientific Discovery* (London: Hutchinson, 1959).
32 Cf. E. D. Hirsch, *Validity in Interpretation* (New Haven: Yale University Press, 1967).
33 Cf. Paul Ricoeur, 'The question of proof in Freud's psychoanalytic writings', in *HHS*, pp. 247–73.
34 Ibid., p. 271.
35 Cf. Martin Heidegger, 'On the essence of truth', trans. R. Hall and Alan Crick, in Heidegger's *Existence and Being* (London: Vision Press, 1949), pp. 317–51.
36 Ibid., p. 338.
37 Paul Ricoeur, 'Existence and hermeneutics', trans. Kathleen McLaughlin, in *CI*, p. 11.
38 Jürgen Habermas, 'A postscript to *Knowledge and Human Interests*', trans. Christian Lenhardt, *Philosophy of the Social Sciences*, 3 (1973), p. 173.
39 Ibid., p. 174.
40 Jürgen Habermas, 'Wahrheitstheorien', in *Wirklichkeit und Reflexion: Walter Schulz zum 60. Geburtstag*, edited by Helmut Fahrenbach (Pfullingen: Neske, 1973), p. 240 (my translation, although 'warranted assertability' appears in English in the original). Weaker versions of Habermas's thesis are suggested by Thomas McCarthy on pages 149–50 of 'A theory of communicative competence', *Philosophy of the Social Sciences*, 3 (1973), pp. 135–56. However, if my interpretation of Habermas is correct, then such attenuations do not obviate the present difficulty, which is that the truth of a statement is not settled when its assertion has been justified, irrespective of whether that justification is characterised as the 'meaning', 'condition' or 'criterion' of truth.
41 It might be said, in Habermas's defence, that the foregoing argument overlooks a distinction between the justification of the assertion of a statement and the justification of the validity claim connected with the speech-act by which the statement is asserted. However, Habermas himself constantly elides the distinction (see, for example, 'Wahrheitstheorien', p. 212), and he never elucidates in any detail the idea of 'the validity claim connected with the speech-act'. At a later stage, I shall attempt to defend a justificatory analysis of truth by emphasising a somewhat similar distinction.
42 Jürgen Habermas, 'Postscript', p. 168.
43 Ibid., p. 170.
44 Ibid., p. 169.
45 For example, see Y. Bar-Hillel, 'On Habermas' hermeneutic philosophy of language', *Synthese*, 26 (1973), pp. 1–12.
46 Jürgen Habermas, 'What is universal pragmatics?' in *CES*, p. 3.
47 Ibid., p. 1 (translation modified).
48 I criticise Habermas's restriction of his analysis to speech-acts in the 'standard form', as well as other aspects of his theory of language, in my essay on

'Universal pragmatics', in *Habermas: Critical Debates*, edited by John B. Thompson and David Held (London: Macmillan, forthcoming). Habermas replies to these criticisms in his contribution to the same volume; unfortunately, this contribution did not arrive in time for it to be taken into consideration here.

49 Habermas's claim that the construction of an ideal speech situation implies a model of pure communicative action (see above, p. 93) does not mitigate the problem, because communicative action is defined so as to exclude considerations of interest and strategy, of power and persuasion; thus the latter are not thematised and suspended by the model of pure communicative action, but simply ignored.

50 For a perceptive analysis of these connections, see Anthony Giddens, 'Habermas's critique of hermeneutics', in his *Studies in Social and Political Theory* (London: Hutchinson, 1977), pp. 135–64, especially p. 152.

51 Keith Donnellan, 'Speaking of nothing', *Philosophical Review*, 83 (1974), p. 16.

52 Cf. Saul Kripke, 'Naming and necessity'.

53 Cf. Roland Barthes, *Mythologies*, trans. Annette Lavers (St Albans: Paladin, 1973); and Judith Williamson, *Decoding Advertisements: Ideology and Meaning in Advertising* (London: Marion Boyars, 1978). See also the suggestive study by Bisseret, who argues that expressions employed by members of the dominated sex and class have a 'hidden social referent', namely the individualised male of the dominant class; Noëlle Bisseret, *Education, Class Language and Ideology*, trans. Diana Barker et al. (London: Routledge & Kegan Paul, 1979).

54 Roland Barthes, *Mythologies*, p. 119.

55 In adopting this approach to the status of social structure, I wish to steer a course between a reductionist account of social structure which would treat it as a mere heuristic device, and a crude realist view which would regard it as some sort of 'thing' erected in the social world. As a series of elements which define the conditions for the persistence of a social formation and for the variation of its component institutions, social structure has the status of *conditions of possibility*. Whether this approach could be characterised as a form of 'transcendental realism', to borrow a label from Roy Bhaskar, is a question which I cannot pursue here. See Roy Bhaskar, *A Realist Theory of Science* (Hassocks, Sussex: Harvester, 1978).

56 Cf. Richard M. Martin, 'Truth and its illicit surrogates', *Neue Hefte für Philosophie*, 2 (1972), pp. 95–110; and Hilary Putnam, 'Reference and understanding', in his *Meaning and the Moral Sciences* (London: Routledge & Kegan Paul, 1978), pp. 97–119.

57 Cf. Stephen Toulmin, *The Uses of Argument* (Cambridge: Cambridge University Press, 1958), chapter III.

58 For a typical example of institutional analysis, see Alvin W. Gouldner, *Patterns of Industrial Bureaucracy* (New York: The Free Press, 1954). A more provocative discussion of similar issues may be found in Pierre Bourdieu, *Outline of a Theory of Practice*, trans. Richard Nice (Cambridge: Cambridge University Press, 1977).

59 Cf. V. I. Lenin, *The Development of Capitalism in Russia* (Moscow: Progress Publishers, 1972).

60 Cf. Mary Hesse, *The Structure of Scientific Inference* (London: Macmillan, 1974); and 'Theory and value in the social sciences', in *Action and Interpretation:*

Studies in the Philosophy of the Social Sciences, edited by Christopher Hookway and Philip Pettit (Cambridge: Cambridge University Press, 1978), pp. 1–16.

61 It may be objected that to appeal to the conditions for understanding statements, and thence to grant truth a privileged position in the analysis of meaning, is to begin from a linguistic basis which is even narrower than Habermas's. Perhaps this objection could be averted if, first, principles could be established which would show how utterances in different moods were related to indicative sentences; and second, the notion of truth could be freed from reference to a pre-given object domain.

62 See Donald Davidson, 'Meaning and truth', *Synthese,* 17 (1967), pp. 304–23. For discussions of some of the questions arising from this article, see *Truth and Meaning: Essays on Semantics,* edited by Gareth Evans and John McDowell (Oxford: Oxford University Press, 1976); and *Reference, Truth and Reality: Essays on the Philosophy of Language,* edited by Mark Platts (London: Routledge & Kegan Paul, 1980). My cursory comments on the relation between meaning and truth skate over the issues which divide 'realists' like Davidson from 'anti-realists' such as Dummett. Without wishing here to take a specific stand on these issues, I believe that many of Dummett's objections are sound.

63 Jürgen Habermas, 'Postscript', p. 184.

64 In a recent discussion, Habermas acknowledged that the reconstruction of the conditions of action and speech is a task which cannot be accommodated within the epistemological framework of *Knowledge and Human Interests* (seminar in Cambridge, 23 February 1979).

65 Paul Ricoeur, 'A philosophical interpretation of Freud', trans. Willis Domingo, in *CI,* p. 172.

66 Jürgen Habermas, 'Vorbereitende Bemerkungen zu einer Theorie der kommunikativen Kompetenz', in Jürgen Habermas and Niklas Luhmann, *Theorie der Gesellschaft oder Sozialtechnologie – Was leistet die Systemforschung?* (Frankfurt: Suhrkamp, 1971), p. 120 (my translation).

Select bibliography

The bibliography contains a selection of the works cited in the notes and references. The items selected are those which are of particular importance for the issues discussed in the text. No attempt is made to provide an exhaustive list of the writings of Ricoeur and Habermas, nor to mention the many works which examine their views. For a full bibliography of Ricoeur's writings up to 1972, see:

Vansina, Dirk F. 'Bibliographie de Paul Ricoeur (jusqu'au 30 juin 1962)', *Revue philosophique de Louvain*, 60 (1962), pp. 394–413
  'Bibliographie de Paul Ricoeur, compléments (jusqu'à la fin de 1967)', *Revue philosophique de Louvain*, 66 (1968), pp. 85–101
  'Bibliographie de Paul Ricoeur, compléments (jusqu'à la fin de 1972)', *Revue philosophique de Louvain*, 72 (1974), pp. 156–81

An abridged and updated version of this bibliography may be found on pages 180–94 of:

Reagan, Charles E., ed. *Studies in the Philosophy of Paul Ricoeur*. Athens, Ohio: Ohio University Press, 1979

The secondary literature on Ricoeur's work is compiled in:

Lapointe, Francois H. 'Paul Ricoeur and his critics: a bibliographic essay', in *Studies in the Philosophy of Paul Ricoeur*, pp. 164–77

For a complete bibliography of Habermas's writings up to 1978, see:

Görtzen, Rene and van Gelder, Frederik. 'Jürgen Habermas: the complete oeuvre. A bibliography of primary literature, translations and reviews', *Human Studies*, 2 (1979)

This bibliography will be reprinted in the second edition of:

McCarthy, Thomas. *The Critical Theory of Jürgen Habermas*. London: Hutchinson, 1978

Some of the secondary literature on Habermas's work is cited in the bibliography to:

Thompson, John B. and Held, David, eds. *Habermas: Critical Debates*. London: Macmillan, forthcoming

If an article mentioned in the notes and references is reprinted in a collection of papers by the same author, then the collection alone is cited in the bibliography. When an article is published in a volume which includes relevant papers by other authors, the article and the volume are listed separately. Where an English translation exists of material originally published in French or German, only the English version is given; but in the case of books by Ricoeur and Habermas, the original date of publication is added in square brackets.

241

Adorno, Theodor et al. *The Positivist Dispute in German Sociology*, tr. Glyn Adey and David Frisby. London: Heinemann, 1976

Althusser, Louis and Balibar, Etienne. *Reading Capital*, tr. Ben Brewster. London: New Left Books, 1972

Anscombe, G. E. M. 'Causality and determination', in *Causation and Conditionals*, ed. Ernest Sosa, pp. 63–81. Oxford: Oxford University Press, 1975
Intention. Oxford: Basil Blackwell, 1972

Anthony, E. James. 'Emotions and intelligence', in *Piaget, Psychology and Education*, ed. Ved P. Varma and Philip Williams, pp. 43–54. London: Hodder & Stoughton, 1976

Apel, Karl-Otto. *Analytic Philosophy of Language and the Geisteswissenschaften*, tr. H. Holstelilie. Dordrecht: D. Reidel, 1967
'Communication and the foundations of the humanities', *Acta Sociologica*, 15–16 (1972–3), pp. 7–26
Towards a Transformation of Philosophy, tr. Glyn Adey and David Frisby. London: Routledge & Kegan Paul, 1980

Austin, J. L. *How to do Things with Words*, second edition, ed. J. O. Urmson and Marina Sbisà. Oxford: Oxford University Press, 1976
Philosophical Papers, ed. J. O. Urmson and G. J. Warnock. Oxford: Oxford University Press, 1970
Sense and Sensibilia, ed. G. J. Warnock. Oxford: Oxford University Press, 1962

Ayer, A. J. *Language, Truth and Logic*, second edition. London: Victor Gollancz, 1967
ed. *Logical Positivism*. New York: The Free Press, 1959
et al. *The Revolution in Philosophy*. London: Macmillan, 1956

Bar-Hillel, Y. 'On Habermas' hermeneutic philosophy of language', *Synthese*, 26 (1973), pp. 1–12

Barthes, Roland. *Elements of Semiology*, tr. Annette Lavers and Colin Smith. London: Jonathan Cape, 1967
Mythologies, tr. Annette Lavers. St Albans: Paladin, 1973

Beardsmore, R. M. *Moral Reasoning*. London: Routledge & Kegan Paul, 1969

Bell, Roderick et al., eds. *Political Power: A Reader in Theory and Research*. New York: The Free Press, 1969

Benveniste, Emile. 'La forme et le sens dans le langage', in *Le Langage*, ii: *actes du XIIIᵉ congrès des sociétés de philosophie de langue française*, pp. 29–40. Neuchâtel: Editions de la Baconnière, 1967
Problems in General Linguistics, tr. Mary Elizabeth Meek. Florida: University of Miami Press, 1971

Bernstein, Eduard. *Evolutionary Socialism: A Criticism and Affirmation*, tr. Edith C. Harvey. New York: Schocken, 1961

Bhaskar, Roy. *The Possibility of Naturalism: A Philosophical Critique of the Contemporary Human Sciences*. Hassocks, Sussex: Harvester, 1979
A Realist Theory of Science. Hassocks, Sussex: Harvester, 1978

Binkley, Robert et al., eds. *Agent, Action, and Reason*. Oxford: Basil Blackwell, 1971

Bisseret, Noëlle. *Education, Class Language and Ideology*, tr. Diana Barker et al. London: Routledge & Kegan Paul, 1979

Black, Max. *Models and Metaphors: Studies in Language and Philosophy*. New York: Cornell University Press, 1962

Borger, Robert and Cioffi, Frank, eds. *Explanation in the Behavioural Sciences.* Cambridge: Cambridge University Press, 1970

Bourdieu, Pierre. *Outline of a Theory of Practice,* tr. Richard Nice. Cambridge: Cambridge University Press, 1977

Bukharin, Nikolai. *Historical Materialism: A System of Sociology.* Ann Arbor: University of Michigan Press, 1969

Carnap, Rudolf. *The Logical Structure of the World,* tr. Rolf A. George. London: Routledge & Kegan Paul, 1967

Cavell, Stanley. *Must We Mean What We Say? A Book of Essays.* Cambridge: Cambridge University Press, 1976

Cicourel, Aaron V. *Method and Measurement in Sociology.* New York: The Free Press, 1964

  The Social Organization of Juvenile Justice. New York: John Wiley & Sons, 1968

Connerton, Paul, ed. *Critical Sociology.* Harmondsworth: Penguin, 1976

Connolly, William E. *The Terms of Political Discourse.* Lexington, Mass.: D. C. Heath, 1974

Davidson, Donald. 'Action, reasons, and causes', in *The Philosophy of Action,* ed. Alan R. White, pp. 79–94. Oxford: Oxford University Press, 1968

  'Agency', in *Agent, Action, and Reason,* ed. Robert Binkley et al., pp. 3–25. Oxford: Basil Blackwell, 1971

  'Causal relations', in *Causation and Conditionals,* ed. Ernest Sosa, pp. 82–94. Oxford: Oxford University Press, 1975

  'The logical form of action sentences', in *The Logic of Decision and Action,* ed. Nicholas Rescher, pp. 81–95. Pittsburgh: University of Pittsburgh Press, 1966

  'Meaning and truth', *Synthese,* 17 (1967), pp. 304–23

  and Harman, Gilbert, eds. *Semantics of Natural Languages.* Dordrecht: D. Reidel, 1972

Derrida, Jacques. *Speech and Phenomena and Other Essays on Husserl's Theory of Signs,* tr. D. B. Allison. Evanston: Northwestern University Press, 1973

Dilthey, Wilhelm. *Selected Writings,* ed. and tr. H. P. Rickman. Cambridge: Cambridge University Press, 1976

Donnellan, Keith. 'Proper names and identifying descriptions', in *Semantics of Natural Languages,* ed. Donald Davidson and Gilbert Harman, pp. 356–79. Dordrecht: D. Reidel, 1972

  'Speaking of nothing', *Philosophical Review,* 83 (1974), pp. 3–31

Dreitzel, Hans Peter, ed. *Recent Sociology,* no. 2. New York: Macmillan, 1970

Dufrenne, Mikel. *Language and Philosophy,* tr. Henry B. Veatch. New York: Greenwood Press, 1968

Engels, Frederick. *Herr Eugen Dührings Revolution in Science (Anti-Dühring),* tr. Emile Burns. London: Martin Lawrence, n.d.

  'Introduction to Karl Marx's work *The Class Struggles in France, 1848–1850*', in *Karl Marx and Frederick Engels, Selected Works,* pp. 641–58. London: Lawrence & Wishart, 1968

Ermarth, Michael. *Wilhelm Dilthey: The Critique of Historical Reason.* Chicago: University of Chicago Press, 1978

Evans, Gareth and McDowell, John, eds. *Truth and Meaning: Essays on Semantics.* Oxford: Oxford University Press, 1976

Feyerabend, Paul. *Against Method: Outline of an Anarchistic Theory of Knowledge.* London: New Left Books, 1975

Flew, Antony. 'Psycho-analytic explanation', in *Philosophy and Analysis*, ed. Margaret MacDonald, pp. 139–48. Oxford: Basil Blackwell, 1954

Freud, Sigmund. *The Interpretation of Dreams*, tr. James Strachey. Harmondsworth: Penguin, 1976

Gadamer, Hans-Georg. *Truth and Method*. London: Sheed & Ward, 1975

Gellner, Ernest. 'Concepts and society', in *Rationality*, ed. Bryan R. Wilson, pp. 18–49. Oxford: Basil Blackwell, 1970

'The new idealism – cause and meaning in the social sciences', in *Positivism and Sociology*, ed. Anthony Giddens, pp. 129–56. London: Heinemann, 1974

Giddens, Anthony. *Central Problems in Social Theory: Action, Structure and Contradiction in Social Analysis*. London: Macmillan, 1979

'Labour and interaction', in *Habermas: Critical Debates*, ed. John B. Thompson and David Held. London: Macmillan, forthcoming

New Rules of Sociological Method: A Positive Critique of Interpretative Sociologies. London: Hutchinson, 1976

Studies in Social and Political Theory. London: Hutchinson, 1977

ed. *Positivism and Sociology*. London: Heinemann, 1974

Godelier, Maurice. *Rationality and Irrationality in Economics*, tr. Brian Pearce. London: New Left Books, 1972

'Structure and contradiction in *Capital*', in *Ideology in Social Science: Readings in Critical Social Theory*, ed. Robin Blackburn, pp. 334–68. London: Fontana/Collins, 1972

Grice, H. P. '"Meaning"', in *Philosophical Logic*, ed. P. F. Strawson, pp. 39–48. Oxford: Oxford University Press, 1967

Habermas, Jürgen. 'The analytical theory of science and dialectics', in Theodor Adorno et al., *The Positivist Dispute in German Sociology*, tr. Glyn Adey and David Frisby, pp. 131–62. London: Heinemann, 1976

Communication and the Evolution of Society, tr. Thomas McCarthy. London: Heinemann, 1979

Knowledge and Human Interests, tr. Jeremy J. Shapiro. London: Heinemann, 1972 [1968]

Kultur und Kritik. Frankfurt: Suhrkamp, 1973

Legitimation Crisis, tr. Thomas McCarthy. London: Heinemann, 1976 [1973]

'On communicative action', unpublished paper

'A postscript to *Knowledge and Human Interests*', tr. Christian Lenhardt, *Philosophy of the Social Sciences*, 3 (1973), pp. 157–89

'Summation and response', tr. Martha Matesich, *Continuum*, 8 (1970), pp. 123–33

Theory and Practice, tr. John Viertel. London: Heinemann, 1974 [1963]

Toward a Rational Society: Student Protest, Science, and Politics, tr. Jeremy J. Shapiro. London: Heinemann, 1971

'Toward a theory of communicative competence', in *Recent Sociology*, no. 2, ed. Hans Peter Dreitzel, pp. 115–48. New York: Macmillan, 1970

'Wahrheitstheorien', in *Wirklichkeit und Reflexion: Walter Schulz zum 60. Geburtstag*, ed. Helmut Fahrenbach, pp. 211–65. Pfullingen: Neske, 1973

Zur Logik der Sozialwissenschaften. Frankfurt: Suhrkamp, 1970

Zur Rekonstruktion des Historischen Materialismus. Frankfurt: Suhrkamp, 1976

and Luhmann, Niklas. *Theorie der Gesellschaft oder Sozialtechnologie – Was leistet die Systemforschung?* Frankfurt: Suhrkamp, 1971 et al., eds. *Hermeneutik und Ideologiekritik*. Frankfurt: Suhrkamp, 1971

Hacker, P. M. S. *Insight and Illusion: Wittgenstein on Philosophy and the Metaphysics of Experience*. Oxford: Oxford University Press, 1972

Hare, R. M. *The Language of Morals*. Oxford: Oxford University Press, 1952

Hart, H. L. A. 'The ascription of responsibility and rights', *Proceedings of the Aristotelian Society*, 49 (1948–9), pp. 171–94

Hegel, G. W. F. *The Phenomenology of Mind*, tr. J. B. Baillie. New York: Harper & Row, 1967

Heidegger, Martin. *Being and Time*, tr. John Macquarrie and Edmund Robinson. Oxford: Basil Blackwell, 1967

Existence and Being, tr. Alan Crick et al. London: Vision Press, 1949

On the Way to Language, tr. Peter D. Hertz. New York: Harper & Row, 1971

Poetry, Language, Thought, tr. Albert Hofstadter. New York: Harper & Row, 1971

Held, David. *Introduction to Critical Theory: Horkheimer to Habermas*. London: Hutchinson, 1980

Hesse, Mary. 'In defence of objectivity', *Proceedings of the British Academy*, 58 (1972), pp. 275–92

Models and Analogies in Science. Indiana: University of Notre Dame Press, 1966

'Science and objectivity', in *Habermas: Critical Debates*, ed. John B. Thompson and David Held. London: Macmillan, forthcoming

The Structure of Scientific Inference. London: Macmillan, 1974

'Theory and value in the social sciences', in *Action and Interpretation: Studies in the Philosophy of the Social Sciences*, ed. Christopher Hookway and Philip Pettit, pp. 1–16. Cambridge: Cambridge University Press, 1978

Hindess, Barry. *The Use of Official Statistics in Sociology: A Critique of Positivism and Ethnomethodology*. London: Macmillan, 1973

Hirsch, E. D. *Validity in Interpretation*. New Haven: Yale University Press, 1967

Hjelmslev, Louis. *Prolegomena to a Theory of Language*, tr. Francis J. Whitfield. Madison: University of Wisconsin Press, 1966

Hook, Sidney, ed. *Psychoanalysis, Scientific Method, and Philosophy*. New York: New York University Press, 1959

Hookway, Christopher and Pettit, Philip, eds. *Action and Interpretation: Studies in the Philosophy of the Social Sciences*. Cambridge: Cambridge University Press, 1978

Horkheimer, Max. *Critical Theory: Selected Essays*, tr. Matthew J. O'Connell et al. New York: Herder & Herder, 1972

Eclipse of Reason. New York: Oxford University Press, 1947

and Adorno, Theodor. *Dialectic of Enlightenment*, tr. John Cumming. London: Allen Lane, 1973

Hudson, W. D., ed. *The Is/Ought Question*. London: Macmillan, 1969

Hughes, H. Stuart. *Consciousness and Society: The Reorientation of European Social Thought 1890–1930*. St Albans: Paladin, 1974

Husserl, Edmund. *Cartesian Meditations: An Introduction to Phenomenology*, tr. Dorion Cairns. The Hague: Martinus Nijhoff, 1960

The Crisis of European Sciences and Transcendental Phenomenology: An Introduction to Phenomenological Philosophy, tr. David Carr. Evanston: Northwestern University Press, 1970

Ideas: General Introduction to Pure Phenomenology, tr. W. R. Boyce Gibson. London: George Allen & Unwin, 1931

Ihde, Don. *Hermeneutic Phenomenology: The Philosophy of Paul Ricoeur*. Evanston: Northwestern University Press, 1971

Jarvie, I. C. 'Understanding and explanation in sociology and social anthropology', in *Explanation in the Behavioural Sciences*, ed. Robert Borger and Frank Cioffi, pp. 231–48. Cambridge: Cambridge University Press, 1970

Jay, Martin. *The Dialectical Imagination: A History of the Frankfurt School and the Institute of Social Research, 1923–50*. London: Heinemann, 1973

Kautsky, Karl. *The Class Struggle (Erfurt Program)*, tr. William E. Bohn. New York: W. W. Norton, 1971

Kenny, Anthony. *Action, Emotion and Will*. London: Routledge & Kegan Paul, 1963

Kohlberg, Lawrence. 'From is to ought: how to commit the naturalistic fallacy and get away with it in the study of moral development', in *Cognitive Development and Epistemology*, ed. Theodore Mischel, pp. 151–235. New York: Academic Press, 1971

  'Stage and sequence: the cognitive-developmental approach to socialization', in *Handbook of Socialization Theory and Research*, ed. David A. Goslin, pp. 347–480. Chicago: Rand McNally, 1969

Kovesi, Julius. *Moral Notions*. London: Routledge & Kegan Paul, 1967

Kripke, Saul. 'Naming and necessity', in *Semantics of Natural Languages*, ed. Donald Davidson and Gilbert Harman, pp. 253–355. Dordrecht: D. Reidel, 1972

Kuhn, Thomas. *The Structure of Scientific Revolutions*. Chicago: University of Chicago Press, 1970

Ladrière, Jean. *Language and Belief*, tr. Garrett Barden. Dublin: Gill & Macmillan, 1972

Lakatos, Imre and Musgrave, Alan, eds. *Criticism and the Growth of Knowledge*. Cambridge: Cambridge University Press, 1970

Lenin, V. I. *The Development of Capitalism in Russia*. Moscow: Progress Publishers, 1972

Lévi-Strauss, Claude. 'Réponses à quelques questions', *Esprit*, 31 (1963), pp. 628–53

Lichtheim, George. *The Concept of Ideology and Other Essays*. New York: Random House, 1967

Locke, Don. 'Action, movement, and neurophysiology', *Inquiry*, 17 (1974), pp. 23–42

Lorenzer, Alfred. 'Symbols and stereotypes', tr. Thomas Hall, in *Critical Sociology*, ed. Paul Connerton, pp. 134–52. Harmondsworth: Penguin, 1976

Louch, A. R. *Explanation and Human Action*. Oxford: Basil Blackwell, 1966
  'The very idea of a social science', *Inquiry*, 6 (1963), pp. 273–86

Lukes, Steven. 'Of gods and demons: Habermas and practical reason', in *Habermas: Critical Debates*, ed. John B. Thompson and David Held. London: Macmillan, forthcoming
  Power: A Radical View. London: Macmillan, 1974

McCarthy, Thomas. *The Critical Theory of Jürgen Habermas*. London: Hutchinson, 1978
  'Rationality and relativism: on Habermas's "overcoming" of hermeneutics', in *Habermas: Critical Debates*, ed. John B. Thompson and David Held. London: Macmillan, forthcoming

'A theory of communicative competence', *Philosophy of the Social Sciences*, 3 (1973), pp. 135–56

MacIntyre, Alasdair. 'The idea of a social science', in *Rationality*, ed. Bryan R. Wilson, pp. 112–30. Oxford: Basil Blackwell, 1970

'Is understanding religion compatible with believing?', in *Rationality*, ed. Bryan R. Wilson, pp. 62–77. Oxford: Basil Blackwell, 1970

The Unconscious: A Conceptual Analysis. London: Routledge & Kegan Paul, 1958

Mackie, J. L. *The Cement of the Universe: A Study of Causation*. Oxford: Oxford University Press, 1975

Malcolm, Norman. 'Knowledge of other minds', in *Wittgenstein: The 'Philosophical Investigations'*, ed. George Pitcher, pp. 371–83. London: Macmillan, 1966

'Wittgenstein's *Philosophical Investigations*', in *Wittgenstein: The 'Philosophical Investigations'*, ed. George Pitcher, pp. 65–103. London: Macmillan, 1966

Mannheim, Karl. *Ideology and Utopia: An Introduction to the Sociology of Knowledge*, tr. Louis Wirth and Edward Shils. London: Routledge & Kegan Paul, 1936

Marcuse, Herbert. *Negations*, tr. Jeremy J. Shapiro. Harmondsworth: Penguin, 1968

One Dimensional Man. London: Sphere, 1972

Reason and Revolution. London: Routledge & Kegan Paul, 1955

Martin, Richard M. 'Truth and its illicit surrogates', *Neue Hefte für Philosophie*, 2 (1972), pp. 95–110

Marx, Karl. *Capital: A Critique of Political Economy*, tr. Samuel Moore and Edward Aveling. London: Lawrence & Wishart, 1974

The Economic and Philosophic Manuscripts of 1844, tr. Martin Milligan. New York: International Publishers, 1964

and Engels, Frederick. *The German Ideology*. London: Lawrence & Wishart, 1970

Melden, A. I. *Free Action*. London: Routledge & Kegan Paul, 1961

Mueller, Claus. 'Notes on the repression of communicative behavior', in *Recent Sociology*, no. 2, ed. Hans Peter Dreitzel, pp. 101–13. New York: Macmillan, 1970

The Politics of Communication: A Study in the Political Sociology of Language, Socialization, and Legitimation. New York: Oxford University Press, 1973

Nabert, Jean. *Elements for an Ethic*, tr. William J. Petrek. Evanston: Northwestern University Press, 1969

Nagel, Ernest. 'Methodological issues in psychoanalytic theory', in *Psychoanalysis, Scientific Method, and Philosophy*, ed. Sidney Hook, pp. 38–56. New York: New York University Press, 1959

Neurath, Otto. 'Protocol sentences', tr. George Schlick, in *Logical Positivism*, ed. A. J. Ayer, pp. 199–208. New York: The Free Press, 1959

'Sociology and physicalism', tr. Morton Magnus and Ralph Raico, in *Logical Positivism*, ed. A. J. Ayer, pp. 282–317. New York: The Free Press, 1959

Offe, Claus. 'The abolition of market control and the problem of legitimacy, ɪ and ɪɪ', *Kapitalistate*, 1 and 2 (1973), pp. 109–16 and 73–5

'Political authority and class structures', in *Critical Sociology*, ed. Paul Connerton, pp. 388–421. Harmondsworth: Penguin, 1976

'The theory of the capitalist state and the problem of policy formation', unpublished paper presented at a conference in Florence, 1975

Outhwaite, William. *Understanding Social Life: The Method Called 'Verstehen'*. London: George Allen & Unwin, 1975

Palmer, Richard. *Hermeneutics: Interpretation Theory in Schleiermacher, Dilthey, Heidegger, and Gadamer.* Evanston: Northwestern University Press, 1969

Peters, Richard. 'Cause, cure and motive', in *Philosophy and Analysis*, ed. Margaret MacDonald, pp. 148–54. Oxford: Basil Blackwell, 1954

The Concept of Motivation. London: Routledge & Kegan Paul, 1958

Phillips, D. Z. and Mounce, H. O. 'On morality's having a point', in *The Is/Ought Question*, ed. W. D. Hudson, pp. 228–39. London: Macmillan, 1969

Piaget, Jean. *The Moral Judgement of the Child.* London: Routledge & Kegan Paul, 1932

Six Psychological Studies. London: University of London Press, 1968

Structuralism, tr. Chaninah Maschler. London: Routledge & Kegan Paul, 1971

Pitcher, George, ed. *Truth.* New Jersey: Prentice-Hall, 1964

ed. *Wittgenstein: The 'Philosophical Investigations'.* London: Macmillan, 1966

Pitkin, Hanna Fenichel. *Wittgenstein and Justice: On the Significance of Ludwig Wittgenstein for Social and Political Thought.* Berkeley: University of California Press, 1972

Pivčević, Edo, ed. *Phenomenology and Philosophical Understanding.* Cambridge: Cambridge University Press, 1975

Platts, Mark, ed. *Reference, Truth and Reality: Essays in the Philosophy of Language.* London: Routledge & Kegan Paul, 1980

Popper, Karl R. *The Logic of Scientific Discovery.* London: Hutchinson, 1959

Putnam, Hilary. *Meaning and the Moral Sciences.* London: Routledge & Kegan Paul, 1978

Rescher, Nicholas, ed. *The Logic of Decision and Action.* Pittsburgh: University of Pittsburgh Press, 1966

Ricoeur, Paul. 'The antinomy of human reality and the problem of philosophical anthropology', tr. Daniel O'Connor, in *Readings in Existential Phenomenology*, ed. Nathaniel Lawrence and Daniel O'Connor, pp. 390–402. New Jersey: Prentice-Hall, 1967

The Conflict of Interpretations: Essays in Hermeneutics, ed. Don Ihde, tr. Willis Domingo et al. Evanston: Northwestern University Press, 1974 [1969]

Cours sur l'herméneutique. Unpublished manuscript, delivered as a series of lectures at the Institut Supérieur de Philosophie, Louvain, 1971–2

'Le discours de l'action', in Paul Ricoeur et al., *La Sémantique de l'action*, pp. 1–137. Paris: Editions du Centre National de la Recherche Scientifique, 1977

Fallible Man, tr. Charles Kelbley. Chicago: Henry Regnery, 1965 [1960]

'Foreword', in Don Ihde, *Hermeneutic Phenomenology: The Philosophy of Paul Ricoeur.* Evanston: Northwestern University Press, 1971

Freedom and Nature: The Voluntary and the Involuntary, tr. Erazim V. Kohák. Evanston: Northwestern University Press, 1966 [1950]

Freud and Philosophy: An Essay on Interpretation, tr. Denis Savage. New Haven: Yale University Press, 1970 [1965]

'The hermeneutical function of distanciation', tr. David Pellauer, *Philosophy Today*, 17 (1973), pp. 129–41

Hermeneutics and the Human Sciences: Essays on Language, Action and Interpretation, ed. and tr. John B. Thompson. Cambridge: Cambridge University Press, 1981

'History and hermeneutics', tr. David Pellauer, *Journal of Philosophy*, 73 (1976), pp. 683–95

History and Truth, tr. Charles A. Kelbley. Evanston: Northwestern University Press, 1965 [1955]

Husserl: An Analysis of His Phenomenology, tr. E. G. Ballard and L. E. Embree. Evanston: Northwestern University Press, 1967

'Husserl and Wittgenstein on language', in *Phenomenology and Existentialism*, ed. E. N. Lee and M. Mandelbaum, pp. 207–17. Baltimore: Johns Hopkins University Press, 1967

Interpretation Theory: Discourse and the Surplus of Meaning. Fort Worth: Texas Christian University Press, 1976

'New developments in phenomenology in France: the phenomenology of language', tr. P. G. Goodman, *Social Research*, 34 (1967), pp. 1–30

'Phenomenology of freedom', in *Phenomenology and Philosophical Understanding*, ed. Edo Pivčević, pp. 173–94. Cambridge: Cambridge University Press, 1975

The Philosophy of Paul Ricoeur: An Anthology of His Work, ed. Charles Reagan and David Stewart. Boston: Beacon Press, 1978

Political and Social Essays, ed. David Stewart and Joseph Bien, tr. Donald Siewert et al. Athens, Ohio: Ohio University Press, 1974

'The problem of the will and philosophical discourse', tr. Peter McCormick, in *Patterns of the Life-World: Essays in Honor of John Wild*, ed. James M. Edie et al., pp. 273–89. Evanston: Northwestern University Press, 1970

The Rule of Metaphor: Multi-Disciplinary Studies of the Creation of Meaning in Language, tr. Robert Czerny with Kathleen McLaughlin and John Costello, SJ. London: Routledge & Kegan Paul, 1978 [1975]

The Symbolism of Evil, tr. Emerson Buchanan. New York: Harper & Row, 1967 [1960]

'The unity of the voluntary and the involuntary as a limiting idea', tr. Daniel O'Connor, in *Readings in Existential Phenomenology*, ed. Nathaniel Lawrence and Daniel O'Connor, pp. 93–108. New Jersey: Prentice-Hall, 1967

Russell, Bertrand. 'On denoting', in *Contemporary Readings in Logical Theory*, ed. Irving M. Copi and James A. Gould, pp. 93–105. New York: Macmillan, 1967

'The philosophy of logical atomism', in *Russell's Logical Atomism*, ed. David Pears, pp. 31–142. London: Fontana/Collins, 1972

Ryle, Gilbert. *Collected Papers*, vol. ii. London: Hutchinson, 1971

The Concept of Mind. Harmondsworth: Penguin, 1949

Schmid, Michael. 'Habermas's theory of social evolution', tr. Nicholas Saul, in *Habermas: Critical Debates*, ed. John B. Thompson and David Held. London: Macmillan, forthcoming

Schutz, Alfred. *Collected Papers*, vol. i, ed. Maurice Natanson. The Hague: Martinus Nijhoff, 1962

Scriven, Michael. 'The experimental investigation of psychoanalysis', in *Psychoanalysis, Scientific Method, and Philosophy*, ed. Sidney Hook, pp. 226–51. New York: New York University Press, 1959

Searle, John R. *Speech Acts: An Essay in the Philosophy of Language*. Cambridge: Cambridge University Press, 1970

Seliger, Martin. *Ideology and Politics*. London: George Allen & Unwin, 1976

Skinner, Quentin. '"Social meaning" and the explanation of social action', in *Philosophy, Politics and Society*, fourth series, ed. Peter Laslett et al., pp. 136–57. Oxford: Basil Blackwell, 1972

Sosa, Ernest, ed. *Causation and Conditionals*. Oxford: Oxford University Press, 1975

Specht, Ernst Konrad. *The Foundations of Wittgenstein's Late Philosophy*, tr. D. E. Walford. Manchester: Manchester University Press, 1969

Strawson, P. F. 'Construction and analysis', in A. J. Ayer et al., *The Revolution in Philosophy*, pp. 97–110. London: Macmillan, 1956

Individuals: An Essay in Descriptive Metaphysics. London: Methuen, 1959

Logico-Linguistic Papers. London: Methuen, 1971

ed. *Philosophical Logic*. Oxford: Oxford University Press, 1967

Taylor, Charles. *The Explanation of Behaviour*. London: Routledge & Kegan Paul, 1964

'Interpretation and the sciences of man', *Review of Metaphysics*, 25 (1971), pp. 3–51

Thompson, John B. 'Universal pragmatics', in *Habermas: Critical Debates*, ed. John B. Thompson and David Held. London: Macmillan, forthcoming

and Held, David, eds. *Habermas: Critical Debates*. London: Macmillan, forthcoming

Toulmin, Stephen. 'The logical status of psychoanalysis', in *Philosophy and Analysis*, ed. Margaret MacDonald, pp. 132–9. Oxford: Basil Blackwell, 1954

The Uses of Argument. Cambridge: Cambridge University Press, 1958

Warnock, G. J. 'A problem about truth', in *Truth*, ed. George Pitcher, pp. 54–67. New Jersey: Prentice-Hall, 1964

Wellmer, Albrecht. *Critical Theory of Society*, tr. John Cumming. New York: Seabury Press, 1974

White, Alan R., ed. *The Philosophy of Action*. Oxford: Oxford University Press, 1968

Williamson, Judith. *Decoding Advertisements: Ideology and Meaning in Advertising*. London: Marion Boyars, 1978

Willis, Paul. *Learning to Labour: How Working Class Kids Get Working Class Jobs*. Farnborough, Hants.: Saxon House, 1977

Wilson, Bryan R., ed. *Rationality*. Oxford: Basil Blackwell, 1970

Winch, Peter. 'Comment', in *Explanation in the Behavioural Sciences*, ed. Robert Borger and Frank Cioffi, pp. 249–59. Cambridge: Cambridge University Press, 1970

Ethics and Action. London: Routledge & Kegan Paul, 1972

The Idea of a Social Science and its Relation to Philosophy. London: Routledge & Kegan Paul, 1958

'Mr. Louch's idea of a social science', *Inquiry*, 7 (1964), pp. 202–8

'Understanding a primitive society', in *Rationality*, ed. Bryan R. Wilson, pp. 78–111. Oxford: Basil Blackwell, 1970

Wittgenstein, Ludwig. *Lectures and Conversations on Aesthetics, Psychology and Religious Belief*, ed. Cyril Barrett. Oxford: Basil Blackwell, 1966

On Certainty, ed. G. E. M. Anscombe and G. H. von Wright, tr. Denis Paul and G. E. M. Anscombe. Oxford: Basil Blackwell, 1974

Philosophical Grammar, ed. Rush Rhees, tr. Anthony Kenny. Oxford: Basil Blackwell, 1974

Philosophical Investigations, third edition, tr. G. E. M. Anscombe. Oxford: Basil Blackwell, 1968

Philosophical Remarks, ed. Rush Rhees, tr. Raymond Hargreaves and Roger White. Oxford: Basil Blackwell, 1975

Preliminary Studies for the 'Philosophical Investigations', Generally Known as the Blue and Brown Books. Oxford: Basil Blackwell, 1969

'Remarks on Frazer's *Golden Bough*', tr. A. C. Miles and Rush Rhees, *The Human World* (1971), pp. 28–41

'Some remarks on logical form', in *Essays on Wittgenstein's 'Tractatus'*, ed. Irving M. Copi and Robert W. Beard, pp. 31–7. London: Routledge & Kegan Paul, 1966

Tractatus Logico-Philosophicus, tr. D. F. Pears and B. F. McGuinness. London: Routledge & Kegan Paul, 1961

Zettel, ed. G. E. M. Anscombe and G. H. von Wright, tr. G. E. M. Anscombe. Oxford: Basil Blackwell, 1967

Wright, Georg Henrik von. *Explanation and Understanding*. London: Routledge & Kegan Paul, 1971

Index